EVERYONE WANTS TO BE
ON THE SOAPS

Take a look at the variety of celebrities who have acted or appeared at least once in a favorite soap opera:

Roy Rogers, cowboy star: *As the World Turns* and *Guiding Light*

Russell Baker, *New York Times* columnist: *All My Children*

Aretha Franklin, The Queen of Soul: *The Young and the Restless*
   As the World Turns, and *Guiding Light*

Kate Pierson, singer with the B-52s: *All My Children*

Janet Dailey, romance novelist: *Days of Our Lives*

Shelby Foote, Civil War historian: *As the World Turns*

The Artist Formerly Known as Prince, singer/musician: *General Hospital*

The
Soap Opera
BOOK of LISTS

Gerard J. Waggett

HarperPaperbacks
A Division of HarperCollinsPublishers

HarperPaperbacks *A Division of* HarperCollins*Publishers*
10 East 53rd Street, New York, N.Y. 10022

HarperPaperbacks may be purchased for educational, business, or sales promotional use. For information please write: Special Markets Department, HarperCollins*Publishers*, 10 East 53rd Street, New York, N.Y. 10022.

Cover photograph of Linda Dano by E. J. Carr; Jeanne Cooper and Susan Lucci by Michael Ferguson/Globe Photos, Inc.; Tony Geary by Jonathan Green/Globe Photos, Inc.; Deidre Hall by Ralph Dominguez/Globe Photos, Inc.; Michael Nader, Christian Slater and Marisa Tomei, Alec Baldwin and Meg Ryan by Rangefinders/Globe Photos, Inc.

First printing: May 1996

Printed in the United States of America

HarperPaperbacks and colophon are trademarks of HarperCollins*Publishers*

Designed by Michele Bonomo

Library of Congress Cataloging-in-Publication Data

Waggett, Gerard J.
        The soap opera book of lists / Gerard J. Waggett.
            p.   cm.
        ISBN 0-06-100985-7 (pbk.)
            1. Soap operas—United States—Miscellanea.   I. Title.
PR1992.8.S4W35   1996
791.45'6--dc20   95-48028
                                                       CIP

❖ 10 9 8 7 6 5 4 3 2

for my parents,
Barbara and Frederick Waggett

Acknowledgments

This is my own personal list of people I need to thank, people who played a role in bringing this book about. I don't feel guilty about being thorough in my gratitude because unlike acceptance speeches at the Daytime Emmys, no one who doesn't want to has to sit through these "thank you's."

To Gretchen Young, my editor, thanks for taking a chance. I hope I made this book what you envisioned it could be. To my agents, Frank Coffey and Frank Weimann, thanks for taking care of the business end of things so I could concentrate on the writing.

To the contributors, thank you for your time and your help. I hope you enjoyed our interviews/conversations as much as I did. In reverse alphabetical order, you are: Jacklyn Zeman, Gary Warner, Mimi Torchin, Angela Shapiro, Louise Shaffer, Kathryn Leigh Scott, R. Scott Reedy, Martha Nochimson, Dawn Mazzurco, Robin Mattson, Bill Lieberman, Karen Lindsey, Jean LeClerc, Lynn Leahy, Susan Seaforth Hayes, Bill Hayes, Freeman Günter, Eileen Fulton, Linda Dano, Jeanne Cooper, Alan Carter, Peter Bergman, and Julia Barr.

To the publicists and managers who helped me get to the contributors and to those people who provided me with information and feedback, your help was invaluable: Johnathan Zaleski, Bill Timmoney, Janet Storm, Vivien Stern, Cynthia Sneider, Sally Shoneboom, Charles Sherman, Jonathan Reiner, Virginia Piccolo, Henry Newman, Irene Keene, Sharon Kearns, Judy Katz, David Johnson, David Granoff, Cheryl Fuchs, Amy Farina, Carol Dickson, Brenda Dickson, John Beradino, and Scott Barton.

Despite all the time I've spent in front a TV set, I have been able to obtain a level of education all parents dream of their children acquiring. Five English teachers in particular need to be singled out for that: Bill Collins, Kevin Kynock, Fr. Lawrence Corcoran, Lee Grove, and Chris Leland.

A number of people have supported me emotionally through the years. I owe them for seeing that something inside myself that a rejection letter occasionally blinded me to. At the top of that list is Eileen Maher, an incredible support system in and of herself, enhanced by being of an amazing family. As John Michael Montgomery puts it, "She thinks I can rope the moon." Up there too are: the Woods (Kathy, Charlie, C. J., Kim, and Julie); Anne Walsh; Cathy Tately; Jerry Stonehouse; Kathy Stauner; Jill Stanley; the Sheas (Genevieve, Leo, Young Leo, Barbara, and Jackie); Mike Roche; Ellie Roche; Marie and Jay Princiotto; Beth Pratt; Kim Ovaitte Gonzales; Darragh Murphy; Nance Movsesian; Roseanne Montgomery; Tom Maher; Mark Lund; Mary and Joe Lee; Matt Law; Dianne Kennedy; Jane Hansen; the Flynns (Joe, Anne Marie, Jen, Chris, and Katie); Robin Di Carlo; Don Casali; and Paul Bonaceto.

Lastly, the people who have been there the longest, my family. Thank you for supporting for so long what had to seem at times like little more than a dream and an excuse not to get a real job. Thank you to my mother and father, Barbara and Fred Waggett; my brothers Freddie, Michael, and Kevin; my sisters-in-law Keri and Christine; my aunt Margaret Connolly; my uncles Jackie and Eddie Connolly; and my cousin Mabel Waggett.

To everyone who has played a part in the creation of this book and in my evolution as a writer, I wish you the same sense of self-satisfaction that I am feeling right at this very moment.

Table of Contents

CONTENTS

CONTENTS

CONTENTS

Introduction

Soap operas have long been linked with lists in my mind because of the game show *Family Feud*, (which remains my all-time favorite game show.) As a Valentine's Day special back in the late '70s, the show pitted a "family" of five actors from *One Life to Live* against five from *General Hospital*. Thirteen years old at the time, I was only vaguely familiar with *One Life to Live* and had never seen more than a commercial or two for *General Hospital*. Within a couple of years, though, I got hooked on the entire ABC line-up. Once I was, I really looked forward to those sweeps months when *Family Feud* would bring on the castmembers from the different soaps. Susan Lucci, who plays Erica Kane on *All My Children*, impressed the hell out of me the time she racked up two hundred points in the bonus round all by herself.

The seed for this book must have been planted during those specials. When my agent wanted some angle for a soap opera trivia book I was proposing, *The Soap Opera Book of Lists* sprang immediately to mind. Credit must also be given to the late Irving Wallace and his family for literally creating the genre with that original *Book of Lists* back in 1977. (After wearing the cover off that first paperback, I made sure to buy the subsequent editions in hardcover.)

Lists, I've come to realize, do seem to hold a certain appeal for soap fans. Almost every back issue of *Soap Opera Digest* I researched through included some kind of list: the hottest love triangles on daytime; the most difficult stars to work with; the sexiest men and most beautiful women. *Soap Opera Weekly* has its F.Y.I. column that lists varied actors' favorite movies, books, TV shows, etc. *Soap Opera Magazine* runs a similar column it calls Star Stats.

I think that soap operas create a list mentality in their fans. Part of it comes from the division of attention fans develop while watching their favorite shows, jumping from Plot A to Plot B to Plot C to a string of commercials and back to Plot A. Soap fans have had to become quite adept at absorbing information in brief segments. Beyond that, major characters on the soaps become walking lists of a sort. In 1995, *As the World Turns'* Lisa (played by Eileen Fulton) married her seventh husband; when he died, she was comforted by Husband #1 Bob Hughes (Don Hastings). *One Life to Live*'s Vicki Buchanan (played by four-time Emmy winner Erika Slezak) has had a total of six alternate personalities. And on *Days of Our Lives*, the ever-villainous Stefano DiMera (Joseph Mascolo), nicknamed The Phoenix, has "come back from the dead" at least half a dozen times. To keep track of character history that sometimes spans more than twenty years, a mind has to think in terms of lists.

Unfortunately, some entries on different lists will become inevitably outdated by the time the book hits the stores. Given actor turnover, some of the names on the list of best-looking men and women may actually be gone, while a name or two on the list of most sorely missed actors may actually have returned to daytime. One character on my list of oddest deaths actually had to be demoted to an honorable mention because she recently came back from the dead. But if an audience can accept a character's sudden resurrection as easily as it does, I don't think a seemingly outdated reference to the death will bother too many people. Just as soaps have trained their audiences to think in terms of lists, they have also forced their fans to learn a great deal of forgiveness. For a sampling of just how much soaps have expected fans to simply accept and move on, check out the lists of 12 Odd Recasting Choices and 5 Cases Where Actors Returned to Their Roles after Their Characters Had Gone through Major Reconstructive Plastic Surgery.

Of course, as I write this introduction, I realize that few people will have bothered reading it. As many times as I picked up *The Book of Lists*, I can't remember if I ever read the introduction. And back when I was watching *Family Feud*, I never cared much for the beginning where Richard Dawson would chat with (and, in those days, kiss) the two families; I always saw it as time where the show could have squeezed in another question.

The
Soap Opera
BOOK *of* LISTS

1

Opening Credits

25 SOAPS THAT BEGAN ON THE SAME DAY AS OTHER SOAPS

1–3. General Hospital (ABC), The Doctors (NBC), and Ben Jerrod (NBC)
Premiered: April 1, 1963
Ben Jerrod ran less than three months. *The Doctors* aired its last episode on December 31, 1982, the same day that *Texas* went off the air. *General Hospital* remains one of the top soap operas on the air. Gerald Gordon has appeared on all three soaps over the years: as Sam Richardson on *Ben Jerrod*, as Dr. Nick Bellini on *The Doctors*, and as Dr. Mark Dante on *General Hospital*.

4–5. The Edge of Night and As the World Turns (both CBS)
Premiered: April 2, 1956
The Edge of Night and *As the World Turns* were the first two soap operas to run a full half hour each on a major network. Although *The Edge of Night* was more popular in its first year, *As the World Turns* climbed to the top of the daytime ratings by the end of 1959.

6–7. Three Steps to Heaven and Follow Your Heart (both NBC)
Premiered: August 3, 1953
Three Steps to Heaven and *Follow Your Heart* filled the 11:30 and 11:45 time slots

1

respectively. They followed *The Bennetts*, which had debuted a month previously and which was cancelled the same day as *Follow Your Heart* (January 8, 1954). *Three Steps* survived till the end of 1954.

8–12. *The Seeking Heart* (CBS), *First Love* (NBC), *A Time to Live* (NBC), *Concerning Miss Marlowe* (NBC), and *Golden Windows* (NBC)
  Premiered: July 5, 1954
  July 5, 1954 holds the record for the largest number of soap operas to debut in one day. A year later, however, not one of those five soaps was still on the air.

13–16. *Morning Star* (NBC), *Paradise Bay* (NBC), *Never Too Young* (ABC), and the daytime version of *The Nurses* (ABC)
  Premiered: September 27, 1965
  Morning Star and *Paradise Bay* were both given late-morning time slots and both went off the air on the same day, July 1, 1966. *Never Too Young* was given a late-afternoon time slot (4:00 P.M.) to appeal to a younger audience but was also cancelled in the summer of 1966. A daytime serial version of the CBS prime-time drama *The Nurses* also debuted this day; the prime-time version of the show had debuted on September 27 exactly three years earlier.

17–19. *Best of Everything* (ABC), *A World Apart* (ABC), and *Another World: Somerset* (NBC)
  Premiered: March 30, 1970
  This day may best be described as something of a grudge match in soap opera circles. *Somerset* was spun off from *Another World*, a show which Irna Phillips had created and then been fired from. *A World Apart*, whose title may have been a play on *Another World*, was created by Phillips's adopted daughter, Katherine, and was inspired by the life of Irna Phillips. (Irna Phillips served as story editor for the show.) *Best of Everything* (based on the Rona Jaffe novel and Joan Crawford movie of the same name) had been created by James Lipton, who like Irna Phillips had been fired as headwriter of *Another World*. *Somerset* emerged as the most popular of the three soaps that debuted on March 30. *Best of Everything* was the lowest rated soap of 1970. When it was cancelled, that dubious distinction fell on *A World Apart*.

20–21. *The Secret Storm* and *Woman with a Past* (both CBS)
  Premiered: February 1, 1954
  Woman with a Past began at 4:00, and *The Secret Storm* followed at 4:15. Despite

the poor lead-in *Woman with a Past* provided in its initial months—it was cancelled by mid-summer—*The Secret Storm* survived exactly twenty years and one week.

22–23. Search for Tomorrow and *The Egg and I* (both CBS)
Premiered: September 3, 1951
Search for Tomorrow had originally been scheduled to premiere in May of 1951 but was pushed back to September 3, which coincided with Labor Day that year as well as the debut of *The Egg and I*. While *The Egg and I* didn't last a year, *Search for Tomorrow* quickly rose to the top of the Nielsen ratings.

24–25. Bright Promise (NBC) and *The Survivors* (ABC)
Premiered:September 29, 1969
Bright Promise debuted at 3:30 in the afternoon and *The Survivors* at 9:00 that evening. Both shows were headed by former Hollywood movie stars: Dana Andrews starred on *Bright Promise* as college president Thomas Boswell and Lana Turner as Tracy Carlyle Hastings, daughter of banker Baylor Carlyle (Ralph Bellamy), on *The Survivors*.

THE 12 LONGEST RUNNING DAYTIME SOAPS

1. *Guiding Light*
   June 30, 1952–present
   Note: List refers to run on television only. *Guiding Light* began as a radio soap in 1937.

2. *As the World Turns*
   April 2, 1956–present

3. *Search for Tomorrow*
   September 3, 1951–December 26, 1986

4. *General Hospital*
   April 1, 1963–present

5. *Another World*
   May 4, 1964–present

6. *Days of Our Lives*
   November 8, 1965–present

7. *The Edge of Night*
   April 2, 1956–December 28, 1984

8. *Love of Life*
   September 24, 1951–February 1, 1980

9. *One Life to Live*
   July 15, 1968–present

10. *All My Children*
    January 5, 1970–present

11. *The Young and the Restless*
    March 26, 1973–present

12. *The Secret Storm*
    February 1, 1954–February 8, 1974

THE 8 LONGEST RUNNING PRIME-TIME SOAPS

1. *Knots Landing*
   December 27, 1979–May 14, 1993

2. *Dallas*
   April 2, 1978–May 3, 1991

3. *Falcon Crest*
   December 4, 1981–May 17, 1990

4. *Dynasty*
   January 12, 1981–May 11, 1989

5. *Beverly Hills 90210*
   October 4, 1991–present

6. *Peyton Place*
   September 15, 1964–June 2, 1969

7. *Melrose Place*
   July 8, 1992–present

8. *Soap*
   September 13, 1977–April 20, 1981

8 DAYTIME SOAPS THAT DIDN'T SURVIVE SIX MONTHS

1. *These Are My Children* (26 days: January 31 to February 25, 1949)

The first soap opera to be broadcast on a major network (NBC) was also its shortest-lived. It was also the first soap opera created for TV by the legendary Irna Phillips, who three years later would bring to TV its longest running soap opera, *Guiding Light*. Action on *These Are My Children* centered around a boarding house run by the Widow Henehan (Alma Platts).

2. *Ben Jerrod* (2 months, 27 days: April 1 to June 28, 1963)

Roy Winsor, who had created the highly rated *Search for Tomorrow* and *Love of Life* did not fare so well with this legal soap opera. Because of the show's short run, Ben only got to defend one client, a socialite accused of murdering her husband.

3. *Woman with a Past* (5 months, 1 day: February 1 to July 2, 1954)

Woman with a Past was daytime veteran Constance Ford's (Ada Davis, *Another World*) first soap opera. She played the title character of Lynn Sherwood, a dress designer living in New York City. *Woman with a Past* also featured *All in the Family*'s Jean Stapleton in her first TV series.

4. *Follow Your Heart* (5 months, 5 days: August 3, 1953 to January 8, 1954)

Creator Elaine Carrington borrowed the premise for *Follow Your Heart* from the radio soap she created, *When a Girl Marries*: a young socialite defying her family to marry beneath her station. Because the show was pulled before the six-month mark, viewers never got to see Julie Fielding (Sallie Brophy) actually marry the beneath-her-station Peter Davis (Grant Williams) as was planned.

5. *The Seeking Heart* (5 months, 5 days: July 5 to December 10, 1954)

At the center of *Seeking Heart* was a love triangle involving police doctor John Adam (Scott Forbes), his unhappy wife, Grace (Dorothy Lovett), and his female assistant, Dr. Robinson McKay (Flora Campbell). The soap was replaced with a TV version of Irna Phillips's long-running radio soap *The Road of Life*, which fared only marginally better in the ratings.

6. *A Time to Live* (5 months, 26 days: July 5 to December 31, 1954)

A Time to Live debuted on the same day as *The Seeking Heart* and outlasted it by only three weeks. The action centered around the romance between two newspaper reporters, Julie Byron (Pat Sully) and Don Riker (who was played in the show's short time on the air by two actors, John Himes and Larry Kerr).

7. *Best of Everything* (5 months, 26 days: March 30 to September 25, 1970)

Best of Everything was preceded by a best-selling novel by Rona Jaffe and a 1959 film starring Joan Crawford. Neither the movie recognition nor the casting of movie actresses Geraldine Fitzgerald and Gayle Sondergaard brought in a sufficient audience to keep the show alive. The soap opera did, however, mark Susan Sullivan's (Lenore Moore, *Another World*; Maggie Gioberti, *Falcon Crest*) first foray into the medium.

8. *Today Is Ours* (5 months, 26 days: June 30 to December 26, 1958)

When it was decided that *Today Is Ours* was going to be cancelled and replaced with a TV version of the radio soap *Young Doctor Malone*, characters and storylines were introduced on *Today Is Ours* that would carry into *Young Doctor Malone*. *Young Doctor Malone* ran three and a half years.

6 SOAPS THAT HAVE RANKED NUMBER #1 IN THE YEAR-END RATINGS

1. *As the World Turns*: 20 years (1958–1978)

2. *The Young and the Restless*: 9 years (1987–present)

3. *General Hospital*: 8 years (1979–1987)

4. *Search for Tomorrow*: 4 years (1952–1956)

5. *Guiding Light*: 2 years (1956–1958)

6. *All My Children*: 1 year (1978–1979)

ORIGINAL TITLES FOR 12 SOAP OPERAS

1. *The Young and the Restless*
   Original title: *The Innocent Years*

2. *Falcon Crest*
   Original title: *The Vintage Years*

3. *Dynasty*
   Original title: *Oil*

4. *Search for Tomorrow*
   Original title: *Search for Happiness*
   Search for Happiness was rejected as a title because it did not sound serious enough.

5. *Ryan's Hope*
   Original title: *A Rage to Love*
   ABC could not clear the rights to use the title *A Rage to Love*.

6. One Life to Live
   Original title: *Between Heaven and Hell*

7. The Secret Storm
   Original title: *The Storm Within*
   The Storm Within had to be changed when an antacid company signed on as one of the show's major sponsors.

8. The Bold and the Beautiful
   Original title: *Rags*
   The Bold and the Beautiful's creator Bill Bell used *Rags* as the working title for his project. He never intended for the show to air under that title.

9. Homefront
   Original title: *1945*
   The title was changed in part so that the show would not have to be renamed year after year if it became a hit.

10. Texas
    Original title: *Reunion*
    In its planning stages, *Texas* was conceived as a period drama, set in the pre–Civil War South.

11. Beverly Hills 90210
    Original title: *The Class of Beverly Hills.*

12. Dark Shadows
    Original title: *Shadows on the Wall*
    Also considered for the title were: *Castle of Darkness, The House on Widow's Hill,* and *Terror at Collinwood.*

11 SOAPS THAT CHANGED THEIR TITLES AFTER THEY DEBUTED

1–2. Another World and Somerset
   When *Another World* launched its spin-off *Somerset* in 1970, *Another World*

became *Another World: Bay City* while *Somerset* was introduced as *Another World: Somerset.* Eventually *Another World* dropped its *Bay City* suffix, and *Somerset* dropped its *Another World* prefix.

3. Dynasty II: The Colbys

Before it aired, the show was titled *Dynasty II: The Colbys of California.* By the first episode, that title was trimmed to *Dynasty II: The Colbys.* It was trimmed yet again during its run to simply *The Colbys.*

4. Lovers and Friends

Lovers and Friends ran on NBC from January 3, 1977, to May 6 of the same year and was pulled because of low ratings. A revamped version of the show, titled *For Richer, for Poorer,* returned seven months later. The character of Rhett Saxton himself also underwent a name change and was called "Bill." As *For Richer, for Poorer,* the show lasted another ten months.

Note: The original title for the show was to be *Into This House.*

5. Mary Hartman, Mary Hartman

Louise Lasser had become too identified as Mary Hartman for the role to be recast. When she left after the second season, it no longer made sense for the show to be called *Mary Hartman.* The title was changed to *Forever Fernwood,* referring to the show's fictional locale.

6. Flame in the Wind

In mid-1965, six months after *Flame in the Wind* premiered, Irna Phillips took over as story editor. Among the sweeping changes she made was a greater focus on younger characters. She also changed the name of the show to *A Time for Us* and changed the name of the core family from Skerba to the far less ethnic Driscoll.

7. Guiding Light

Including its time both on radio and TV, it had been known as *The Guiding Light* for forty years. Then in 1977, shortly after expanding the show from thirty minutes to an hour, the producers removed the *The* from its title as part of their plan to modernize the show's image.

8. Portia Faces Life

Although successful as a radio soap—it ran eleven years on the CBS network—*Portia Faces Life* did not fare nearly so well on television. One move the network took to increase ratings was to pick a new, more romantic title: *The Inner Flame*. The new title may have been modeled after *The Guiding Light*, which had made a successful transition from radio to TV two years previously.

9. *Miss Susan*

Miss Susan had been created as a star vehicle for wheelchair-bound film actress Susan Peters. In the soap, Peters played wheelchair-bound lawyer Susan Martin. When it was learned that some potential viewers found the premise exploitative of Peters's disability, the show was renamed *Martinsville, U.S.A.*

10. *Fairmeadows, U.S.A.*

Fairmeadows, U.S.A. began as a Sunday-afternoon serial. When it moved to a daily schedule as part of *The Kate Smith Hour*, the title was changed to *The House in the Garden*.

11. *Loving*

In 1995, ABC decided to completely overhaul the perennially low-rated *Loving*. A serial killer plotline was introduced to wipe out the show's core family, the Aldens, and a majority of the remaining castmembers were subsequently moved from the fictional town of Corinth, Pennsylvania, to the Soho section of New York City. Morgan Fairchild was also added to the cast. When the changes were first announced, ABC had proposed that the show would be called LOV♥NYC, an awkward title that was ultimately scrapped in favor of *The City*.

8 SOAPS SPUN OFF FROM OTHER SOAPS

1. *Knots Landing* (from *Dallas*)

Ironically, *Knots Landing* had been conceived of before *Dallas* but was not thought of as epic enough for a TV series. When *Dallas* creator David Jacobs was called upon to come up with a spin-off of the number-one-rated *Dallas*, he reintroduced the idea of *Knots Landing*, using the rarely seen third Ewing son, Gary, and his ex-wife, Valene, as a springboard for the series. After Bobby's death on *Dallas* turned out to be a dream, *Knots Landing*, which had incorporated Bobby's death into their plotlines, cut off all ties with the show: only the most tangential mentions of Gary's family were made. Ted Shackleford and Joan Van Ark, who played Gary and Val, did, however, appear in *Dallas*'s final episode. Clearly the most successful of all soap spin-offs, *Knots* ended up lasting fourteen seasons, one more than its parent show.

2. *Our Private World* (from *As the World Turns*)

Inspired by ABC's success with the prime-time serial *Peyton Place* and fueled by Eileen Fulton's popularity as Lisa Hughes on *As the World Turns*, CBS launched the prime-time serial *Our Private World* in 1965, starring Fulton as Lisa. The character of Lisa was transplanted from Oakdale to Chicago and given a new set of characters to torment. Like *Peyton Place*, *Our Private World* aired for a half hour two nights a week. It lasted only one summer. After the series was cancelled, Lisa returned to Oakdale. A recent storyline on *As the World Turns* drew from the events that happened on *Our Private World* and reintroduced characters from the spin-off.

Note: Nicholas Coster, who played Lisa's second husband, John Eldridge, on *Our Private World*, was recently cast on *As the World Turns* as Eduardo Grimaldi, who became Lisa's seventh husband.

3. *Another World* (from *As the World Turns*)

As the World Turns was the number one soap in the country when its creator Irna Phillips came up with the idea for a spin-off. On radio, she had had great success spinning off *The Right to Happiness* from *The Guiding Light*. Phillips conceived of *Another World*'s Bay City as one town over from Oakdale, and she planned for *Another World*'s Matthews family to be friends with the Hughes family from *As the World Turns*. While Procter & Gamble, who owned *As the World Turns*, gave her the green light, CBS didn't have room in its schedule for another soap opera; it already had six in its afternoon line-up. NBC, which at that time only had *The Doctors*, jumped at the chance to put an Irna Phillips soap opera on the air. Given the fact that *Another World* would be airing on a different network, Phillips ultimately abandoned the idea of connecting the two shows in any major way. Only a minor character on *As the World Turns*, a lawyer named Mitchell Dru (Geoffrey Lumb), was moved to Bay City. (Mitchell had also been used on Phillips's *The Brighter Day*.) The title *Another World* was chosen as an homage to its origin as an *As the World Turns* spin-off. Currently, the shows air opposite each other in most markets across the country.

Note: While Phillips saw the different networks as an obstacle to bringing *As the World Turns* characters onto *Another World*, in 1966, *The Guiding Light*'s Mike Bauer (Gary Pillar) and his daughter, Hope (Elissa Leeds), moved to Bay City for about a year.

4. *Somerset* (from *Another World*)

At its peak of popularity, *Another World* spun off *Somerset*, sending three of its characters to live in the title town, which was roughly fifty miles away from Bay City: Missy Matthews (Carol Roux), who been with *Another World* since the first episode, Sam Lucas (Jordan Charney) and his wife, Lahoma (Ann Wedgeworth). The two shows were shown back to back and titled *Another World: Bay City* and *Another World: Somerset*, making for a full hour of *Another World* and thereby paving the way for the hour-long soap. Unfortunately, *Another World* lost almost an entire ratings point the year *Somerset* debuted. By the following year, *Another World* began distancing itself from the spin-off: Robert Cenedella, who had been headwriter on both shows, was cut down to working on *Somerset* alone and was eventually let go altogether; Missy Matthews was written out of *Somerset*—but not back into *Another World*; and the title *Another World: Somerset* was trimmed down to simply *Somerset*. *Somerset* bore even less of a resemblance to its parent show when *The Edge of Night*'s Henry Slesar took over headwriting duties and turned the soap into a continuing crime drama. Although the show moved back to more traditional soap opera territory when Slesar left in 1974, *Somerset* was eventually cancelled in late 1976.

5. *Texas* (from *Another World*)

Hoping, no doubt, to capitalize on the *Dallas* phenomenon, NBC spun *Texas* off from *Another World*. *Another World*, which was airing for ninety minutes a day in 1979, cut back to an hour to make room for the hour-long *Texas*. NBC toyed with the idea of moving the show into prime-time to compete head-on with *Dallas* if the soap proved popular enough—which it never did. Fan favorite Beverlee McKinsey was recruited to pioneer the new show and was promised star billing in the opening credits. In 1980, Iris and her maid, Vivien (Gretchen Oehler), traveled West to Houston (not Dallas) where Iris's son, Dennis Carrington (Jim Poyner), lived. McKinsey's departure hurt *Another World* deeply. The show lost two whole ratings points the year *Texas* debuted. McKinsey stayed with the spin-off only a year. As had happened when McKinsey left *Another World*, her departure from *Texas* was followed by a two point drop in the show's ratings. Unlike its parent show, however, the already low-rated *Texas* couldn't weather such a drop. It was off the air by the end of 1982.

6. The Colbys (from Dynasty)

The success of *Dynasty*, which had surpassed *Dallas* to finish first for the 1984–1985 season, led to the inevitable spin-off. The *Dallas* spin-off *Knots Landing* was, after all, doing quite well, itself ending up among the year's top ten series. *The Colbys*, originally titled *Dynasty II: The Colbys*, sent Jeff Colby (John James) and Fallon Carrington (with Emma Samms replacing Pamela Sue Martin) to California, where Jeff's family hailed from. The producers decided to "ensure" the spin-off's success by casting top-name movie actors Charlton Heston, Barbara Stanwyck, and Katherine Ross. Stanwyck left after the first season. The show made it through a second season, but was not picked up for a third. Jeff and Fallon subsequently moved back to *Dynasty*. *Colbys* regulars Stephanie Beacham and Tracy Scoggins reprised their roles as Sable and Monica Colby during *Dynasty*'s last season.

7. Melrose Place (from Beverly Hills 90210)

In the last two episodes of the 1992 season, *Beverly Hills 90210* introduced the character of Jake Hansen (Grant Show) who had been Dylan's (Luke Perry) surfing "mentor." Kelly (Jennie Garth) fell for Jake and pursued him for a couple of episodes in the crossover storyline that launched *Melrose Place*. In the beginning, *Melrose Place* played like early *90210*. There were four males paired off in some way, not necessarily romantic, with the four female leads, but all eight were friends with one another. Each week, they dealt with social issues ranging from unwanted pregnancy to hate crimes and unemployment. Just like *90210*, *Melrose* evolved into a real prime-time soap opera. As it did so, it bore less and less resemblance to *90210*. While *90210* occasionally drifted into stories of organized crime and espionage, *Melrose* made a weekly practice of going to extremes with tales of drug smuggling, prostitution, and attempted murder.

8. Models, Inc. (from Melrose Place)

The connection between *Models, Inc.* and *Melrose Place* was actually closer than the one between *90210* and *Melrose* even though *90210* and *Melrose Place* creator Darren Starr had nothing to do with *Models*. During the last few weeks of *Melrose Place*'s 1994 season, Linda Gray was introduced as Hillary Michaels, owner of Models, Inc., a Los Angeles–based modeling agency, and the long-absent mother of *Melrose Place*'s Amanda Woodward (Heather Locklear). Photographer Jo Reynolds (Daphne Zuniga) had also taken in model Sarah Owens (Cassidy Rae), who would become a major character on the spin-off. Zuniga and *Melrose Place*–castmate Grant Show showed up briefly in the first episode of *Models, Inc.*

Locklear, though, never surfaced on the show. *Models* did learn one valuable lesson from its parent show. When producer Aaron Spelling realized that *Melrose Place* needed a seasoned soap opera bitch to kick some storylines into high gear, he hired Locklear, whom he had worked with on *Dynasty*, and gave her character control of the show's core, having Amanda buy the apartment building where everybody lived. In an almost identical fashion, Spelling hired former *Dynasty* star Emma Samms to energize *Models, Inc.* and gave her character, Grayson Louder, a classic soap bitch, half ownership of the modeling agency that served as *Models, Inc.*'s core.

Notes: The comedy soap opera *Soap* spun the character of Benson (Robert Guillaume) off into his own series *Benson*, which was a non-continuing sitcom. Although the show did not feature continuing stories as a rule, the final episode ended on a cliffhanger with Benson and series regular Governor Gatling (James Noble) awaiting the results of a gubernatorial election that pitted the two men against each other. The show had lasted a total of seven seasons while *Soap* had lasted four.

The soap spoof *Mary Hartman, Mary Hartman* spun off a talk-show spoof titled *Fernwood 2-Night*. Hosting *Fernwood 2-Night* was Barth Gimble (played by Martin Mull), twin brother to *Mary Hartman's* Garth Gimble. The show ran during the summer hiatus between *Mary Hartman's* first and second seasons. It returned the next summer as *America 2-Night*.

8 PROPOSED SPIN-OFFS THAT NEVER HAPPENED

1-2. *The Doug and Julie Show* and *The Roman and Marlena Show*

In the 1970s, Doug and Julie Williams (Bill Hayes and Susan Seaforth Hayes) were the reigning supercouple on *Days of Our Lives*. They had made the cover of *Time* magazine and were appearing on game shows like *Hollywood Squares*. Come the early '80s, that crown passed on to Roman Brady and Marlena Evans (Wayne Northrop and Deidre Hall). The producers naturally wanted to capitalize on each couple's success and spin them off into a series all their own. Both projects died in the boardroom. Maybe the NBC executives felt the network had been burned by spinning shows off from *Another World*, whose quality and ratings suffered tremendously from writers spreading themselves too thin and the show losing key players.

3. Calliope

In the late '80s, Arleen Sorkin was incredibly popular as Calliope Jones, the comic heroine of *Days of Our Lives.* Her popularity gave way to speculation that maybe the public might enjoy a comic soap opera. There had not been a successful soap opera comedy since *Soap* had gone off the air in 1981. *Calliope* would have sent Calliope and her husband, Eugene Bradford (John de Lancie), back to Queens, where Calliope had grown up. Unlike with Doug and Julie and then Roman and Marlena, Calliope and Eugene were not front-burner characters. Their departure might hurt but would not devastate the show. Unfortunately, the writers' strike delayed the project. By the time it ended, NBC had already set in motion plans to launch *Generations* and had no room on its schedule for another new soap opera.

Note: After *Calliope* went south, Sorkin developed a comic soap opera for HBO titled *Dirty Laundry.* She described the series as a cross between *thirtysomething* and *Mary Hartman, Mary Hartman.* The lead character was an out-of-work soap opera actor. Like *Calliope*, though, *Dirty Laundry* never made it on the air.

4. Pacific Lives

Rather than steal characters from *Days of Our Lives*, *Pacific Lives* would have revived characters who had already left the show. Fronting the cast was to have been Tom Horton, Jr., who had been written off *Days* in 1979. Also expected to be included were Tom, Jr.'s daughter, Sandy, as well as his brother, Bill, and their sister, Marie. While the show would have been set in Hawaii, action would have extended to Tokyo and Tahiti. *Days* executive producer Ken Corday felt that the Hawaiian setting would have lent itself quite nicely to frequent crossovers between the shows, with characters going on vacation or on the lam. The producers had hoped to coincide the launch date of *Pacific Lives* with the twenty-fifth anniversary of *Days of Our Lives*, November 8, 1990.

5. Manhattan Lives

(Also considered as a title was *Body and Soul.*)

In 1991, when *Days of Our Lives* was trying to lure Deidre Hall back to the show, one of the perks it offered was the development deal for a series of her own. Hall was unsure what kind of show to develop for herself until she remembered the Roman and Marlena spin-off that had been proposed in the early '80s. The original bible for *Manhattan Lives*, however, did not include Roman. The title *Manhattan Lives* was chosen to play off the New York setting and to denote the show as a *Days of Our Lives* spin-off. As part of the development deal, Hall was to have been executive producer of the show. *Manhattan Lives* and another soap-in-development titled *Coming of Age* were seen as rivals for the time slot that *Santa Barbara* would be vacating, but NBC decided to go with non-soap programming for the hour.

6. *The Girl from Peyton Place*

The title role *Girl from Peyton Place* was to be Betty Anderson, as played by Barbara Parkins. Although Parkins had stayed with *Peyton Place* for its entire run, she didn't want to continue with the character when it ended. Having made *The Valley of the Dolls* in 1967, she wanted to break into feature films as her former leading man, Ryan O'Neal (Rodney Harrington), was doing. Without Parkins as Betty, the producers didn't think the series would fly.

7. *The Young Loves of General Hospital*

The mania surrounding *General Hospital*'s Luke and Laura (Tony Geary and Genie Francis) had naturally given rise to talk of a spin-off. Ultimately, ABC cancelled the project because it worried that a spin-off would cut too deeply into *General Hospital*'s quality and its ratings. Neither did the network go for the idea of introducing a set of new characters into Port Charles merely to spin them off into a new series.

8. A *Knots Landing* Summer Series

During the late '80s, prime-time soap operas were losing viewers over the course of the summer hiatus. Not all the fans left hanging in May were coming back in September. The producers of *Knots Landing* wondered whether a summer-time spin-off might keep viewers from switching their allegiance to *L.A. Law* over the summer. The benefits of focusing a summer spin-off on a younger cast would have been twofold: The show could appeal to a younger audience who, without homework to do, would be staying up later during the summer months; and a younger cast would cost less than the older established actors. Nicollette Sheridan as Mack's newfound daughter, Paige, was growing into an audience favorite, and the producers expected *Days of Our Lives* superstar Peter Reckell, who had joined the show midseason, to achieve similar popularity with prime-time audiences. Reckell's character, however, petered out early during the next season, and Reckell left the show. As the show's ratings continued to shrink so did producers' interest in any spin-offs.

10 PROPOSED SOAP OPERAS THAT NEVER AIRED

1. *Scruples*

Judith Krantz's novel about the fashion industry had been turned into a popular mini-series on CBS during the late '70s. Former *General Hospital* and *Days of Our Lives* headwriter Pat Falken Smith got Krantz's permission to base a soap opera on the book. Although the *Scruples* mini-series had done well on CBS, NBC was the network interested in running it as a daytime soap. Falken Smith intended to move the story's setting to Los Angeles and film scenes on Rodeo Drive. In the end, NBC opted to air another California-based soap, *Santa Barbara*.

2. *Apartment 3-G*

In the mid-'60s, ABC made plans to bring the comic strip *Apartment 3-G* to television as a daily soap opera. The strip, which had begun in 1961, followed the lives of three working women who shared the same apartment. While the setting was a natural, and the potential for cross-promotion enviable, the show was one of the casualties when a proposed merger between ABC and AT&T was shot down by the government. Over the past thirty years, the comic strip has been optioned a number of times for adaptation as prime-time series and movies-of-the-week.

3. *Heart and Soul*

Back in the '80s, O. J. Simpson was working with Columbia Pictures to develop the first black daytime soap opera. The show would have been set in Los Angeles and would have revolved around the music industry, opening up the opportunity for singers to guest star on the show. That series never came to pass, but in 1989, NBC did launch *Generations*, the first fully integrated soap opera on television.

4. *The Soul Survivors*

When the late Doug Marland took over the headwriting duties on *As the World Turns*, part of his agreement with CBS was that he would develop a new soap opera for the network. Up till the time of his death, he had been working on *The Soul Survivors*, which he set in an industrial New England community. The show, he had said, would have a harder edge than other shows he had written.

5. *Casino*

In the early '80s, the Washington DC–based *Capitol* started something of a trend among daytime soaps, moving away from fictional towns in the East and

Midwest: *Santa Barbara*, *The Bold and the Beautiful* (set in Los Angeles), and *Generations* (set in Chicago). Continuing that trend, *Capitol*'s executive producer John Conboy and writer Peggy O'Shea developed *Casino*, which would be set in Las Vegas. Conboy felt that the location lent itself to a great deal of drama and glamour. ABC agreed and optioned the project but never found space for another half hour of soaps in its afternoon schedule.

6. Salem's Children

Salem's Children was created by Stephen and Elinor Karpf (who created *Capitol*) along with their son Jason. Set on an island off the coast of Massachusetts, the show spanned several centuries. The Gothic nature of the show, coupled with the varying time frames, led some insiders to compare the show with *Dark Shadows*. It was also said that the show was the most expensive soap opera ever to be produced, a distinction which may very well have steered networks away from picking it up. The show did, however, go further than most soaps-in-development. A pilot episode for the series was actually filmed.

7. Wild Palms

While writing *The Edge of Night*, Henry Slesar developed a crime drama of his own for Procter & Gamble which he titled *Wild Palms*. The show would have been set in a small town in Florida that was run by a ruthless mobster. Years previously, Slesar had submitted to Procter & Gamble the outline for a soap he wanted to create, a spy serial titled *Cannon*.

8. Coming of Age

Although the Bell family has done well on CBS—Bill Bell and his wife created *The Young and the Restless* and *The Bold and the Beautiful*— *The Bold and the Beautiful* producer Bill Bell, Jr., created the soap opera *Coming of Age* for NBC. As with *The Bold and the Beautiful*, Los Angeles served as the setting for *Coming of Age*. Despite the image the title implies, the show would not have dealt with teenagers but with characters in their 20s and early 30s. Unlike traditional daytime soaps, *Coming of Age* would not have revolved around a core family but rather a core group of friends the way prime-time serials like *Beverly Hills 90210* and *Melrose Place* do. *Coming of Age* and the *Days of Our Lives* spin-off *Manhattan Lives* were both considered as replacements for *Another World*, which has long been threatened with cancellation. Ultimately, NBC decided to renew its contract with *Another World*.

9. *Jackie Collins's Sunset West*

In 1991 Jackie Collins fused two of her best-selling novels, *Chances* and *Lucky*, into a successful NBC mini-series that starred a number of soap opera actors. On the strength of that project, coupled with Collins's continuing appeal on the best-seller lists, CBS gave her the go-ahead to create a prime-time soap opera of her own. Collins was more than a little familiar with the prime-time soap genre; her sister, Joan, starred on *Dynasty*, and Collins herself was a great fan of *Knots Landing*. *Sunset West* would have been populated with the types of Hollywood characters that made Collins's novels so popular: the male model, the aging actress, the limo driver, the photojournalist—all of them living in the same Los Angeles apartment building. Despite CBS's commitment to a pilot film and six subsequent episodes, the show never made it on the air. The show was expected to run during the 1992–93 season—the same year that Fox launched *Melrose Place*, a prime-time soap focusing on the lives of eight tenants living in a Los Angeles apartment complex.

10. *The Women's Group*

The Women's Group was developed for ABC by best-selling novelist Erica Jong (*Fear of Flying*) and Linda Yellen, who had worked on a number of TV projects as director, producer, and writer. Neither woman had ever worked on daytime, but both were attracted to do one because of the number of people soaps reach. The show would have focused on the way women communicate when they are alone with each other. To get a feel for the genre and an inside look at the way soaps are produced the women visited sets of the ABC soaps filmed in New York.

2

In Character

ORIGINS OF 10 CHARACTERS' NAMES

1. Mike Bauer, *Guiding Light*

Charita Bauer, who played Bert Bauer on *Guiding Light*, requested that the writers name Bert's son, Mike, after Charita's own son. With the soaps being taped live at the time, Charita was afraid that she might slip and call her onscreen son by her real-life son's name.

2. Dean Frame, *Another World*

Envisioned as a teen rebel, Dean Frame (Ricky Paull Goldin) was named after *Rebel without a Cause* star James Dean.

3. Laura Palmer, *Twin Peaks*

David Lynch filled *Twin Peaks* with countless movie references. Laura Palmer's (Sheryl Lee) first name is one such reference, taken from the Otto Preminger film *Laura* in which the title character is found dead at the beginning of the film. The name Waldo Laedecker, given to a minor character on the show, also comes from the movie *Laura*.

4. Lauralee Brooks, *The Young and the Restless*

Bill Bell named Lauralee after his daughter, Lauralee Bell, who would grow up to star on the show as Christine ("Cricket") Blair.

5. Macy Alexander, *The Bold and the Beautiful*

Given Sally Spectra's (Darlene Conley) background as a knockoff designer from New York, it made perfect sense that her daughter Macy's (Bobbie Eakes) name would be borrowed from two department stores back East: the world-famous Macy's and the lesser-known (and now bankrupt) Alexander's.

6. Edmund Grey, *All My Children*

The writers for *All My Children* dug into Shakespeare for Edmund Grey's (John Callahan) name. In *King Lear*, Edmund is the bastard son of the Duke of Gloucester just as *All My Children*'s Edmund is the bastard son of Hungarian royal Hugo Marrick.

7. Tess Wilder, *The City* (played by Catherine Hickland)

Tess was named after the title heroine in Thomas Hardy's *Tess of the d'Urbervilles*.

8. Holden Snyder, *As the World Turns* (played by Jon Hensley)

The first name Holden was chosen after Holden Caulfield, the main character in J. D. Salinger's classic novel *Catcher in the Rye*. Douglas Marland, who created the Snyder clan, loved the name Holden and at one point intended to use it as the family name for the Snyders. Snyder is the family name of Marland's mother.

9. Andrew Carpenter, *One Life to Live*

Reverend Carpenter's (Wortham Krimmer) last name was chosen in homage to Jesus Christ's being a carpenter.

10. Sly Donovan, *The Bold and the Beautiful*

The show capitalized on Brent Jasmer's resemblance to superstar Sylvester "Sly" Stallone, by giving his character the nickname Sly. Donovan's real, but seldom-mentioned, first name is Irving.

12 CHARACTERS WHO WERE TRANSPLANTED FROM ONE SOAP TO ANOTHER

1. Jeremy Hunter (Jean LeClerc)
   From *All My Children* to *Loving*

   Jeremy and Ceara Connor (Genie Francis) paid a sweeps month visit to *Loving*'s Corinth in 1992. After Francis left *All My Children*, Jeremy was transferred to *Loving* on a full-time basis to bring LeClerc's fans over to that show, which lagged far behind *All My Children* in the ratings. (Ceara, who had been living in London, was killed off to free Jeremy up for romantic adventures with the women in Corinth.) On his way from Pine Valley to Corinth, Jeremy stopped off briefly in *One Life to Live*'s Llanview.

2. Austin Cushing (Rod Arrants)
   From *Lovers and Friends* to *Another World* to *For Richer, for Poorer*

   In May of 1977, the three-month-old *Lovers and Friends* went off the air to undergo major renovations. The show resurfaced six months later with a new title, *For Richer, for Poorer*. During the renovation, the show's star Rod Arrants had been asked to stay on, and his character, Austin Cushing, was written into *Another World*. (*Lovers and Friends* co-creator Harding Lemay was *Another World*'s headwriter at the time.) It was hoped that Arrants would make an impression on *Another World* and bring some of its audience over to *For Richer, for Poorer*.

3–4. Angie and Frankie Hubbard (Debbi Morgan and Alimi Ballard)
   From *All My Children* to *Loving/The City*

   Debbi Morgan left *All My Children* in 1990 to join *Generations*, and the role of Angie Hubbard was recast. When the recast didn't work out, Angie and her son, Frankie, were written out of the show. Morgan returned to the role of Angie in 1993, but not to *All My Children*. The character resurfaced on *Loving* with her now teenaged son, Frankie. In 1995, Darnell Williams, who had played Angie's husband, Jesse Hubbard, on *All My Children*, joined the cast of *Loving* as a Jesse look-alike.

5–6. Mike and Hope Bauer (Gary Pillar and Elissa Leeds)
   From *Guiding Light* to *Another World*

   Mike and Hope didn't just move from one show to another, they moved from one network to another (from CBS to NBC). They stayed in *Another World*'s Bay

City for only a year, just long enough for Mike to get romantically tangled between the married Pat Randolph (Beverly Penberthy) and her stepdaughter, Lee (Barbara Rodell). When that triangle ended badly, he and Hope headed back to *Guiding Light*'s Springfield.

7. Mitchell Dru (Geoffrey Lumb)

From *The Brighter Day* to *As the World Turns* to *Another World*

Irna Phillips, who had created all three shows, shipped Lumb as Mitchell Dru, a minor character, from show to show.

8–9. Melinda and Sal Lopez (Jennifer Lopez and Pepe Serna)

From *Second Chances* to *Hotel Malibu*

The audience had responded well to the Hispanic father and daughter Melinda and Sal Lopez when Lynn Marie Latham and Bernard Lechowick introduced them on the short-lived *Second Chances*. So Latham and Lechowick moved the two of them over to their follow-up series, *Hotel Malibu*, which also proved to be short-lived.

10. Marco Dane (Gerald Anthony)

From *One Life to Live* to *General Hospital*

Anthony left *One Life to Live* in 1986 but paid occasional, short-term visits back to the show. In 1992, the character resurfaced in *General Hospital*'s Port Charles. Anthony, who had been nominated for an Emmy for playing Marco on *One Life to Live*, picked up the trophy for playing him on *General Hospital*.

11–12. Sheila Carter (Kimberlin Brown) and Lauren Fenmore (Tracey E. Bregman)

From *The Young and the Restless* to *The Bold and the Beautiful*

After Sheila switched Lauren Fenmore's baby with one who died and then tried to kill not only Lauren but her own mother too, *The Young and the Restless* creator Bill Bell didn't see how he could keep the evil nurse around town. But he didn't want to lose the character either. She was too good a villain and too popular with the audience. So, instead of sending her off to prison or to her death, he sent her to Los Angeles, writing her into the cast of *The Bold and the Beautiful* (which Bell had also created). Sheila has occasionally snuck back to Genoa City to harass Lauren, and Lauren has chased her back to Los Angeles. Crossover storylines have increased ratings on both shows. In 1995, Bregman herself moved from frequent guest star to official castmember on *The Bold and the Beautiful* as Lauren relocated to Los Angeles to work with Eric Forrester on an exclusive fashion line for her department store.

12 REAL PEOPLE UPON WHOM SOAP CHARACTERS WERE MODELED

1. Irna Phillips

Irna Phillips—who had created such soap operas as *Guiding Light*, *As the World Turns*, and *Another World*—became a soap opera character herself when her adopted daughter, Katherine Phillips, created the soap opera *A World Apart*. The show's lead heroine, Betty Kahlman (played by Augusta Dabney, then Elizabeth Lawrence), was a never-married soap opera writer with two adopted children, Patrice and Chris. In real life, in addition to Katherine, Irna Phillips had adopted a boy named Thomas. Irna Phillips served as story editor for the show. A year after *A World Apart* went off the air, Irna Phillips returned to *As the World Turns* and wrote herself into the show in the character of Kim Reynolds (played by Kathryn Hays). In one interview, recounted in Robert LaGuardia's *Soap World*, Phillips said of Kim: "She's fiercely independent, as I was, and she won't settle for second best. She looks in the mirror and still refers to herself as 'the lady in the mirror.'" (One of the titles Phillips considered for her never-finished autobiography was *The Lady in the Mirror*.) Phillips went on to compare Kim's decision to have Bob Hughes's child out of wedlock with her own decision as a single woman to adopt two children.

2. Eartha Kitt

One Life to Live creator Agnes Nixon saw singer/actress Eartha Kitt on a talk show, discussing the plight of being a light-skinned black in the South, rejected by whites and darker-skinned blacks alike. From that story evolved the character of Carla Gray (played on the show by Ellen Holly), a light-skinned black woman who tried to pass herself off as white.

3. Jackie Collins

As Joan Collins was rising to popularity as *Dynasty*'s Alexis Carrington Colby, her sister Jackie Collins was climbing up the best-seller list with novels like *Chances* and *Hollywood Wives.* In 1986, *Dynasty* introduced the character of Caress Morrell, Alexis's sister, a writer. In the role was cast Kate O'Mara, a Jackie Collins look-alike.

4. Mary Ryan Munisteri

Ryan's Hope co-creator Claire Labine modeled and named the character of Mary Ryan after her friend Mary Ryan Munisteri, who herself eventually became the show's headwriter.

5. Heidi Fleiss

Heidi Fleiss made headlines during the summer of 1993 when she was arrested for being a top Hollywood madam, supplying prostitutes to actors and show business executives. By the fall, *Melrose Place* had its own Hollywood madam, Lauren Etheridge (Kristian Alfonso) who lured Sydney Andrews (Laura Leighton) into the business.

6. Marybeth Whitehead

Surrogate mother Marybeth Whitehead had signed an agreement to conceive a child for William and Elizabeth Stern. After the baby was born, Whitehead changed her mind about giving her baby up, and a custody battle ensued. When *Dynasty*'s Dana Carrington (Leann Hunley) admitted to her husband, Adam (Gordon Thomson), that she was sterile, the two decided to find a surrogate mother. While Karen Atkinson (Stephanie Dunnham) agreed to bear Adam's baby, family enemy Sean Rowan (James Healey) manipulated her to keep the baby and fight for custody.

7. Jacqueline Susann

The late Jacqueline Susann, author of *Valley of the Dolls* and *The Love Machine*, had been friends with *Another World* headwriter Robert Soderberg. He created the role of romance novelist Felicia Gallant (played by Linda Dano) in her image.

8. Livia

In Roman history, Livia killed all her stepsons until her favorite, Tiberius, was the only one left to assume the role of emperor. On *Knots Landing,* Claudia Whittaker was conceived in exactly that mode. Among her varied deeds, she brought about her own son's death in order to ensure that her daughter, Kate, received her full inheritance. The writers named Claudia after Livia's grandson Claudius.

9–10. Peter Bogdanovich and Michael Cimino

Santa Barbara's Stephen Slade (Richard Hatch, John O'Hurley) was created as an amalgam of Peter Bogdonavich and Michael Cimino, filmmakers who had garnered incredible attention early in their careers but whose stars had diminished in recent years.

11. Max Jacobson ("Dr. Feelgood")

In the 1960s, Max Jacobson, known as Dr. Feelgood, worked his way into the jet set by peddling drugs in the form of vitamin pills to celebrities such as Andy Warhol. In the 1990s, *All My Children*'s Dr. Jonathan Kinder (Michael Sabatino) wormed his way into Erica Kane's (Susan Lucci) life by supplying her with pain medication (combined with various other drugs) during her recovery from a near-crippling back injury.

12. John F. Kennedy, Jr.

In *Central Park West*, creator Darren Star combined real-life footage of New York City with characters based on famous New Yorkers. None of the show's characters was more thinly disguised than John F. Kennedy, Jr.–clone Peter Fairchild (John Barrowman): the most eligible bachelor in the city, hounded by the press, and an Assistant District Attorney whose late father was a beloved politician and whose mother has remarried an incredibly rich and powerful businessman.

Note: The Whitney family on *The Edge of Night* and the title family *The Monroes* from the short-lived prime-time serial were both loosely based on the Kennedys.

10 CHARACTERS NAMED AFTER THE ACTORS WHO PLAYED THEM

1. Clint Buchanan, *One Life to Live*

Clint Ritchie didn't think the proposed name of Chris Logan was cowboy enough for his character, so the writers relented and named him after the nearest cowboy in sight, Ritchie himself.

2. Carolee Simpson Aldrich, *The Doctors*

When Carolee Campbell began on *The Doctors*, the nurse she played was known simply as Miss Simpson. As the writers expanded the roll and needed a first name for the character, they found Campbell's own first name so interesting that they decided to use it for her character as well.

3. Nathan "Kong" Hastings, *The Young and the Restless*

Nathan Purdee's performance as mob enforcer Kong inspired *The Young and the Restless*'s writers to expand the role. In expanding his name, the writers chose the first name Nathan after Nathan Purdee himself.

4. Steve "Patch" Johnson, *Days of Our Lives*

Like Kong, Patch (played by Stephen Nichols) was originally conceived of as a short-term villain, a henchman of Victor Kiriakis (John Aniston). As such, no last name or real first name had been imagined for the character. When the role was expanded because the audience had taken a liking to Nichols, the character was given the last name Johnson and the first name Steve.

5. Apollonia, *Falcon Crest*

In the mid-'80s, *Falcon Crest* wanted to capitalize on the popularity of Prince's movie *Purple Rain*, and on the growing popularity of music videos in general. (In 1985, when Kotero came on the show, *Falcon Crest* was up against the music-driven crime show *Miami Vice*.) To infuse *Falcon Crest* with music, the show hired Apollonia Kotero to play a rising singer named Apollonia.

6. Brenda McGillis, *One Life to Live*

Brenda Brock so impressed the producers with her turn as Mae McGillis during *One Life to Live*'s Wild West storyline that they created the role of look-alike descendant Brenda McGillis to bring Brock into the current storylines.

7. Keith Jasper, *General Hospital*

Singer Keith Washington was basically playing himself when he played Keith Jasper, a singer at the Outback. As such, the writers didn't bother creating a different name for his character.

8. John Silva, *The Young and the Restless*

John Castellanos, who plays John Silva, found the first names the writers were picking too ethnic-sounding for his character. Under the gun to come up with a name, the writers called him John after John Castellanos, not taking into consideration that there was already a prominently featured John on the show (John

Abbott) as well as a prominently featured Jack (Jack Abbott). As a result, John Silva is usually referred to by his whole name when not being directly addressed in a scene.

9. Elmira Cleebe, *Hawkins Falls*

Elmira Roessler's first name fit in so well with the names of the show's other characters—Clate Weathers, Laif Flaigle, Spec Bassett—that the writers decided to have Roessler use it as her character's name as well.

10. Frank Cooper, *Guiding Light*

The character of garage mechanic Frank Cooper originated on *Guiding Light* as Todd Bauer. When Pam Long came in as a headwriter, she decided not to expand the Bauer family and reshaped the role into Frank Cooper, which she named after Frank Dicopoulos.

6 COUPLES WHO HAVE MARRIED EACH OTHER 3 OR MORE TIMES

1. Cliff Warner and Nina Cortlandt, *All My Children*

Cliff (Peter Bergman) and Nina (Taylor Miller) have been married a total of four times. The first time around they married in an elaborate outdoor ceremony complete with horsedrawn carriages. Although Cliff had gotten Sybil Thorne (Linda Gibboney) pregnant during a brief pre-wedding breakup with Nina, it was Nina's repeated infidelities that led to three divorces. In 1983, Nina slept with her father's lawyer, Steve Jacobi (Dack Rambo). Cliff divorced her, but they remarried offscreen in 1985. During a subsequent bout of amnesia, Nina couldn't remember her marriage to Cliff and had an affair with another of her father's employees, groundskeeper Benny Sago (Vasili Bogazianos). Soon thereafter, Nina was written off the show. Taylor Miller returned in 1986 to facilitate Peter Bergman's departure. They remarried and left for Hong Kong. When Miller decided to come back to the show, Cliff was "killed off," and a grief-stricken Nina threw herself into marriage with ex-mercenary Matt Connolly (Michael Tylo). Cliff turned up alive and divorced Nina for remarrying so quickly after his presumed death—but not before making love to her once, which was enough to get her pregnant. Miller left the show in 1988 and returned the following year to facilitate Bergman's second departure from the show. A medical crisis for Michael (Cliff and Nina's son) brought them back together. The fourth time, they married in a simple ceremony on the grounds of Cortlandt Manor with only immediate family present and have stayed together off-camera ever since.

2. Mac Cory and Rachel Davis, *Another World*

Despite everyone's warnings about what a schemer Rachel Davis (Victoria Wyndham) was, millionaire Mac Cory (Douglass Watson) fell in love with her and married her. They broke up several times but never divorced until gold digger Janice Frame (Christine Jones) came into their lives. After one too many arguments about Janice and about Rachel's problems with her son, Jamie, Mac and Rachel divorced. Janice married Mac and soon began plotting his death. Rachel slept with Janice's partner-in-crime, Mitch Blake (William Gray Espy), to find out exactly what Janice planned to do. Mac and Rachel remarried soon after she saved his life, but Rachel was pregnant by Mitch and eventually left Mac for him. She subsequently left Mitch for her first love, Steve Frame (David Canary), who then died on their honeymoon. Rachel found her way back into Mac's life, and they married a third time, sharing the ceremony with Mac's son, Sandy (Chris Rich), and Rachel's ex-daughter-in-law, Blaine Ewing (Laura Malone). As if three times for real wasn't enough, Mac and Rachel renewed their vows in 1987 shortly before Mac's (and Watson's) death in 1988.

3. Cord Roberts and Tina Lord, *One Life to Live*

When cowboy Cord Roberts (John Loprieno) came into Tina Lord's (Andrea Evans) life, she was torn between him, whom she loved, and her wealthy cousin, Richard Abbott (Jeffrey Byron), who could support her financially. Finding out that Cord was Clint Buchanan's (Clint Ritchie) son and heir to the Buchanan fortune tipped the scale in Cord's favor. (At the time, even Cord didn't know the truth.) Cord eloped with Tina, but their marriage fell apart when Cord discovered that Tina knew he was Clint's son when she married him and said nothing. Their second attempt at marriage fell apart because of another secret: Tina knew that Gabrielle Medina (Fiona Hutchison) had switched Brenda McGillis's (Brenda Brock) baby with a dead one. (Gabrielle bribed Tina into keeping her mouth shut.) Cord's "death" ruined their third marriage. While Cord was presumed dead, Tina fell in love with con artist Cain Rogan (Christopher Cousins). Even when Cord "came back from the dead," Tina was so infatuated with Cain that she couldn't make a go of things with Cord. The marriage to Cain lasted only a few months as did her rebound marriage to David Vickers (Tuc Watkins), who had been masquerading as her long-lost brother. Through it all, Cord and Tina keep coming back to each other and will probably end up married at least a fourth time.

Note: Cord's father, Clint, and Tina's older sister, Vicki (Erika Slezak), have been married to and divorced from each other twice already. Too much of the audience wants a reconciliation between them for a third marriage not to be in their future.

4. Doug Williams and Julie Olson, *Days of Our Lives*

Although con artist/lounge singer Doug Williams (Bill Hayes) and Julie Olson (Susan Seaforth Hayes) fell in love at first sight, it took them five years and various marriages to other people before they finally became husband and wife. Their happiness was spoiled when a grease fire left Julie's face scarred. Afraid that Doug couldn't love her anymore, she ran away to Mexico and got herself a quickie divorce. Doug in turn married his late brother's widow, Lee Dumonde (Brenda Benet), and refused to take Julie back after her plastic surgery. Eventually, they fell back in love. After trying to have Julie killed, Lee changed her mind and consented to a divorce. The two stayed married until Bill Hayes and Susan Seaforth Hayes left the show in 1984. While in Europe, Doug and Julie split, allowing the characters to come back on the show at separate times. When Susan Seaforth Hayes was written off the show in 1993, Julie rejoined Bill, and the couple remarried offscreen.

5. Valene Clements and Gary Ewing, *Knots Landing*

Gary (Ted Shackleford) and Valene (Joan Van Ark) had married as teenagers and were long divorced when *Dallas* first began its run on TV. (The two were occasional guest stars on the show.) They remarried on *Dallas* and were spun off onto *Knots Landing.* Their marriage lasted three full seasons on that show. Valene divorced Gary after his affair with Abby Cunningham. Even while married to other people, Gary and Val remained entwined in each other's life. The show took eight years to bring them back together as husband and wife, which is how they were left when the show went off the air in 1993.

6. Shannon O'Hara and Duncan McKechnie, *As the World Turns*

Shannon (Margaret Reed) was drunk the first time she married Duncan McKechnie (Michael Swan), who she thought died in an avalanche. Duncan showed up alive in Oakdale to break up her wedding to Brian McColl (Mark Pinter). Although they divorced, Duncan was in love with Shannon. He wooed her back and married her in a full ceremony. After she was presumed killed by his first wife, Lilith, Duncan married his lawyer and friend Jessica Griffin (Tamara Tunie). When Shannon showed up alive, Duncan divorced Jessica to remarry Shannon. The two soon discovered that the third marriage was not legal.

6 PAIRS OF IDENTICAL COUSINS

1. Luke Spencer and Bill Eckert, *General Hospital*

When Tony Geary agreed to come back to *General Hospital* in 1991, he wanted to do something different, so producer Gloria Monty created for him the role of Bill Eckert, a look-alike cousin of Luke's. At one point, Bill and Luke's sister, Bobbie Jones (Jacklyn Zeman), shared a passing flirtation. When Genie Francis decided to come back to the show as Laura, and Geary agreed to revive Luke, plans were made to write Bill off. Bill and Luke shared one scene together before Bill was killed by hit men gunning for Luke.

2. Laura Palmer and Maddie Ferguson, *Twin Peaks*

While Laura Palmer was already dead in the first episode of the series, Sheryl Lee, who played the corpse, was soon cast as Laura's look-alike brunette cousin, Maddie Ferguson. A few episodes into the second season, Maddie was killed by her uncle, Leland Palmer (Ray Wise), who was possessed by a demon and had also killed Laura. Like Laura, Maddie's dead body was discovered wrapped in plastic.

3. Mary Frances Sumner and Kate Whittaker, *Knots Landing*

Although Danielle Brisebois (from *All in the Family*) originated the role of Greg Sumner's (William Devane) daughter Mary Frances, Stacy Galina played the role for a couple of episodes in 1990—just long enough for the character to be killed off. Galina resurfaced the following season as Greg's niece Kate Whittaker, a red-haired ringer for his dead daughter. Eventually, the show let Galina's hair go back to its natural color.

4. Frannie Hughes and Sabrina Fullerton, *As the World Turns*

Frannie and Sabrina were not simply first cousins; they were half-sisters as well. They shared a father, Bob Hughes, and their mothers were sisters, Jennifer Hughes and Kim Reynolds. Although Kim believed that the baby she had with Bob died at birth, the girl had in truth been stolen and put up for adoption. Frannie discovered her sister/cousin while traveling in Europe. Julianne Moore, who was playing Frannie at the time, originated the role of Sabrina, but after Moore left, the roles were given to two different actresses.

5. André and Tony DiMera, *Days of Our Lives*

During the Salem Slasher storyline, everyone was shocked to see hero Roman Brady (Wayne Northrop) commit one of the murders. At one point, the villain pulled off a Roman Brady face mask to reveal the face of Tony DiMera (Thaao Penghlis), another audience favorite. As it turned out, the killer was not Tony but rather Tony's evil cousin, André, who had had plastic surgery to make himself look like Tony. While they were trapped on a deserted island together, Tony ended up killing André.

6. Jack Stanfield Lee and Jerry Cooper, *Santa Barbara*

During one of *Santa Barbara*'s earliest and oddest storylines, Jack Stanfield Lee (Joel Crothers) had had an unsuspecting Amy Perkins (Kerry Sherman) impregnated with the sperm of a dead prince—all part of a grand plot to take over the kingdom of New Stailand. In a plot twist inspired by *The Prisoner of Zenda*, Jack turned out not to be Jack but rather an evil cousin named Jerry Cooper, who had undergone plastic surgery to look like Jack. The real Jack, who was locked away back in New Stailand, was rescued by Amy and her boyfriend, Brick Wallace (Richard Eden).

11 GAY, LESBIAN, AND BISEXUAL CHARACTERS

1–2. Ed and Howard McCullough, *Mary Hartman, Mary Hartman*

1976: Although Ed and Howard McCullough were originally introduced on *Mary Hartman* as brothers, the audience and the neighborhood soon learned the real truth about them: they weren't brothers, they were lovers. It was one more controversy the show's many protesters could complain about.

3. Sharon Duval, *Days of Our Lives*

1976: Sharon (Sally Stark) arrived in Salem with her husband, Karl (Alejandro Rey), as a friend of Julie Williams (Susan Seaforth Hayes). The audience no doubt expected Sharon's husband to be attracted to Julie, which he was. What came as a shock, though, was that Sharon herself shared those same feelings. After she admitted those feelings to both Julie and Karl, Sharon and her husband were quickly written off the show.

4. Jodie Dallas, *Soap*

1977: *Soap* wasn't sure what it wanted to do with Jodie (Billy Crystal) at first. Not only was he gay, he was a cross-dresser and a preoperative transsexual. By the end of the season, though, he ended up in bed with a woman. After that, Jodie had no serious boyfriends on the show. Instead, he became involved emotionally but not sexually with his lesbian roommate, and during the show's final season, he fell in love with a female detective (Barbara Rhoades), with whom he enjoyed a sexual relationship.

5. Steven Carrington, *Dynasty*

1981: Stephen (Al Corley, later Jack Coleman) started off as a homosexual, the first lead gay character in a drama series. Before the end of the first season, however, he slept with a woman, Claudia Blaisdel (Pamela Bellwood). During the second season, he married Sammy Jo Dean (Heather Locklear). From then on, Steven fluctuated between men and women.

6. Lynn Carson, *All My Children*

1983: In the beginning, Jackie Smith, head of ABC Daytime, wanted to do a gay storyline involving a male character. Since it had already been done on *Dynasty*, the producers decided to do a lesbian story instead. Donna Pescow, who had starred in the sitcom *Angie*, came on the show as a doctor who befriended Devon McFadden (Tricia Pursley) and ultimately revealed to her that she was gay. Although Devon developed a same-sex crush on Lynn, Lynn made Devon realize that she (Devon) was not gay. The storyline won Pescow and *All My Children* awards from the gay and lesbian community.

7. Lindsay Smith, *Santa Barbara*

1985: While Cruz Castillo (A Martinez) was investigating the murder of Channing Capwell, he discovered a love letter written to Channing by a Lindsay

Smith. Cruz and the audience were more than a little shocked to discover that Lindsay Smith (Joel Bailey) was a man and that Channing had led a secret homosexual life. Mason Capwell (Lane Davies) couldn't wait to break the news to his father, C. C. (then Charles Bateman), that his beloved son Channing was gay.

8. Hank Eliot, *As the World Turns*

1988: Doug Marland had long wanted to bring a gay character onto daytime. He'd wanted to do it on *The Doctors* and again on *Another World*. He finally got his chance when he was headwriter for *As the World Turns*. Originally, Marland intended for Hank (Brian Starcher) to die of AIDS. (Up till that point, daytime's only AIDS victims had been women.) Marland changed his mind when he realized that giving daytime's only gay character AIDS would perpetuate the myth that all gay men had AIDS. Instead, Hank's out-of-town (and off-the-show) lover, Charles, discovered he was HIV positive, but Hank himself was not infected.

9. Billy Douglas, *One Life to Live*

1992: *One Life to Live* took a risk not only in introducing a homosexual character but a teenaged one at that during the summer of 1992. *One Life to Live* headwriter Michael Malone originally wanted Joey Buchanan (then played by Chris McKenna), a character with whom the audience was already familiar, to be gay. Billy's (Ryan Phillippe) sexual orientation sparked a plotline that found Reverend Andrew Carpenter (Wortham Krimmer) accused both of child molestation and of being gay himself. The dual climax to the homophobia storyline came when the AIDS quilt was brought to town and Billy announced to the community that he was gay. Billy was given a boyfriend but was written off the show by the next summer.

10. Matt Fielding, *Melrose Place*

1992: As Matt Fielding, Doug Savant has gone through a slew of gay storylines: he's been gay-bashed; he's lost his job because of his sexual preference twice and had to sue to get it back; his love interest Jeffrey, a military man, had to keep his sexuality secret or risk court-martial; and later Jeffrey revealed to Matt that he was HIV positive. During a storyline where Matt was helping Dr. Michael Mancini (Thomas Calabro) with his varied illegal schemes, Savant wanted to play the story as though Matt was falling in love with Michael, but the producers didn't go for it.

11. Michael Delaney, *All My Children*

1995: It struck many people as suspicious that *All My Children* would hire former

Another World heartthrob Chris Bruno (Dennis Wheeler) to play history teacher Michael Delaney and not bother pairing him up with any of the show's leading ladies. Six months after the character debuted, Michael revealed to Dixie Martin (Cady McLain) that he was gay.

Notes: In the mid-'70s, Mike Horton on *Days of Our Lives* (then played by Wesley Eure) worried that he might be gay because he couldn't make love to his girlfriend, Trish Clayton (Patty Weaver). An affair with Linda Patterson (Margaret Mason) quickly got that idea out of his head. Katherine Chancellor (Jeanne Cooper) at one point grew a little too close to her assistant Joann Curtis (Kay Heberle) on *The Young and the Restless*. A kiss between the two women sent the ratings tumbling, and their friendship was ended right before the two were to take a trip to Hawaii together. Although *Dallas* had introduced a gay character for one episode in the second season—Lucy (Charlene Tilton) almost married him—the show scrapped its much publicized plans to make Angelica Nero (Barbara Carrera) and her female assistant lovers.

3 BLACK CHARACTERS WHO MASQUERADED AS WHITE

1. Carla Gray, *One Life to Live*

One of *One Life to Live*'s first storylines concerned the light-skinned Carla Gray (Ellen Holly), who attempted to pass herself off as white in Llanview society. Using the name Benari, Carla let people believe she was Italian. For the first few months that *One Life* was on the air, not even the TV audience was clued into Carla's true identity. A kiss between her and Dr. Price Trainor (Thurman Scott, later Peter DeAnda), a black intern, was therefore perceived as interracial and set the switchboards at ABC lighting up with complaints from viewers. In addition to Price, Carla had also become involved with Jim Craig (Robert Milli), a white doctor for whom she worked as a secretary. Although Carla eventually chose Price, his family rejected her, in an ironic turn of events, because of the lightness of her skin color.

2. Tyrone Jackson, *The Young and the Restless*

Law student Tyrone Jackson (Phil Morris) went undercover twice to break up the mob that was ruling Genoa City. Mob kingpin Mr. Anthony (Logan Ramsey) discovered his plan the first time around and put a contract out on

Tyrone's life. In order to stay alive, Tyrone pretended to be dead and—with an extensive make-up job—disguised himself as a white man. A second opportunity to infiltrate the mob soon presented itself when Mr. Anthony's daughter, Alana (Amy Gibson), moved into Tyrone's building and became infatuated with Tyrone's white alter ego, Robert. While exploiting Alana's infatuation as a means to get back into her father's organization, Tyrone ended up falling in love. He did not reveal his true identity to her until their wedding night. Even after Alana shot him, Tyrone wanted to make things work, but Alana couldn't deal with his betrayal and left town.

3. Taylor Roxbury Cannon, *All My Children*

Rookie cop Taylor Roxbury Cannon (then Ingrid Rodgers) wanted to break up a white racist group that was operating on the campus of Pine Valley University. With a blonde wig and an extensive make-up job, she transformed herself into a Greek shipping heiress. While in disguise, she attracted the attention of two of the group's core members. Using romance to find out their secrets backfired when Taylor's wig came off while she was kissing one of them. Taylor managed to escape and warn her stepbrother, Terrence (Dondre Whitfield), that his house was rigged to blow up. Although she herself didn't get out of the house in time, she did survive the explosion.

10 RAPISTS WHO EVOLVED INTO LEADING MEN

1. Luke Spencer, *General Hospital*

In one of the most famous soap opera scenes of all time, Luke Spencer (Tony Geary) gave in to his obsession with newlywed Laura Baldwin (Genie Francis) and raped her on the floor of his disco. Not only did Laura not name Luke as her attacker, she ended up leaving her husband for him. As they fell in love, Luke and Laura's popularity as a couple soared. When Tony Geary made personal appearances promoting the show, women in the audience would often shout, "Rape me, Luke." (Geary found such cries more than a little disconcerting.) At one point, some time after the rape happened, Laura referred to the incident as "the first time we made love." More than just a romantic leading man, Luke became a superhero, saving Port Charles from mobsters and mad scientists.

2. Todd Manning, *One Life to Live*

As happened with Tony Geary, Roger Howarth, who played gang rapist Todd Manning, has been met with shouts of "Rape me, Todd!" while making personal appearances. At a fraternity party, Todd and two of his fraternity brothers cornered Marty Saybrooke (Susan Haskell) in a bedroom, and Todd initiated a gang rape. It was later revealed that Todd once had date-raped another student. And when Todd escaped from prison, he tried to rape his lawyer, Nora Gannon (Hillary B. Smith), while she was blind. Despite the horrible things his character did, the audience saw something good in him and demanded to see more of it. The writers, who originally envisioned Todd as a short-term villain, put the character through a series of heroic redemptions: pulling children out of a burning car, rescuing a blind woman from muggers, and helping the police catch a rapist who had been stalking Llanview Hospital. Howarth's personal objection to Todd's transformation into a romantic lead prompted the actor to seek an early release from his contract, which the show granted him.

3. Jack Deveraux, *Days of Our Lives*

Although Kayla Brady (Mary Beth Evans) was in love with Steve "Patch" Johnson (Stephen Nichols), Patch convinced her to marry his long-lost brother, Jack Deveraux (Joseph Adams, later Matthew Ashford), who was suffering from Hodgkin's disease. Infuriated by Kayla's unending love for Patch and her refusal to make love, Jack forcibly consummated the marriage. Because Kayla was such a popular character, *Soap Opera Digest* once ran a photo of Matthew Ashford on its cover naming him "The Most Hated Man on Daytime." Rather than send Jack off to prison or turn him into an out-and-out villain, the show took a decidedly different route. It paired him with the virginal Jennifer Horton (Melissa Reeves). Through the pairing, Jack soon evolved into both a romantic lead and a comic hero. Even Patch and Kayla forgave the new, improved Jack and invited him to be best man at their second wedding.

4. Lawrence Alamain, *Days of Our Lives*

While posing as Katarina Von Leuschner, Jennifer Horton (Melissa Reeves) "married" the villainous Lawrence Alamain (Michael Sabatino). On their wedding night, Lawrence caught Jennifer snooping around in his room and took that as her consent to have sex with him despite her protests to the contrary. During the next few years, the real Katarina (Crystal Chappell), who called herself Carly, found herself caught in a triangle between Lawrence, who had raped her best friend, and the heroic Bo Brady (Peter Reckell, later Robert Kelker-Kelly), who had saved her life on more than occasion. While the choice would seem obvious, the audience, like Carly herself, was torn between Bo and Lawrence. Many fans wanted to see Carly with the handsome and charming Lawrence despite the sins he had committed in the past. Carly ended up leaving Salem with Lawrence and a long-lost son they had recently discovered.

5. Roger Thorpe, *Guiding Light*

By the time, Roger Thorpe (Michael Zaslow) had been "killed off" in 1980, he had raped his own wife, Holly (Maureen Garrett), as well as Ed Bauer's (then Peter Simon) wife, Rita (Lenore Kasdorf). When Roger returned to life nine years later, he tried time and again to win back his ex-wife, Holly. The majority of the people watching in the '90s either had not seen the scenes in which Roger forced himself on Holly or didn't care because the audience was actually rooting for a reconciliation between the two, which eventually happened.

6. Jake McKinnon, *Another World*

Jake McKinnon (Tom Eplin) raped his ex-wife, Marley Love (then Anne Heche), after she broke off their reconciliation. When Jake was subsequently shot by a blond woman, Marley went on trial for it. She did not, however, press charges against Jake when he came out of his coma. As a way of penance, Jake made a large contribution to the rape crisis center where Marley worked. Soon thereafter he was paired with Paulina Cory (Calli Timmons, Judi Evans Luciano), who happened to be the blonde who shot him. The two became one of the show's favorite couples. Their storylines ranged from comedy to action adventure. When Jake was presumed dead and written off the show, his funeral—a hero's sendoff—was attended by most of the show's major characters, including Marley's mother, Donna Hudson (Anna Stuart), and Marley's twin sister, Vicky (played now by Jensen Buchanan), who had remained best friends with Jake despite what he had done.

7. Ross Chandler, *All My Children*

In a moment of anger over losing his wife, Ellen (Kathleen Noone), Ross Chandler (Robert Gentry) raped his former mistress Natalie Cortlandt (Kate Collins), who happened to be married at the time to his father, Palmer Cortlandt (James Mitchell). Ross eventually confessed to the crime and went to prison for it for a few months. He escaped from prison long enough to rescue his daughter, Julie (Lauren Holly), from a kidnaper; a few months later, while on a furlough, he saved his family from a bomb that had been planted at his uncle Stuart's (David Canary) wedding. Prior to the rape, Ross had never been so heroic nor so adventurous. After he was released from prison, he even managed to become Natalie's confidante, listening to the problems she was having with her new husband, Jeremy Hunter (Jean LeClerc).

8. Josh Snyder, *As the World Turns*

When the character of Iva Snyder (Lisa Brown) was introduced on *As the World Turns*, it was revealed that she was Lily Walsh's (Martha Byrne) biological mother, the result of having been raped at age thirteen by her cousin Josh. Eventually, Josh (William Fichtner) showed up in town. He himself eventually admitted that he had been molested as a child and underwent treatment. Josh was paired first with Betsy Andropolous (Lindsay Frost), one of the show's lead heroines, and later with Meg Snyder (Jennifer Ashe), Iva's adopted sister.

9. Adam Carrington, *Dynasty*

During a dinner date with Kirby Anders (Kathleen Beller), Adam Carrington (Gordon Thomson) forced himself on her. Kirby married Jeff Colby (John James) and didn't tell him about the rape until she realized she was pregnant by Adam. When Kirby miscarried the baby, a devastated Adam stood by her, and they got engaged. Although separated by the machinations of Adam's mother, Alexis (Joan Collins), the two reunited during the *Dynasty* reunion movie.

10. Miles Colby, *The Colbys*

The *Dynasty* reunion movie also saw a loving reunion between yet another rapist and victim, Miles Colby (Maxwell Caulfield) and Fallon Carrington (Emma Samms). In a near carbon copy of the Adam/Kirby plotline, Miles had raped Fallon, who became pregnant and didn't know whether the baby was his or his brother Jeff's. (It turned out to be Jeff's.) Despite the rape, the *Dynasty* reunion started off with Fallon back together with Miles and spurning Jeff's attempts at reconciliation.

Note: Todd Manning was not the only gang rapist whom *One Life to Live*'s audience was willing to forgive. Powell Lord (Sean Moynihan), the penitent rapist, seemed on his way to becoming a romantic leading man. He was, in fact, on the other side of a love triangle from Todd; both wanted Rebecca Lewis (Reiko Aylesworth), the woman who brought them God in prison. In a bizarre twist, Powell was revealed to be the ski-masked stalker who had raped two nurses at the hospital.

10 CHARACTERS WHO SLEPT WITH 3 OR MORE MEMBERS OF THE SAME FAMILY

1. Reva Shayne, *Guiding Light*

Although Reva (Kim Zimmer) loved Josh Lewis (Robert Newman), she married his brother, Billy (Jordan Clarke), and his father, H.B. (Larry Gates), before she ended up tying the knot with him. When she had fallen in love with Kyle Sampson (Larkin Malloy), she thought she'd broken free from the Lewises—until he revealed himself to be H.B.'s son by prostitute Sally Gleason (Patricia Barry). Although he turned out not to be H.B.'s son, he did turn out to be Billy's half-brother.

2. Erica Kane, *All My Children*

When Erica Kane (Susan Lucci) became involved in a relationship with the much younger Charlie Brent (then played by Charles Van Eman), his grandfather Nick Davis (Larry Keith) congratulated her for hitting the trifecta. Erica had once been married to Charlie's father, Phil Brent (Richard Hatch, Nicholas Benedict), and, later had fallen in love with Phil's father, Nick, whom she almost married. Although Charlie asked her to marry him, she turned him down.

3. Dorian Lord, *One Life to Live*

In the spring of 1994, Dorian Lord (Robin Strasser) was sentenced to death for the murder of her late husband, Victor Lord, some eighteen years previously. By autumn, she was in bed with his grandson Joey Buchanan (Nathan Fillion). In between, she also had a short-lived affair with Clint Buchanan (Clint Ritchie) before he married Vicki Lord (Erika Slezak) and became Joey's adoptive father. Along the way, Dorian made unsuccessful attempts to win Joey's biological father, Joe Riley (Lee Patterson), and Clint's father, Asa Buchanan (Phil Carey).

Note: Niece Blair Daimler (Mia Korf, Kassie Wesley) is learning well from Aunt Dorian. She has already married Asa and seduced his grandson Cord Roberts (John Loprieno) as well as Max Holden (James De Paiva), who once believed himself to be Asa's son.

4. Scott Eldridge, *As the World Turns*

Scott Eldridge (Joseph Breen, later Doug Wert) did not realize that he was sleeping his way through Lucinda Walsh's (Elizabeth Hubbard) family. After his affair with Lucinda went bust, Scott took up with artistic designer Neal Alcott

(Mary Kay Adams), whom he—and Lucinda—learned months later was really Lucinda's half-sister. Two years later, Scott discovered that another of his former flames, con artist Samantha Markham (Brooke Alexander), was also another of Lucinda's long-lost half-sisters.

5. Delia Reid, *Ryan's Hope*

When *Ryan's Hope* premiered, Delia Reid (Ilene Kristen) was married to Frank Ryan (then played by Michael Hawkins). After divorcing him, she moved on to his brother, Dr. Pat Ryan (Malcolm Groome), whom she also married. When Frank and Pat's father, Johnny (Bernard Barrow), discovered that he had a third son he never knew about by the name of Dakota Smith (Christopher Durham), Delia went after him. She got him into bed but not into a marriage.

6. Blake Lindsey, *Guiding Light*

Before Blake Lindsey (originated by Elizabeth Dennehy and later played by Sherry Stringfield and Liz Keifer) arrived in Springfield, she had had an affair with Alan Spaulding (Chris Bernau). Within her first two years on the show, she married Alan's adopted son, Phillip (Grant Aleksander). Almost immediately upon her divorce from Phillip, she married Alan's biological son, Alan-Michael (Carl Evans, Rick Hearst). She is currently married to Phillip's uncle Ross Marler (Jerry ver Dorn), whom she stole from her own mother, Holly (Maureen Garrett).

7. Jake McKinnon, *Another World*

As if it wasn't bad enough that Jake McKinnon (Tom Eplin) ping-ponged back and forth between twin sisters Vicky and Marley Love (played by Ellen Wheeler, Anne Heche, and Jensen Buchanan), he also went and slept with their mother, Donna Hudson (Anna Stuart).

8. Angel Lange, *As the World Turns*

Before Angel Lange's (Alice Haining) character was introduced on the show, she had been involved with Caleb Snyder (Michael David Morrison) while he'd been living in Chicago. When Jon Hensley (Holden Snyder) left the show, the audience learned that he had married Angel. After Holden returned, their marriage broke up, and Angel got back together with Caleb. The two of them left the show together. Their relationship lasted only until they were brought back on the show. Angel finally married the eldest Snyder, Seth (Steve Bassett), and moved to New York—and off the show—with him.

9. Ava Rescott, *Loving*

Alden-wannabe Ava Rescott (Roya Megnot, later Lisa Peluso) started off with Jack Forbes (Perry Stephens), grandson to Cabot Alden. When Jack dumped her for Stacey Donovan (Lauren-Marie Taylor), Ava married Jack's cousin Curtis Alden (played then by Linden Ashby). Not long after Curtis dumped her, Ava found herself involved with Alex Masters (Randolph Mantooth), an impostor claiming to be Curtis's presumed-dead father, Clay Alden. When the real Clay (James Horan) showed up alive, Ava briefly wound up in bed with him. She has also attempted to seduce Jack's father, Dane Hammond (Anthony Herrera).

10. Craig Montgomery, *As the World Turns*

Craig Montgomery (Scott Bryce) had a one-night stand with Lucinda Walsh (Elizabeth Hubbard) while he was working for her. He then fell in love with her daughter, Sierra Esteban (Finn Carter), whom he eventually married. During a recent estrangement from Sierra, Craig fell into bed with Lucinda's half-sister, Samantha Markham (Brooke Alexander). Craig scores extra points for sleeping with Iva Snyder (Lisa Brown), the biological mother of Lucinda's adopted daughter, Lily (Martha Byrne), and with Iva's sister, Ellie (Renee Props).

10 OF SOAP OPERA'S ODDEST PREGNANCIES

1. Gina Timmons, *Santa Barbara*

Obsessed with being connected to the Capwell family, Gina Timmons (Robin Mattson) stole ex-husband C. C. Capwell's (Jed Allan) deposit from a sperm bank and impregnated herself with it. In keeping with the theme of immaculate conception, Gina gave birth on Christmas Eve in a veterinarian's office, surrounded by farm animals.

2. Vivian Alamain, *Days of Our Lives*

Vivian Alamain (Louise Sorel) believed that giving birth to Victor Kiriakis's (John Aniston) child would help win her ex-lover back. To that end, she switched petri dishes at the fertility clinic where Victor and his fiancée, Kate Roberts (Deborah Adair), were clients and wound up pregnant with Victor and Kate's child. Although Victor and Kate were horrified, there was no legal way they could make Vivian give back the fertilized egg. Vivian used the pregnancy to maneuver her way into Victor's mansion.

3. Amy Perkins, *Santa Barbara*

When Amy Perkins (Kerry Sherman) discovered she was pregnant, she mistakenly thought the baby belonged to an old boyfriend. Why would she suspect that she had secretly been impregnated with the sperm of a dead prince? It was one of those bizarre plots to overtake one of those mythical European monarchies, New Stailand. Although Amy had originally been told that the baby died at birth, she and her current boyfriend, Brick Wallace (Richard Eden), traveled to New Stailand and rescued her baby from having to rule the country.

4. Victoria Lord, *One Life to Live*

While it is a mainstay of the soaps to have men discover children they never knew even existed, *One Life to Live* found a way for Vicki Buchanan (Erika Slezak) to discover a daughter she never knew about. During the pregnancy, Vicki's split personality Nikki Smith emerged and carried the baby to term. Although Victoria's personality returned during childbirth, her domineering father had all traces of the pregnancy and birth hypnotized out of her mind.

5–6. Ava Rescott, *Loving*

A complicated woman, Ava Rescott has had two of daytime's most complicated pregnancies. After Ava (played at the time by Roya Megnot) suffered a miscarriage, she padded her clothes, kept her husband, Jack Forbes (Perry Stephens), at arm's length, and bought her sister's baby to pass off as her own. She suffered a second miscarriage a few years later while pregnant with Alex Masters's child. It wasn't until a few weeks after the miscarriage that the doctor realized that Ava had been pregnant with twins, the second of whom was still alive.

7. Brenda McGillis, *One Life to Live*

As with Ava Rescott, *One Life to Live*'s Brenda McGillis (Brenda Brock) also suffered a miscarriage and learned weeks later that she had in fact been pregnant with twins, the second of whom was still alive. As if that story twist weren't cruel enough for Brenda, when her baby was born, it was switched in the nursery with a baby who had died.

8. Nadine Lewis/Bridget Reardon, *Guiding Light*

Nadine Lewis (Jean Carol) wanted a baby to win back her estranged husband, Billy (Jordan Clarke). Bridget Reardon (Melissa Hayden) was pregnant, and the baby's father, Hart Jessup (Jeff Phillips), had recently left town. Nadine came up with the perfect solution to both their problems: Nadine faked a pregnancy by padding her clothes and hid Bridget upstairs in the attic until she gave birth and handed the boy over to Nadine. To make matters a little more complicated, the baby's grandfather was Roger Thorpe (Michael Zaslow), Billy Lewis's archenemy.

9. Suzi Wyatt, *Search for Tomorrow*

In mid-March of 1984, Suzi Wyatt (Teri Eoff) discovered that she was pregnant. For plotline reasons, the writers couldn't be bothered with a prolonged pregnancy (meaning one that ran the natural nine months). So Suzi gave birth at the end of April.

10. Corrine Tate Flotsky, *Soap*

Like Suzi Wyatt, Corrine Tate Flotsky (Diana Canova) had had one of those fast-forward pregnancies. But at least the writers came up with a "plausible" explanation for that one: the baby was possessed by Satan.

13 OF THE ODDEST DEATHS WRITERS HAVE DREAMED UP

1. David Kimball, *The Young and the Restless*

While dressed up like the Big Bad Wolf, David Kimball (Michael Corbett) stalked Nina Webster (Tricia Cast), Cricket Blair (Lauralee Bell), and Danny Romalotti (Michael Damian) around a costume ball. After shooting all three of them, he realized that he'd been set up. The bullets in his gun had been replaced with blanks, and the police were on to him. While trying to escape them, David slipped into what he thought was a closet. It was in fact the garbage chute. As he slid down the chute, David accidentally turned on the trash compactor.

2. David Gray, *General Hospital*

David Gray (Paul Rossilli) had kidnaped and presumably murdered Laura Spencer (Genie Francis) in his pursuit of the Sword of Malkuth, a symbol of power that would let him rule his native country. All during the storyline, Luke Spencer (Tony Geary) had been displaying varied psychic abilities, but the writers were saving the best for last. In a final confrontation with David Gray, Luke took hold of the sword and pointed it in David's direction. That was all it took to send David toppling backward out a window.

3. Kathy Holden, *Guiding Light*

Right before Irna Phillips left *Guiding Light* to work on *As the World Turns*, she decided to kill off the character of Kathy Holden (Susan Douglas). In the show's initial storyline, Kathy's husband, Bob, had been killed in a car accident. Kathy herself was later in a car accident that left her confined to a wheelchair. While Kathy was in her wheelchair, some kids on bicycles accidentally knocked her into the street and into the path of oncoming traffic. Kathy's death did not sit well with viewers, who had not wanted Kathy to die, especially not in such a brutal manner.

4. Liz Talbot, *As the World Turns*

This was another of Irna Phillips's classic death scenes. The day after Liz Talbot (played then by Judith Milligan) married Dan Stewart (played then by John Colenback), she tripped on the hem of her nightgown and fell *up— not down*— a flight of stairs. The impact of the fall ruptured her liver. By the following commercial break, she was dead. Phillips had originally planned to burn Liz to death on her wedding night but Emily Hunter on *Search for Tomorrow*, another Procter & Gamble soap, was already slated to die in a fire around that same time.

5. Lesley Ann Andrews, *Guiding Light*

Dr. Jim Reardon (Michael Woods) was researching a mysterious tropical virus called The Dreaming Death that turned its victims into virtual zombies before killing them. One of the mice Jim had infected with the disease escaped from the lab and found its way into Lesley Ann Andrews's (Carolyn Ann Clark) kitchen. After the mouse bit her, she contracted the illness and died.

6. Mary McCormack, *Santa Barbara*

After all the heartache Mason Capwell (Lane Davies) and Mary McCormack (Harley Jane Kozak) had gone through to be together, the audience had expected them to enjoy a little bit of happiness. Unfortunately, the writers didn't want Mason getting too complacent with his life. Mary and her husband, Mark (Jon

Lindstrom), had headed to the roof of the Capwell hotel on a particularly windy night. The wind was so strong it knocked the letter "C" off the hotel sign. When it fell, it landed right on top of Mary.

7. Grant Todd, *Another World*

One of Carl Hutchins's (Charles Keating) more Byzantine plots to kill Mac Cory (Douglass Watson) involved an amphora filled with poisonous dust. Unfortunately for Hutchins's plans, it was Grant Todd (John Dewey-Carter) who first inhaled the dust, which triggered a massive and fatal heart attack. By the time Mac and Rachel (Victoria Wyndham) had been exposed to the poisonous dust, Dr. Chris Chapin (Don Scardino) had developed an antidote.

8. Chip Roberts, *Knots Landing*

Killer Chip Roberts (Michael Sabatino) was hiding out in Gary Ewing's (Ted Shackleford) stable when he came face to face with Cathy Geary (Lisa Hartman), who bore an uncanny resemblance to Chip's murder victim, Ciji Dunne (who was also played by Hartman). Stunned, Chip fell backward, impaling himself on a pitchfork.

9. Walker Daniels, *Falcon Crest*

Falcon Crest's final season saw its share of odd deaths, including one villain being stabbed to death by his teenaged wife under the tree on Christmas Eve. But the oddest death of all was Walker Daniels's (Robert Ginty). Blaming Richard Channing (David Selby) and Michael Sharpe (Gregory Harrison) for all the misfortunes in his life, he strapped sticks of dynamite to his body and took the men and his wife, Lauren (Wendy Phillips), hostage. Just as he decided against killing anyone, he accidentally dropped the timing device, which triggered the countdown mechanism. Unable to remove the dynamite in time, he went running into the woods where he blew up all by himself.

10. Rex Allingham, *Another World*

Stephen Schnetzer actually got to kill himself while playing the dual role of Cass Winthrop and Rex Allingham on *Another World*. For months, Allingham (who had undergone extensive plastic surgery) had held Cass prisoner and taken his place in Bay City. When Cass escaped, he hunted Rex down to a disco. Rex pulled out a gun and tried to take Nicole Love (Anne Howard) hostage. Cass in turn cut a rope and dropped a chandelier right on top of his impostor.

11–12. Cabot and Isabelle Alden, *Loving*

The 1995 serial killer storyline allowed its writers to get creative with ways to murder victims as gently as possible. Stacey Forbes (Lauren Marie Taylor) suffered heart failure after using a poisoned powder puff; Clay Alden (Dennis Parlato) drank poisoned brandy; and a sedated Curtis Alden (Chris Marcantel) drowned in a sensory deprivation tank. But the killer outdid herself with the dual murder of Cabot and Isabelle Alden (Wesley Addy and Augusta Dabney). On their Golden Wedding Anniversary, the two of them died in their own bed after inhaling the gas emitted by a pair of poisoned candles.

13. Jeremy Hunter, *Loving*

Another victim of *Loving*'s serial killer, artist Jeremy had the most fitting murder of any hero on daytime. A vat of caustic and quick-drying plaster was dumped on top of him, turning him into an instant statue.

Honorable Mention. Shannon McKechnie, *As the World Turns*

This was one of the oddest deaths until Margaret Reed returned to the show, and Shannon "came back from the dead." Duncan McKechnie's (Michael Swan) deranged ex-wife, Lilith (Sarah Botsford), refused to let Duncan find happiness with another woman and kidnaped his present wife, Shannon. When Duncan tracked Lilith down to Africa, she presented him with a token of her twisted obsession: Shannon's shrunken head. (The writers have avoided mention of the shrunken head since Shannon's return.)

Note: *Mary Hartman, Mary Hartman* deserves special attention for the way in which it disposed of varied characters: one passed out face first into a bowl of chicken soup and drowned; a wife abuser was skewered with an aluminum Christmas tree; and a child evangelist was electrocuted when a television set fell into his bath.

8 LONG-RUNNING CHARACTERS WHO HAD ORIGINALLY BEEN BROUGHT ON TO BE KILLED OFF

1–2. Victor and Julia Newman, *The Young and the Restless*

As originally written, the character of Victor Newman was to have come on *The Young and the Restless* for only a few months—just long enough to kill his wife, Julia (Meg Bennett), and to be killed himself in turn. At the time Eric Braeden was cast as Victor (1980), *The Young and the Restless* had just lost two of its more popular leading men: David Hasselhoff (who played Snapper Foster) and John McCook (who played Lance Prentiss). As soon as Bill Bell heard Braeden's voice, he realized that Braeden could beef up the show's roster of leading men. The storyline was reworked, keeping both Victor and Julia alive. Bennett stayed with the show until 1984 and has occasionally returned for shorter stays. (She has also written for the show.) Braeden has been with the show for sixteen years.

3. Frank Ryan, *Ryan's Hope*

Frank, who was found unconscious at the foot of the stairway in the first episode of *Ryan's Hope*, was not supposed to live much beyond that show. ABC, however, objected to his death, and the storyline was altered, leaving Frank merely temporarily paralyzed. Played by five actors, the character survived throughout the show's entire thirteen-year run.

4. Nick Davis, *All My Children*

Like Rosemary Prinz, who played Amy Tyler, Larry Keith had come on the show for a few months early in *All My Children*'s run as part of the mystery surrounding Phillip Brent's (Richard Hatch) true parentage. Although Nick was supposed to have been killed off, Keith made such an impression on Agnes Nixon and on the *All My Children* audience that he stayed around for eight years. Nick still comes back to visit Pine Valley every now and again.

5. Bobby Ewing, *Dallas*

The five-episode first season of *Dallas* was considered something of a pilot for the series. Series creator David Jacobs intended for Bobby Ewing (Patrick Duffy) to bring home his new wife, Pamela (Victoria Principal), in the first episode and then be killed off at the end of the fifth episode. He saw more dramatic story potential for Pamela, whom he considered the center of the show, if she were living at Southfork without Bobby there to protect her. The idea of some dalliance between her and brother-in-law J.R. (Larry Hagman) had also been toyed with. Unlike Jacobs, CBS saw Bobby as too integral to the show to be killed off. Reluctantly Jacobs gave in, and Bobby lived another six years until Duffy himself decided to leave the show. (The character was "brought back to life" when Duffy decided to return a year later.)

6. Barnabas Collins, *Dark Shadows*

Jonathan Frid, who played vampire Barnabas Collins on *Dark Shadows*, owes his longevity on *Dark Shadows* in part to a typo. The whole Barnabas storyline was originally going to play out like the movie *Dracula*: the vampire would arrive in town, people would be bitten, some would die, and eventually, Barnabas would have a stake driven through his heart. The Van Helsing character who would bring about Barnabas's downfall was to be Dr. Julian Hoffman. In the typewriter, though, Dr. Julian Hoffman became Dr. *Julia* Hoffman. Seeing no reason why Dr. Hoffman couldn't be a woman, producer Dan Curtis hired Grayson Hall to play the part. The chemistry between her and Frid clicked with the viewers; fan mail poured in, and the ratings climbed from 4.3 to 7.3. The producers decided they had to keep both characters (and actors) around. Frid and Hall stayed with the show until its demise in 1971.

7. Audrey Hardy, *General Hospital*

Shortly after Steve Hardy (John Beradino) married Audrey March (Rachel Ames), Beradino let it slip during an interview with a Los Angeles newspaper that Audrey was going to die on the show. Because of negative reaction from the fans, coupled with the fact that the story was given away, the writers decided against going ahead with Audrey's death. Audrey has instead become one of the longest-running characters on daytime (thirty-three years). The writers and producers also learned to keep Beradino in the dark about upcoming stories.

8. Luke Spencer, *General Hospital*

As hard as it is to envision what *General Hospital* would have been like without Tony Geary as Luke Spencer, Luke was never envisioned as a central figure. He wasn't even supposed to be on the show for more than a few months. Luke was supposed to have been killed while try to assassinate the mob-connected politician Mitch Williams. (Ironically, Mitch was the role Geary had originally auditioned for.) By the time the hit was to take place, however, the audience had grown fascinated with Luke. Rather than hate him for raping Laura Baldwin (Genie Francis), the viewers actually wanted him to get together with her. Recognizing Geary's star potential, producer Gloria Monty had the scripts changed so that Roy DeLuca (Asher Brauner), Luke's best friend, was the one to be killed in mid–assassination attempt. Seventeen years later, Luke is married to Laura and still tied up with the underworld.

3

Out of Character

REAL NAMES OF 20 SOAP STARS

1. Eric Braeden (Victor Newman, *The Young and the Restless*)
   Born: Hans Gudegast
   Note: Braeden, who had appeared in several films and on the TV series *Combat* under the name Hans Gudegast, was convinced by executives at Universal Studios to change his name because of lingering anti-German sentiment in the United States.

2. Eileen Fulton (Lisa Mitchell, *As the World Turns*)
   Born: Margaret Elizabeth McLarty
   Note: Fulton is a family name. She chose the name Eileen because she misunderstood her first husband, who had suggested the name Aileen.

3. Steve Bond (Jimmy Lee Holt, *General Hospital*; Mack Blake, *Santa Barbara*)
   Born: Shlomo Goldberg
   Note: Shlomo is the Hebrew equivalent to Steve.

4. Katherine Kelly Lang (Brooke Logan, *The Bold and the Beautiful*)
   Born: Katherine Wegeman
   Note: Lang is her mother's family name.

5. Robert Tyler (Trucker McKenzie, *Loving*)
   Born: Barry Kaufman

6. Victoria Wyndham (Rachel Cory, *Another World*)
   Born: Victoria Camargo
   Note: Wyndham is a family name.

7. Rory Calhoun (Judge Judson Tyler, *Capitol*)
   Born: Francis Timothy Durgin

8. Marie Masters (Susan Stewart, *As the World Turns*)
   Born: Marie Mastruserio

9. Maurice Bernard (Sonny Corinthos, *General Hospital*)
   Born: Mauricio Morales
   Note: Bernard comes from his grandmother's family name.

10. Mary Stuart (Jo Gardner, *Search for Tomorrow*)
    Born: Mary Houchins
    Note: Stuart is her mother's family name.

11. David Hedison (Spencer Harrison, *Another World*)
    Born: Ara Heditsian

12. Emma Samms (Holly Scorpio, *General Hospital*; Fallon Colby, *Dynasty*; Grayson Louder, *Models Inc.*)
    Born: Emma Samuelson

13. Grayson Hall (Dr. Julia Hoffman, *Dark Shadows*; Euphemia Ralston, *One Life to Live*)
    Born: Shirley Grossman

14. Michael Damian (Danny Romalotti, *The Young and the Restless*)
    Born: Michael Weir
    Note: Damian is his middle name.

15. Susan Seaforth Hayes (Julie Williams, *Days of Our Lives*)
    Born: Susan Seabold

16. Kathryn Hays (Kim Hughes, *As the World Turns*)
    Born: Kathryn Piper
    Note: Hays is her mother's family name.

17. Russell Todd (Jamie Frame, *Another World*; Jerry Birn, *The Bold and the Beautiful*)
    Born: Russell Todd Goldberg

18. Linda Evans (Krystle Carrington, *Dynasty*)
    Born: Linda Evanstad

19. Rick Hearst (Alan-Michael Spaulding, *Guiding Light*)
    Born: Rick Herbst

20. Anna Lee (Lila Quartermaine, *General Hospital*)
    Born: Joan Boniface Winnifrith

10 ACTRESSES WHO TOOK THEIR HUSBANDS' NAMES *AFTER* THEY WERE ALREADY FAMOUS

Actresses have long made an exception to the practice of wives taking their husbands' names. It takes too many years to establish a recognizable name to risk changing it. The following actresses, though, have taken that risk and their husbands' names.

1. Melissa Reeves *née* Brennan (Jennifer Deveraux, *Days of Our Lives*)
    Married to actor Scott Reeves (Ryan McNeil, *The Young and the Restless*).

2. Kristina Wagner *née* Malandro (Felicia Jones, *General Hospital*)
    Married to former *General Hospital* co-star Jack Wagner (Frisco Jones).

3. Hillary B. Smith *née* Bailey (Nora Gannon, *One Life to Live*; Margo Hughes, *As the World Turns*; Kit McCormack, *The Doctors*)
    Went by Hillary Bailey Smith for several years.

4. Cynthia Jordan *née* Eilbacher (April Stevens, *The Young and the Restless*)

Cynthia Eilbacher left *The Young and the Restless* in 1982 and returned ten years later as Cynthia Jordan.

5. Debrah Farentino *née* Deborah Mullowney (Sloane Denning, *Capitol*)

Although now divorced from James Farentino (Nick Toscanni, *Dynasty*), she has kept his name.

6. Krista Tesreau (Mindy Lewis, *Guiding Light*; Tina Roberts, *One Life to Live*)

Briefly took her husband's surname, Mione, but reverted to Tesreau after separating from him.

7. Rosa Nevin *née* Langshwadt (Cecily Davidson, *All My Children*)

Found Nevin easier to pronounce than Langshwadt.

8. Amelia Weatherly *née* Heinle (Steffi Brewster, *Loving/The City*)

Married to former co-star Michael Weatherly (Cooper Alden).

9. Gail Ramsey *née* Gail Rae Carlson (Susan Moore, *General Hospital*; Laura Whitmore McCallum, *Generations*)

Went by Gail Rae Carlson on *General Hospital* and Gail Ramsey on *Generations*.

10. Hunter Tylo *née* Deborah Hunter (Taylor Hayes, *The Bold and the Beautiful*)

Married to Michael Tylo (Blade and Rick, *The Young and the Restless*), whom she met on *All My Children* when she was using the name Deborah Moorehart. Hunter is her family name.

12 BIRTHDAYS SHARED BY 3 OR MORE SOAP STARS

1. February 18: Michael Nader (Dimitri Marrick, *All My Children*), Anthony Peña (Miguel Rodriguez, *The Young and the Restless*), and Jess Walton (Jill Abbott, *The Young and the Restless*)

2. April 18: Anna Holbrook (Sharlene Frame Hudson, *Another World*), Robert Kelker-Kelly (Bo Brady, *Days of Our Lives*), and Melody Thomas Scott (Nikki Abbott, *The Young and the Restless*)

3. May 16: Brent Jasmer (Sly, *The Bold and the Beautiful*), Scott Reeves (Ryan McNeil, *The Young and the Restless*), Tori Spelling (Donna Martin, *Beverly Hills 90210*), and Carolyn Cromwell (Mary Williams, *The Young and the Restless*)

4. June 11: Stephen Schnetzer (Cass Winthrop, *Another World*), Peter Bergman (Jack Abbott, *The Young and the Restless*; Cliff Warner, *All My Children*), and Michael Swan (Duncan McKechnie, *As the World Turns*)

5. July 18: Darlene Conley (Sally Spectra, *The Bold and the Beautiful*), Jensen Buchanan (Victoria and Marley Love, *Another World*; Sarah Gordon, *One Life to Live*), and Susan Marie Snyder (Julie Snyder, *As the World Turns*)

6. July 31: Susan Flannery (Stephanie Forrester, *The Bold and the Beautiful*; Laura Horton, *Days of Our Lives*), Gerald Anthony (Marco Dane, *General Hospital and One Life to Live*), and Wally Kurth (Ned Ashton, *General Hospital*; Justin Kiriakis, *Days of Our Lives*)

7. August 9: Beverlee McKinsey (Alexandra Spaulding, *Guiding Light*; Iris Carrington, *Another World*), Clint Ritchie (Clint Buchanan, *One Life to Live*), and Michael Storm (Larry Wolek, *One Life to Live*)

8. September 24: Paul Michael Valley (Ryan Harrison, *Another World*), Greg Watkins (Evan Walsh, *As the World Turns*), Louis Edmonds (Roger Collins, *Dark Shadows*; Langley Wallingford, *All My Children*), and Larry Gates (H. B. Lewis, *Guiding Light*)

9. October 15: Vanessa Marcil (Brenda Barrett, *General Hospital*), Teresa Blake (Gloria Chandler, *All My Children*), and Renée Jones (Lexie Carver, *Days of Our Lives*)

10. November 1: Anna Stuart (Donna Love, *Another World*), Lauren-Marie Taylor (Stacey Forbes, *Loving*), and Michael Zaslow (Roger Thorpe, *Guiding Light*)

11. December 23: Martha Burns (Lily Walsh, *As the World Turns*), Susan Lucci (Erica Kane, *All My Children*), and John Callahan (Edmund Grey, *All My Children*)

12. December 31: Rachel Ames (Audrey Hardy, *General Hospital*), Don Diamont (Brad Carlton, *The Young and the Restless*), and Joanna Johnson (Caroline and Karen Spencer, *The Bold and the Beautiful*).

10 SOAP ACTORS WHO STAND 6'3" OR TALLER

1. Vince Williams (Hampton Speakes, *Guiding Light*): 6'5"

2. Rod Arrants (Travis Sentell, *Search for Tomorrow*; Dr. Stephen Lassiter, *The Young and the Restless*): 6'5"

3. Phil Carey (Asa Buchanan, *One Life to Live*): 6'4"

4. Scott Thompson Baker (Connor Davis, *The Bold and the Beautiful*): 6'4"

5. Keith Hamilton Cobb (Noah Keefer, *All My Children*): 6'4"

6. Daniel McVicar (Clarke Garrison, *The Bold and the Beautiful*): 6'4"

7. John Aniston (Victor Kiriakis, *Days of Our Lives*): 6'3"

8. Walt Willey (Jackson Montgomery, *All My Children*): 6'3"

9. Jeff Trachta (Thorne Forrester, *The Bold and the Beautiful*): 6'3"

10. Philip Moon (Keemo Volien, *The Young and the Restless*): 6'3"

10 SOAP ACTRESSES WHO STAND 5'9" OR TALLER

1. Monika Schnarre (Ivana, *The Bold and the Beautiful*): 6'1"

2. Brooke Alexander (Samantha Markham, *As the World Turns*): 5'10 1/2"

3. Maitland Ward (Jessica Forrester, *The Bold and the Beautiful*): 5'10"

4. Tamara Tunie (Jessica Griffin, *As the World Turns*): 5'9"

5. Sharon Wyatt (Tiffany Hill, *General Hospital*): 5'9"

6. Teri Ann Linn (Kristen Forrester, *The Bold and The Beautiful*): 5'9"

7. Brenda Epperson (Ashley Abbott, *The Young and the Restless*): 5'9"

8. Kassie Wesley (Blair Daimler, *One Life to Live*): 5'9"

9. Edie Lehmann (Katherine Delafield, *General Hospital*): 5'9"

10. Allyson Rice-Taylor (Connor Walsh, *As the World Turns*): 5'9"

FORMER JOBS OF 15 SOAP STARS

1. Charles Keating (Carl Hutchins, *Another World*)
   Hairdresser.

2. Dennis Parlato (Clay Alden, *Loving*)
   High school English teacher and a mailman.

3. Maureen Garrett (Holly Lindsey, *Guiding Light*)
   Freelance photographer and editor for an American newspaper in Germany.

4. Eileen Fulton (Lisa Grimaldi, *As the World Turns*)
   Sold hats at Macy's.

OUT OF CHARACTER

5. Ed Fry (Dr. Larry McDermott, *As the World Turns*)
   Butcher.

6. Judi Evans Luciano (Paulina Cory McKinnon, *Another World*)
   Circus clown (as a child).

7. Nathan Purdee (Hank Gannon, *One Life to Live*; Nathan Hastings, *The Young and the Restless*)
   Bounty hunter.

8. James Reynolds (Abe Carver, *Days of Our Lives*)
   Drama critic for a newspaper.

9. Susan Batten (Luna Moody, *One Life to Live*)
   Wearing scuba diving gear, would retrieve golf balls from water traps.

10. Nathan Fillion (Joey Buchanan, *One Life to Live*)
    Delivered singing telegrams dressed as Tarzan.

11. John Callahan (Edmund Grey, *All My Children*)
    Nightclub manager.

12. Kate Linder (Esther Valentine, *The Young and the Restless*)
    Flight attendant.
    Note: She juggled both jobs for a number of years.

13. Eric Braeden (Victor Newman, *The Young and the Restless*)
    Worked on a ranch and in a lumber mill.

14. Deidre Hall (Marlena Evans, *Days of Our Lives*)
    Disc jockey at an all-women radio station.

15. Tony Geary (Luke Spencer, *General Hospital*)
    Sold toys in a department store.

NON-ENTERTAINMENT-RELATED COLLEGE MAJORS OF 15 STARS

1. Stephen Schnetzer (Cass Winthrop, *Another World*)
   French from University of Massachusetts.

2. Peter Simon (Ed Bauer, *Guiding Light*)
   French Literature from Williams College.

3. Susan Haskell (Marty Saybrooke, *One Life to Live*)
   Biopsychology from Tufts University.

4. Wesley Addy (Cabot Alden, *Loving*)
   Economics from UCLA.

5. Stuart Damon (Alan Quartermaine, *General Hospital*)
   Psychology from Brandeis University.

6. Lynn Herring (Lucy Coe, *General Hospital*)
   Psychology from Louisiana State University.

7. Michael Zaslow (Roger Thorpe, *Guiding Light*)
   Political Science from UCLA.

8. Jerry Douglas (John Abbott, *The Young and the Restless*)
   Economics from Brandeis University.

9. Terry Lester (Jack Abbott, *The Young and the Restless*; Mason Capwell, *Santa Barbara*; Royce Keller, *As the World Turns*)
   Political Science from DePauw University.

10. Amelia Marshall (Gilly Grant, *Guiding Light*)
    Business Administration from University of Texas at Austin.

11. Jeff Trachta (Thorne Forrester, *The Bold and the Beautiful*)
    Psychology from St. John's University.

12. Nathan Purdee (Hank Gannon, *One Life to Live*; Nathan Hastings, *The Young and the Restless*)
Mental health from Metropolitan State College in Denver.

13. Anthony Peña (Miguel Rodriguez, *The Young and the Restless*)
Comparative literature and Native American history (double major) from California State University at Fullerton.

14. J. Eddie Peck (Cole Howard, *The Young and the Restless*)
Marketing from Missouri Southern State College.

15. Anthony Herrera (James Stenbeck, *As the World Turns*; Dane Hammond, *Loving*)
English literature and zoology (double major) from the University of Mississippi.

12 IVY LEAGUE GRADUATES WHO HAVE ACTED ON DAYTIME

1. Maeve Kinkead (Vanessa Chamberlain, *Guiding Light*)
Radcliffe

2. Philip Moon (Keemo Volien, *The Young and the Restless*)
Yale

3. Brian Patrick Clarke (Grant Andrews and Grant Putnam, *General Hospital*; Storm Logan, *The Bold and the Beautiful*)
Yale

4. Jessica Tuck (Megan Gordon Harrison, *One Life to Live*)
Yale

5. Elizabeth Hubbard (Dr. Althea Davis, *The Doctors*; Lucinda Walsh, *As the World Turns*)
Radcliffe

6. David Hedison (Spencer Harrison, *Another World*)
   Brown

7. Frank Runyeon (Steve Andropolous, *As the World Turns*; Michael Donnelly, *Santa Barbara*)
   Princeton

8. Paul Anthony Stewart (Casey Bowman, *Loving*)
   Princeton

9. Richard Cox (Giff Bowman, *Loving*)
   Yale

10. Gil Rogers (Ray Gardner, *All My Children*; Hawk Shayne, *Guiding Light*)
    Harvard

11. Adam Lazarre-White (Nathan Hastings, *The Young and the Restless*)
    Harvard

12. Bernard Barrow (Johnny Ryan, *Ryan's Hope*; Louis Slavinsky, *Loving*)
    Yale
    Note: Barrow received a Ph.D. in theater history from Yale.

12 SOAP ACTRESSES WHO COMPETED IN THE MISS AMERICA AND MISS USA PAGEANTS

1. Deborah Shelton (Mandy Winger, *Dallas*)
   Miss USA 1970

2. Laura Herring (Carla Greco, *General Hospital*)
   Miss USA 1985

3. Lynn Herring (Lucy Coe, *General Hospital*)
   As Miss Virginia
   Note: Runner-up for Miss USA 1978

4. Tonya Walker (Alex Olanov Buchanan, *One Life to Live*)
   As Miss Maryland

5. Bobbie Eakes (Macy Alexander, *The Bold and the Beautiful*)
   As Miss Georgia

6. Kimberlin Brown (Sheila Carter Forrester, *The Bold and the Beautiful* and *The Young and the Restless*)
   As Miss California

7. Teri Ann Linn (Kristen Forrester, *The Bold and the Beautiful*)
   As Miss Hawaii

8. Karen Moncrieff (Gabrielle Pascal, *Days of Our Lives*; Cassandra Benedict, *Santa Barbara*)
   As Miss Illinois

9. Sandra Reinhardt (Amanda Cory, *Another World*)
   As Miss Pennsylvania

10. Judith McConnell (Sophia Capwell, *Santa Barbara*)
    As Miss Pennsylvania

11. Mary Ellen Stuart (Frannie Hughes, *As the World Turns*)
    As Miss Arkansas

12. Nancy Stafford (Adrienne Hunt, *The Doctors*)
    As Miss Florida

10 SOAP STARS WHO HAVE PLAYED PROFESSIONAL AND SEMI-PRO SPORTS

1. John Beradino (Steve Hardy, *General Hospital*)
   Played with the St. Louis Browns, the Cleveland Indians (won the 1948 World Series), and the Pittsburgh Pirates baseball teams.

2. Drake Hogestyn (John Black, *Days of Our Lives*)
   Played with a minor league New York Yankees baseball team.

3. Forry Smith (Reese Walker, *Santa Barbara*)
   Played with the Seattle Seahawks.

4. Harry O'Reilly (Charlie Hailey, *Homefront*)
   Played with semi-pro football team the Brooklyn Mariners.

5. James A. Fitzpatrick (Pierce Riley, *All My Children*)
   Played with the Baltimore Colts.

6. Brian Patrick Clarke (Grant Putnam/Grant Andrews, *General Hospital*)
   Played semipro football with the Memphis Southmen of the World Football League, but was cut midway through the season.

7. Jack Scalia (Nicholas Pearce, *Dallas*)
   Played on a minor league Montreal Expos baseball team.

8. Philip Brown (Buck Huston, *Loving*)
   Played semi-pro soccer.

9. Chris Bruno (Dennis Wheeler, *Another World*; Michael Delaney, *All My Children*)
   Played semi-pro baseball.

10. A Martinez (Cruz Castillo, *Santa Barbara*)
    Played semi-pro baseball.

10 ACTORS AND ONE ACTRESS WHO SERVED IN THE MILITARY

1. Phil Carey (Asa Buchanan, *One Life to Live*)
   Marine Corps. Served in both World War II and the Korean War.

2. David Canary (Adam and Stuart Chandler, *All My Children*)
   Army. Named Best Pop Singer in an All-Army Entertainment competition.

3. John Aniston (Victor Kiriakis, *Days of Our Lives*)
   Navy. Lieutenant Major in US Navy Intelligence.

4. John Forsythe (Blake Carrington, *Dynasty*)
   Marines. Spent four years as a medic and was decorated for bravery.

5. Robert S. Woods (Bo Buchanan, *One Life to Live*)
   Green Berets. Served in Vietnam. Bo was brought on *One Life to Live* as a Vietnam veteran. Bo and Woods both wear a Montagnard bracelet, which Woods received from the Vietnamese as a token of their friendship and respect for him.

6. David Forsyth (Dr. John Hudson, *Another World*)
   Marine Corps. Served as a medic in Vietnam and was awarded a medal for bravery.

7. Steve Kanaly (Ray Krebbs, *Dallas*; Seabone Hunkle, *All My Children*)
   Army. Served in Vietnam and wanted *Dallas* to write in a Vietnam story for Ray.

8. Terry Lester (Jack Abbott, *The Young and the Restless*; Mason Capwell, *Santa Barbara*; Royce Keller, *As the World Turns*)
   Army. Taught Russian.

9. Roy Thinnes (General Sloan Carpenter, *One Life to Live*)
   Army. Newscaster for Armed Forces Radio Service.

10. Mark Valley (Jack Deveraux, *Days of Our Lives*)
    Army. Graduated West Point.

And Elizabeth Lawrence (Myra Murdoch, *All My Children*)
   WAVES. Served during World War II as an airplane mechanic and a celestial navigation instructor.

10 FAMOUS PARENTS OF SOAP OPERA ACTORS

1–2. Loretta Young and Clark Gable
    Daughter: Judy Lewis (Susan Ames, *The Secret Storm*; Barbara Vining, *General Hospital*)

3. Elizabeth Taylor
    Son: Michael Wilding (Jackson Freemont, *Guiding Light*; Alex Barton, *Dallas*)

4. Joan Crawford
    Daughter: Christina Crawford (Joan Borman Kane, *The Secret Storm*)

5. John Wayne
    Son: Ethan Wayne (Storm Logan, *The Bold and the Beautiful*)

6–7. Peter Lawford and Patricia Kennedy
    Son: Christopher Lawford (Charlie Brent, *All My Children*)
    Note: This makes Christopher Lawford nephew to President John F. Kennedy.

8. Cloris Leachman
    Son: Morgan Englund (Dylan Lewis, *Guiding Light*)

9. Astronaut Michael Collins
    Daughter: Kate Collins (Natalie Hunter and Janet Green, *All My Children*)
    Note: Guest-hosting *Good Morning America*, Kate Collins once interviewed her father about his 1969 trip to the moon with Buzz Aldrin and Neil Armstrong.

10. President Gerald Ford
    Son: Stephen Ford (Andy Richards, *The Young and the Restless*)

15 FAMOUS ANCESTORS OF SOAP OPERA ACTORS

1. President Andrew Johnson
    Ancestor of James De Paiva (Max Holden, *One Life to Live*)

OUT OF CHARACTER

2. President Andrew Jackson

    Ancestor of Andrew Jackson (Dr. Stephen Hammill, *All My Children*)

3. Robert Burns, Poet

    Ancestor of Ian Buchanan (Dr. James Warwick, *The Bold and the Beautiful*; Duke Lavery, *General Hospital*)

4. Czar Alexander, Russian Emperor

    Ancestor of Stephanie Romanov (Teri Spencer and Monique Durand, *Models Inc.*)

5. Calamity Jane, Cowgirl

    Ancestor of David Canary (Adam and Stuart Chandler, *All My Children*)
    Note: Calamity Jane's real name was Martha Jane Canary.

6–7. Mary, Queen of Scots and John Witherspoon, who signed the Declaration of Independence

    Ancestors of Dane Witherspoon (Joe Perkins, *Santa Barbara*; Tyler McCandless, *Capitol*)

8. Sir Thomas More, British statesman

    Ancestor of Camilla and Carey More (Gillian and Grace Forrester, *Days of Our Lives*)

9. Guy Fawkes, anarchist who tried to blow up the British Parliament

    Ancestor of Conard Fowkes (Don Hughes, *As the World Turns*)

10–12. Pocahontas, Davy Crockett, and Dolly Madison

    Ancestors of Anna Stuart (Donna Hudson, *Another World*)

13. Jeb Stuart, Civil War General

    Ancestor of Mary Stuart (Joanne Gardner, *Search for Tomorrow*)

14–15. Presidents John Adams and John Quincy Adams

    Ancestors of Mary Kay Adams (India Von Halkein, *Guiding Light*; Neal Alcott, *As the World Turns*)

10 ACTRESSES WHO POSED NUDE OR SEMI-NUDE FOR *PLAYBOY*

1. Shannon Tweed (Diana Hunter, *Falcon Crest*; Savannah Wilder, *Days of Our Lives*)

Tweed was the 1982 Playmate of the Year.

2. Joan Collins (Alexis Colby, *Dynasty*)

Collins, nearing 50, posed both in lingerie and completely nude in the 1983 Christmas issue. Two photographers were hired to do the pictorial.

3. Pamela Sue Martin (Fallon Carrington Colby, *Dynasty*)

Martin had posed for *Playboy* shortly after leaving her role as Nancy Drew.

4. Sherilyn Fenn (Audrey Horne, *Twin Peaks*)

Fenn's pictorial featured frontal but not full frontal nudity. She and her *Twin Peaks* leading man, Kyle MacLachlan (Agent Dale Cooper), were listed elsewhere in the same issue among the Sex Stars of 1990.

5. Shannen Doherty (Brenda Walsh, *Beverly Hills 90210*)

Doherty appeared in a 1994 pictorial promoting safe sex that included Sonia Braga, Kelly Lynch, and Mimi Rogers (Blair Harper Venton, *Paper Dolls*). Doherty's own pictures revealed frontal nudity but not full frontal nudity.

6. Linda Evans (Krystle Carrington, *Dynasty*)

Evans first appeared in *Playboy* in 1970. John Derek, her husband at the time, had taken the nude photos of her. In 1982 he put those pictures together with nudes of ex-wife Ursula Andress (who had once guest-starred on *Falcon Crest*) and current wife, Bo Derek, for a pictorial on his wives.

7. Audrey Landers (Heather Lawrence, *Somerset*; Afton Cooper, *Dallas*; Charlotte Hesser, *One Life to Live*)

Landers posed with her younger sister Judy Landers.

8. Roberta Leighton (Dr. Casey Reed, *The Young and the Restless*)

Leighton's see-through teddy barely masked her full frontal nudity. She was part of a 1982 pictorial on the women of daytime television.

9. Jaime Lyn Bauer (Lauralee Brooks, *The Young and the Restless*; Laura Horton, *Days of Our Lives*)

Like Leighton, Jaime Lyn Bauer was part of the 1982 pictorial on soap actresses. Ironically, she told the magazine that she would prefer not to be doing so many sex scenes on *The Young and the Restless*.

10. Kimberly McArthur (Kelly Capwell, *Santa Barbara*)

Future soap actress Kimberly McArthur was Miss January 1982 and toured with *Playboy*'s Girls of Rock 'n' Roll show. Prophetically, her centerfold appeared in the same issue as the pictorial on soap opera actresses.

AND 2 ACTORS WHO POSED NUDE FOR *PLAYGIRL*

1. Steve Bond (Jimmy Lee Holt, *General Hospital*; Mack Blake, *Santa Barbara*)

Nude photos Bond had taken early in his career resurfaced after he landed on *General Hospital*.

2. John Gibson (Jerry Cashman, *The Young and the Restless*)

Gibson not only posed nude for *Playgirl*, he was also a Chippendale dancer. He played a male stripper on *The Young and the Restless*.

12 AUTOBIOGRAPHIES WRITTEN BY SOAP ACTORS

1. *The Bennett Playbill* by Joan Bennett (Elizabeth Stoddard, *Dark Shadows*) with Lois Kibbee (Geraldine Saxon, *The Edge of Night*)

Published by Holt, Rinehart & Winston in 1970.

2. *The Days of My Life* by Macdonald Carey (Tom Horton, *Days of Our Lives*)

Published by St. Martin's Press in 1991.

3. *Diahann: An Autobiography* by Diahann Carroll (Dominique Deveraux, *Dynasty*)

Published by Little, Brown in 1986.

4. *Past Imperfect* by Joan Collins (Alexis Carrington Colby, *Dynasty*)

Published by Simon and Schuster in 1984.

5. *How My World Turns* by Eileen Fulton (Lisa Hughes, *As the World Turns*) with Brett Bolton

Published by Taplinger Publishing Company in 1970.

6. *How My World Still Turns* by Eileen Fulton (Lisa Hughes, *As the World Turns*)

Published by Birch Lane Press in 1995.

7. *Uncommon Knowledge* by Judy Lewis (Susan Ames, *The Secret Storm*; Barbara Vining, *General Hospital*)

Published by Simon & Schuster in 1994.

Note: Lewis's autobiography reveals that Lewis, "adopted" by screen legend Loretta Young, was actually Young's and Clark Gable's biological daughter.

8. *The Quality of Mercy: An Autobiography* by Mercedes McCambridge (veteran of numerous radio soaps: Mary Ruthledge, *The Guiding Light*; Betty Drake, *Betty and Bob*; Ruth Evans Wayne, *Big Sister*; and Peg Martinson, *This Is Nora Drake*)

Published by Times Books in 1981.

9. *Elvis and Me* by Priscilla Beaulieu Presley (Jenna Wade, *Dallas*)

Published by Putnam in 1985.

Note: *Elvis and Me* discusses Priscilla Presley's romance with and marriage to rock and roll legend Elvis Presley.

10. *Both of Me* by Mary Stuart (Jo Gardner Barron, *Search for Tomorrow*)

Published by Doubleday in 1980.

11. *By Emily Possessed* by Mona Bruns (Emily Potter, *The Brighter Day*; Emily Hastings, *Another World*)

    Published by Exposition Press in 1973.

12. *The Confessions of Phoebe Tyler* by Ruth Warrick (Phoebe Tyler, *All My Children*) with Don Preston

    Published by Prentice Hall in 1980.

4

Backstage

10 BACKSTAGE FEUDS AND FIGHTS

1. Peter Bergman and Eric Braeden, *The Young and the Restless*

In a case of life imitating art, the long-running feud between Jack Abbott and Victor Newman, which occasionally erupted into physical violence, extended over to the actors who play them, Peter Bergman and Eric Braeden respectively. In late 1992, an argument came about during the filming of a scene in which Braeden felt that Victor should have the last line. Bergman's comment that Braeden should just follow the script did not sit well with Braeden. The following day, Braeden went to Bergman's dressing room to discuss the matter further. The conversation deteriorated into an argument, and that argument led to a fistfight. Although each pressed criminal charges against the other, the charges were eventually dropped, and the two made a public reconciliation.

2. Lana Turner and Jane Wyman, *Falcon Crest*

The feud between Jane Wyman (Angela Channing) and Lana Turner (Jacqueline Perrault) which took place on *Falcon Crest* actually dated back to their days in Hollywood. Professionally, Wyman had been the critical favorite back then, an Oscar winner for *Johnny Belinda*, while Turner was the commercial success, the box office draw. In their personal lives, Turner had dated Wyman's future husband Ronald Reagan. When Turner was added to *Falcon Crest* for her star appeal, she started making star demands: she had the set closed to visitors while she was filming and demanded that limousines be at the ready to drive her anywhere she wanted to go. Wyman objected to the way Turner was taking over *her* show. At one point, Wyman told the crew to have her chair moved as far away as possible from Turner's, and eventually the two stopped speaking to each other altogether. So as not to risk losing Wyman, the producers decided to let Turner go. By the end of her run on the show, she and Wyman were filming their scenes on different days. Scenes in which both their characters had to appear were also filmed separately and later spliced together.

Note: Wyman also had a running rivalry with co-star Robert Foxworth (Chase Gioberti). According to an insider, when Foxworth discovered that Wyman's trailer was six inches longer than his, he demanded a trailer of equal length. And when Foxworth was allowed to direct episodes of the series, Wyman wanted the same. She never actually directed any of the episodes, but every time Foxworth directed one, Wyman would be paid a director's salary for the episode.

3. Susan Lucci and Sarah Michelle Gellar, *All My Children*

"Susan and I were not best friends, and we're never going to be. Basically, the best I can say is that we worked together—*on top* of each other—for so long that problems were inevitable." That is how Sarah Michelle Gellar (Kendall Hart) summed up the relationship between her and Susan Lucci (Erica Kane) in a farewell interview with *TV Guide*. Trouble between the actresses began shortly after Gellar took on the role of Kendall Hart, the daughter Erica had given up at birth. After the two rehearsed a scene together, the director instructed Gellar to add some "punch" to it during the taping. No one informed Lucci of the change, and she believed that Gellar was trying to upstage her. During Gellar's last year on the air, she and Lucci were given relatively few scenes together. In late May of 1995, three days after Gellar won the Emmy as Best Younger Actress and Lucci lost her fifteenth race for Best Actress, *All My Children* announced it was letting Gellar out of her contract eight months early. While the timing was suspicious, Gellar denied that her leaving had anything to do with Lucci. When questioned about the trouble between her and Gellar, Lucci told *Soap Opera Digest* that she was "very surprised by the rumors . . . [and] didn't know where they came from." The Gellar story aside, Lucci has long maintained a reputation for making new actors feel welcome on the *All My Children* set.

4. Larry Hagman and Philip Capice, *Dallas*

The long-running feud between Larry Hagman (J. R. Ewing, *Dallas*) and executive producer Philip Capice began during the summer of 1980 when the entire world was asking "Who Shot J.R.?" Hagman, recognizing his full value to the show, held out for more money and got it. Thereafter, he and Capice seemed to be vying for control on the set. In front of the cast and crew, Hagman derided Capice's ability to produce the show and held him singularly responsible for the show's declining ratings during the 1985–86 season. He also blamed Capice for driving away producer Leonard Katzman, whom Hagman considered "the real brains behind the show." Hagman vowed that he would get rid of Capice, and at one point he went to the higher-ups at Lorimar and requested that Capice be fired. When Capice finally stepped down as executive producer at the close of the 1986 season, he did not admit that he was leaving because of Hagman, but neither did he deny it.

5. Irna Phillips and Jane House, *As the World Turns*

As the World Turns creator and headwriter Irna Phillips took exceptional exception to the fact that Jane House, who played Liz Talbot on the show during the day, was baring her body nightly on Broadway, playing a stripper in the hit play *Lenny*. What made Phillips's reaction all the more interesting is that Liz was not a paragon of virtue on the show. She had had an affair with Dan Stewart (played then by John Colenback) and bore his child out of wedlock. Regardless, Phillips decided to kill Liz off to punish House for her nude scenes. Unfortunately for Phillips, Liz Talbot did not go quietly. While she lay dying of pneumonia, the CBS switchboard lit up with complaints from viewers; they threatened to stop watching if Liz died. Responding to the calls, CBS ordered Phillips to reverse Liz's condition, which Phillips quite begrudgingly did. None too pleased with what Phillips had tried to pull, House ultimately refused to stay on when her contract came up for renewal. When House left the show, Phillips's vendetta against the actress transferred to Liz Talbot. Even though a new actress (Judith McGilligan) was playing the role, Phillips was determined to kill Liz off and did so in a freak accident.

6. Kimberlin Brown and Hunter Tylo, *The Bold and the Beautiful*

At one point, Kimberlin Brown (Sheila Forrester) and Hunter Tylo (Taylor Hayes) were the best of friends. That friendship started to break down about the same time that Tylo left both *The Bold and the Beautiful* and her husband, Michael Tylo, who played Blade on *The Young and the Restless*. Brown and her husband sided with Michael during the split. Even though Hunter Tylo reunited with Michael and returned to *The Bold and the Beautiful*, she was no longer friends with Brown. The tension between them grew to the point where each actress hired bodyguards to protect herself from the other.

7. James De Paiva and Linda Gottlieb, *One Life to Live*

Although *One Life to Live*'s executive producer Linda Gottlieb was not popular with many actors on the show, James De Paiva (Max Holden) was one of the most vocal in his dislike for the way the woman produced the show. During an interview with *Soap Opera Weekly* conducted after she had left, he said: "When Linda was here, it was a terrible place to be." The tension between them sometimes erupted into shouting matches. During one such shouting match, an insider reports, De Paiva reduced Gottlieb to tears. At another time, De Paiva himself admits to throwing furniture around a set because of the tension Gottlieb created.

8. Vincent Irizarry and Gail Kobe, *Guiding Light*

In 1984, Vincent Irizarry (then playing Lujack on *Guiding Light*) was offered a small but important role as an abusive husband in the Sissy Spacek film *Marie*. The role would have required him to miss only one day of taping. Although then–executive producer Gail Kobe maintains that she tried "very hard to get him the time off," Irizarry believed the exact opposite, that she simply refused to let him go. (Ultimately, he did get the time off to do the movie, but only after the film's producer, Frank Capra, Jr., called to put some pressure on the show.) In an interview with *Soap Opera Digest*, Irizarry cited that incident as "the turning point in my relationship with [Kobe]. I had very little respect for her after that." He also told the magazine: "Kobe had very little respect for the talent on the show . . . and she put everybody at odds with each other." (Kobe denied both those accusations.) Irizarry ended up leaving *Guiding Light* as soon as his contract expired.

9. Jennie Garth and Shannen Doherty, *Beverly Hills 90210*

In the beginning, Shannen Doherty's Brenda Walsh was the centerpiece of *Beverly Hills 90210*. As Jennie Garth's Kelly Taylor emerged as a stronger and stronger character—often with better storylines than Brenda's—Doherty's envy grew. According to the producers, the more popular Garth got, the meaner Doherty acted toward her. Even though Doherty is no longer on the show, the rivalry remains. Doherty refuses to let Garth's name be brought up in her presence.

10. Terry Lester and Bill Bell, *The Young and the Restless*

It is not typical for an Emmy-nominated fan favorite like Terry Lester (Jack Abbott, *The Young and the Restless*) to feel his position threatened by a young *actress*. Yet, during Lester's last two years on *The Young and the Restless*, he believes that Jack Abbott "dwindled from leading man to second banana" directly because of Lauralee Bell, who plays Cricket Blair on the show. Lauralee Bell, it should be noted, is not just any young actress; she is the daughter of *The Young and the Restless* creator and executive producer Bill Bell. According to Lester, Bill Bell cut back the role of Jack Abbott to make more room in the show for his daughter. In a very vocal departure from the show in 1989, Lester told *Soap Opera Digest*: "I think one of [Bell's] aims was to make his daughter Lauralee the centerpiece of the show." Bell dismissed Lester's comments about Cricket cutting into Jack's storyline as "ridiculous," but wished him well nonetheless. Lester and Bell have since mended fences with one another.

10 SOAP OPERA—RELATED LAWSUITS

1. *Days of Our Lives* v. Bill Bell

In 1973, Bill Bell tried to leave his role as headwriter for *Days of Our Lives* to create a new soap, *The Young and the Restless*, for CBS. Corday Productions, which owned *Days of Our Lives*, didn't want to lose him and filed a lawsuit to make him stay. The lawsuit was eventually settled out of court. Bell agreed to stay on *Days* for three years in the capacity of story editor while he also got *The Young and the Restless* up and running.

2. Emmons Carlson v. Irna Phillips

Writer Emmons Carlson claimed that he had helped Irna Phillips create the radio soap *The Guiding Light*. Phillips, in turn, claimed that Carlson was "a lying bastard." According to Phillips, Carlson had done nothing more than write some of the scripts for the early episodes. Although her lawyers advised her to settle the matter out of court, Phillips refused. Carlson won the case and a $250,000 settlement.

3. Gordon Thomson v. *Dynasty*

Gordon Thomson couldn't revive the role of Adam Carrington in the 1991

Dynasty reunion movie because of scheduling conflicts with *Santa Barbara*, where he had recently taken over the role of Mason Capwell. According to Thomson's contract with Spelling, *Santa Barbara* was supposed to have been given sufficient notice of the reunion's production needs so that the show could give him time off. The five days' notice Spelling gave *Santa Barbara* before production began Thomson considered a breach of contract, and he subsequently filed a million-dollar lawsuit against Aaron Spelling Productions. At one point, Thomson claimed that he would drop the lawsuit in exchange for a public apology but quickly changed his mind.

4. The Dobsons v. NBC and New World Productions

Bridget Dobson, who created *Santa Barbara* with her husband, Jerome, became locked in a fierce battle for creative control of the show after she fired Anne Howard Bailey as headwriter. In September that battle took a decidedly nasty turn when Dobson was locked out of the studio by the show's co-owners, NBC and New World Productions. New World then sued the Dobsons for $25 million for breaching their contract by jeopardizing the show's success. Dobson and her husband countersued for $120 million against New World and another $52 million against NBC. Both cases were settled two years later for undisclosed but reportedly generous sums of money. As part of the settlement, the Dobsons returned to the show as headwriters. As soon as their year-long contracts expired though, they stepped down as headwriters and stayed on only as consultants.

5. *General Hospital* v. Tia Carrere

When Tia Carrere's (Jade Soong) appearances on *General Hospital* dwindled down to one a week, she decided to get a second job and auditioned for a role on the prime-time action series *The A-Team*, which aired on NBC. Carrere's contract with *General Hospital*, however, banned her from appearing on a regular basis on any other TV series. Carrere offered to do both series at the same time, but *General Hospital* producer Gloria Monty refused to compromise. Disregarding the contract, Carrere went off to do *The A-Team*. ABC in turn sued her for approximately one million dollars. The lawsuit was dropped after Carrere was let go from *The A-Team* (the producers didn't want to get in the middle of a battle with ABC) and returned to *General Hospital*. The show let her go shortly thereafter.

6. Donna Reed v. *Dallas*

When Barbara Bel Geddes's ill health forced her to retire from *Dallas*, the part of Miss Ellie was recast with Donna Reed of *The Donna Reed Show*. After a year off,

Bel Geddes felt well enough to return, and Reed was promptly fired. She sued the show, and her lawyers tried to get an injunction preventing *Dallas* from shooting any scenes featuring Bel Geddes as Miss Ellie. Reed settled out of court for two years' salary and the freedom to work elsewhere while she was receiving that salary.

7. Anita Clay Cornfeld v. *Falcon Crest*

Anita Clay Cornfeld sued the creators of *Falcon Crest* for copyright infringement, claiming that the show's premise was too similar in nature to her novel *Vintage*. A federal court ruled in *Falcon Crest*'s favor.

8. Brent Jasmer v. *Geraldo*

When the talk show *Geraldo* approached Brent Jasmer (Sly Donovan, *The Bold and the Beautiful*) about coming on to talk about the search for his biological family, he made it clear that he did not want any onscreen reunions. Despite Jasmer's wishes, the producers had his biological mother backstage and brought her out during the course of the show. Jasmer felt betrayed by the setup and hurt for his adoptive parents, both of whom were sitting in the audience. He has sued the show for, among other counts, fraud, negligent misrepresentation, invasion of privacy, and intentional infliction of emotional distress. The case is still pending trial.

9. Eileen Fulton v. *Celebrity Sleuth* Magazine

In the early '90s, *Celebrity Sleuth* ran nude photos of a young woman who it claimed was Eileen Fulton (Lisa Hughes, *As the World Turns*). Fulton sued the magazine, and the case was settled out of court. According to Fulton, the same young woman who posed as her also posed in the magazine as Marilyn Monroe.

10. Brenda Dickson v. Columbia Pictures

In 1987, Brenda Dickson was fired from *The Young and the Restless,* where she, an original castmember, had played the role of Jill Foster Abbott off and on since 1973. Following her dismissal, Dickson filed an unlawful termination lawsuit that named both *The Young and the Restless* executive producer Bill Bell and Columbia Pictures Television. According to the lawsuit, Dickson had not been feeling well while taping an episode of *The Young and the Restless* and made it known that she could not continue. Even though Bell had warned her that she would be fired if she left the studio, she did so anyway. Two days later, she received written notice of her termination. In addition to unlawful termination, Dickson's suit also charges

The Young and the Restless with breach of contract and intentional infliction of emotional distress. Seven years later, the case remains unresolved.

10 OF THE WILDEST RUMORS EVER SPREAD ABOUT SOAP STARS

1. Eileen Davidson Was Once a Man

Despite the fact that Eileen Davidson (formerly Ashley Abbott, *The Young and the Restless* and Kelly Capwell, *Santa Barbara*; currently Kristen DiMera, *Days of Our Lives*) is one of the most beautiful women on television, someone started a potentially career-damaging rumor that she used to be a man. One version of the rumor claimed that Davidson's former leading man, Eric Braeden (Victor Newman, *The Young and the Restless*), had revealed her secret past on *Donahue*. In truth, Braeden had never even gone on *Donahue* until the rumor had long been circulating, and even then, he never addressed the issue. He has however expressed an interest in getting his hands on the person who started the rumor.

2. Margaret Klenck's Death

There is an old saying that if you read it in *The New York Times*, then it has to be true. Margaret Klenck, who played newspaper reporter Edwina Lewis on *One Life to Live*, is literally living proof that that's just not the case. In late 1993, the *Times* ran an obituary for the still-living Klenck. As it turns out, it was not Klenck who died but an actress by the name of Edwina Lewis. The obituary went so far as to say that Klenck had changed her name officially to Edwina Lewis. The *Times* subsequently printed a retraction.

3. Hunter Tylo and Kimberlin Brown's Love Affair

The friendship between *The Bold and the Beautiful*'s Hunter Tylo (Taylor Hayes) and Kimberlin Brown (Sheila Forrester) gave way to speculation that the two were in fact not merely friends but lovers as well. Whoever started the rumor didn't factor Tylo's husband, Michael (who played Rick and Blade on *The Young and the Restless*), or Brown's husband into the equation, or the fact that the couples were friends with each other. Tylo and Brown found the whole rumor so laughable that they posed hugging each other in a photo that accompanied an article in *Soap Opera Digest* on crazy rumors.

4. Tony Geary's Engagement to Elizabeth Taylor

After Elizabeth Taylor guest-starred on *General Hospital* in 1981, she struck up a friendship with the show's leading man, Tony Geary (Luke Spencer). Once they appeared in public together a few times, the talk started that they were having an affair and that Geary would be Taylor's next husband. In *People* magazine, Geary admitted that the whole affair was a fake.

Note: There was also a minor rumor about Taylor being Russell Todd's (Jamie Frame, *Another World*) mother and his father being Taylor's late husband Michael Todd. The story may have had a basis in truth, since Taylor did have a son on a soap opera: Michael Wilding, who played Jackson Freemont on *Guiding Light.*

5. Susan Lucci and Robin Strasser are Phyllis Diller's Daughters

At least once a year, someone writes in to *Soap Opera Digest* asking if Susan Lucci (Erica Kane, *All My Children*) is Robin Strasser's (Dorian Lord, *One Life to Live*) sister and if their mother is Phyllis Diller. Responding to the questions most often asked by *Soap Opera Digest*'s readers, Lucci described the story as "one of those rumors that came out of nowhere. It started so long ago and I have never understood it."

6. Jane Elliot Bought Her Emmy

Shortly after winning her 1981 Emmy as Best Supporting Actress, Jane Elliot (Tracy Quartermaine, *General Hospital*) joined the cast of *Guiding Light.* When she got there, she heard a rumor that she had bought that Emmy. No one could explain to her, though, exactly how one goes about buying an Emmy award. The rumor, it seems, sprang from the fact that everyone "knew" Elliot was going to win the award. When she did, the fact that everyone knew it was going to happen ahead of time led some people to believe that the balloting must have been rigged.

7. Michael Sabatino's Bigamy

Michael Sabatino (Lawrence Alamain, *Days of Our Lives*; Antony Amando, *The Bold and the Beautiful*; Dr. Jonathan Kinder, *All My Children*) once read in one of the celebrity tabloids that he was married to two women simultaneously and living with both of them in the San Fernando Valley. At the time the story was published, Sabatino was not married to anyone, nor was he living in the San Fernando Valley.

8. William Gray Espy Is a Monk

During the four years in between William Gray Espy's (Mitch Blake) stints on *Another World*, his absence from daytime was explained away with a rumor that he'd quit acting to join a monastery. A variation on the rumor had him entering a lamasery in Tibet.

9. Roy Thinnes Urged His Fans to Send Death Threats to Castmates

When word got out that *One Life to Live* was planning to kill off Sloan Carpenter (played by Roy Thinnes), the ABC switchboard lit up with complaints from his fans. Soon thereafter, Thinnes heard and read stories that his castmates were receiving death threats from his fans—the implication being that he was encouraging them to write those letters. Worried about what damage such accusations could have on his career, Thinnes investigated the situation, but he could not find one death threat received by a castmate nor track down the "source at ABC" who had fed the stories to the press.

10. Princess Lauralee

It is true that Prince Albert of Monaco is a fan of *The Young and the Restless*. When Lauralee Bell and Michael Damian (Cricket and Danny) were in Monaco several years ago, Prince Albert did entertain them at his home. Once that story hit the press, rumors immediately followed that Prince Albert would make Bell his wife the way his father had married American actress Grace Kelly.

12 ONSCREEN COUPLES WHO MARRIED IN REAL LIFE

Listed in parentheses are the roles they were playing when they met. Asterisk indicates they have since divorced.

1. Bill Hayes and Susan Seaforth Hayes (Doug and Julie Williams, *Days of Our Lives*)

2. Augusta Dabney and William Prince (Tracey and Jerry Malone, *Young Doctor Malone*)

3. James Kiberd and Susan Keith (Mike Donovan and Shana Sloane, *Loving*)

4. Larry Bryggman and Jacqueline Schultz (John Dixon and Dee Stewart, *As the World Turns*)*

5. Peter Simon and Courtney Sherman Simon (Scott Phillips and Kathy Parker, *Search for Tomorrow*)

6. Justin Deas and Margaret Colin (Tom Hughes and Margo Montgomery, *As the World Turns*)

7. Charles Frank and Susan Blanchard (Jeff Martin and Mary Kennicott, *All My Children*)

8. Mark Pinter and Colleen Zenk Pinter (Brian McColl and Barbara Ryan, *As the World Turns*)

9. Vincent Irizarry and Signy Coleman (Scott Clark and Celeste Dinapoli, *Santa Barbara*)*

10. Tom Eplin and Ellen Wheeler (Jake McKinnon and Marley Love, *Another World*)*

11. Jack and Kristina Wagner (Frisco and Felicia Jones, *General Hospital*)

12. Hunter and Michael Tylo (Robin McCall and Matt Connolly, *All My Children*)

12 OTHER SOAP COUPLES WHO BECAME REAL-LIFE COUPLES

Listed in parentheses are the roles they were playing when they met.

1. Wally Kurth and Rena Sofer (Ned Quartermaine and Lois Cerullo, *General Hospital*)

2. Crystal Chappell and Michael Sabatino (Carly Manning and Lawrence Alamain, *Days of Our Lives*)

3. Lori Loughlin and Mark Arnold (Jody Travis and Gavin Wylie, *The Edge of Night*)

4. Ted Shackleford and Teri Austin (Gary Ewing and Jill Bennett, *Knots Landing*)

5. Beth Ehlers and Mark Derwin (Harley Cooper and A. C. Mallett, *Guiding Light*)

6. Vincent Irizarry and Kimberly Simms (Nick McHenry and Mindy Lewis, *Guiding Light*)

7. Nathan Purdee and Stephanie Williams (Nathan Hastings and Amy Lewis, *The Young and the Restless*)

8. Robert Tyler and Jessica Collins (Trucker McKenzie and Dinah Lee Mayberry, *Loving*)

9. Eddie Cibrian and Julianne Morris (Matt Clark and Amy Wilson, *The Young and the Restless*)

10. Grant Show and Yasmine Bleeth (Rick Hyde and Ryan Fennelli, *Ryan's Hope*)

11. Margaret Reed and Michael Swan (Shannon O'Hara and Duncan McKechnie, *As the World Turns*)

12. Courtney Thorne-Smith and Andrew Shue (Allison Parker and Billy Campbell, *Melrose Place*)

10 POPULAR COUPLES WHO HAD A HARD TIME GETTING ALONG TOGETHER OFFSCREEN

1. Kristian Alfonso and Robert Kelker-Kelly (Hope Williams and Bo Brady, *Days of Our Lives*)

Note: According to *TV Guide*, Alfonso refused to re-sign her contract if she had to play Hope opposite Kelker-Kelly's Bo. The show subsequently replaced him with Peter Reckell, who had originated the role of Bo and with whom Alfonso had also shared a rocky work history. Alfonso and Reckell had, however, since resolved their differences.

2. James Kiberd and Kate Collins (Trevor Dillon and Natalie Hunter, *All My Children*)

3. Luke Perry and Shannen Doherty (Dylan McKay and Brenda Walsh, *Beverly Hills 90210*)

4. Judi Evans Luciano and Vincent Irizarry (Beth Raines and Lujack, *Guiding Light*)

5. Nancy Grahn and Lane Davies (Julia Wainwright and Mason Capwell, *Santa Barbara*)
Note: Grahn and Davies have since resolved their differences.

6 Jessica Tuck and Joe Lando (Megan Gordon and Jake Harrison, *One Life to Live*)
Note: Lando wanted to quit after the first week rather than work with Tuck, who at one point slapped him when he wiped a piece of lint off her shoulder. Eventually, they became very good friends.

7. Tristan Rogers and Sharon Wyatt (Robert Scorpio and Tiffany Hill, *General Hospital*)
Note: The first day they worked together, Rogers informed Wyatt that he had told the producers not to hire her. The actors got along much better after the romance between their characters was shelved.

8. Robert S. Woods and Jacqueline Courtney (Bo Buchanan and Pat Ashley, *One Life to Live*)

9. Susan Lucci and Lee Godart (Erica Kane and Kent Bogard, *All My Children*)

10. Michael E. Knight and Cady McClain (Tad and Dixie, *All My Children*)
Note: During their first stint as Tad and Dixie, Knight and McClain had more than a couple of loud arguments, most of them concerning the issue of courtesy.

Since Knight's return to the show in 1992, McClain considers him one of her closest friends on the set.

10 CASES WHERE ART CONSCIOUSLY IMITATED LIFE

1. Margo Flax's Face Lift, *All My Children*

When Eileen Letchworth decided to undergo plastic surgery, the *All My Children* producers decided that Letchworth's character Margo Flax would have her face lifted as well. Letchworth appeared on the show shortly after her surgery and went through the recovery process on camera.

2. Katherine Chancellor's Face Lift, *The Young and the Restless*

Like *All My Children*, *The Young and the Restless* decided to incorporate Jeanne Cooper's (Katherine Chancellor) real-life cosmetic surgery into her character's storyline. Bridging the gap between reality and fiction, footage from Cooper's actual operation was aired on the show.

3. Charita Bauer's Leg Amputation, *Guiding Light*

An untreatable circulatory problem in Charita Bauer's (Bert Bauer) leg led to its amputation in the fall of 1983. Despite some initial resistance to dramatizing her problem as Bert's, Bauer eventually realized the potential service such a storyline could provide to the viewing public and went ahead with it.

4. Mary Stuart's Pregnancy, *Search for Tomorrow*

When Mary Stuart was pregnant with her second child, *Search for Tomorrow* decided to incorporate the pregnancy into her storyline—the first time that had ever been done on a soap. Actual footage of Stuart and her newborn baby was taken in the hospital and aired on the show.

Note: Actresses' real-life pregnancies have since been incorporated into their storylines for the past four decades.

5. Frannie Hughes's Battle with Anorexia, *As the World Turns*

It was no coincidence that Frannie Hughes and her portrayer Terri VandenBosch both suffered from anorexia nervosa. VandenBosch had gone to the producers, told them what she had gone through and asked if she could play out her battle with anorexia on the show. She saw it as a way to get the information out there. She wanted to show young women in the audience that there was help available to them. VandenBosch found going through the battle a second time in the context of the show scary but therapeutic.

6. Maggie Horton's Myasthenia Gravis Diagnosis, *Days of Our Live*

In 1984, Suzanne Rogers (Maggie Horton) was diagnosed with myasthenia gravis, a life-threatening neuromuscular disease. It was because of symptoms such as fatigue and depression that she originally left *Days of Our Lives*. When she returned to the show, she asked the producers to write the illness into her character, and Maggie Horton was subsequently diagnosed with the disease.

7. Jordy Clegg's Car Accident, *Capitol*

During the spring of 1987, a car accident left Todd Curtis's face badly disfigured. He lost teeth and a cheekbone and suffered extensive facial wounds. Rather than take months off from work while he underwent extensive plastic surgery, Curtis approached the producers about working the accident into his storyline. Jordy Clegg soon suffered a car accident similar to the one Curtis was in, and the audience went through the recovery process with both Jordy and Curtis himself. Curtis talked at length with the writers, discussing the varied emotional traumas he was experiencing so that they could put them into the script. At one point, for dramatic effect, the make-up department added extra scars to Curtis's face.

8. Danny Romalotti's Broadway Career, *The Young and the Restless*

When Michael Damian landed the lead role in the California production of Andrew Lloyd Webber's *Joseph and the Amazing Technicolor Dreamcoat*, Danny Romalotti's stage career was born. *The Young and the Restless* aired scenes of Danny practicing for the show. His busy schedule became the catalyst for problems between him and his wife, Cricket (Lauralee Bell). When *Joseph* moved to Broadway, necessitating Damian's departure from the California-based soap, it was written that Danny too would be taking the show to New York. At one point, Andrew Lloyd Webber himself had agreed to appear on the show but later changed his mind.

9. Lyla's Defense of Sacred Ground, *As the World Turns*

As chair of the American Indian College Fund, Anne Sward (Lyla Peretti, *As the World Turns*) not only raised money for the education of Native Americans, she was also active in efforts to preserve their burial grounds and other sacred sites. Wanting *As the World Turns* to deal with the issue, she put together a treatment for a storyline and presented it to then–headwriter Doug Marland. Sward's character, Lyla, soon found herself at odds with her tycoon boyfriend, Cal Stricklyn (Patrick Tovatt), trying to prevent him from drilling for oil on sacred ground.

10. Clint Buchanan's Plane Crash on *One Life to Live*

During the summer of 1993, Clint Ritchie (Clint Buchanan) was critically injured during an accident with a tractor on his California ranch. Although the circumstances of Clint Buchanan's accident were different (a light-plane crash), his injuries were almost identical in seriousness to those Ritchie sustained. Both Clints spent the summer offscreen recovering.

10 CASES WHERE LIFE IMITATED ART

1. The Santa Barbara Earthquake

During the show's first six months on the air, *Santa Barbara* tried to shake up a few storylines by staging an earthquake. The very same day that the show was taping its earthquake scenes, an earthquake hit the real Santa Barbara, measuring 4.7 on the Richter scale.

2. Felicia Gallant's Romance Novel

On *Another World,* Linda Dano has played romance novelist Felicia Gallant since 1983. In 1985, Dano and Rebecca Flanders co-wrote a Harlequin romance titled *Dreamweaver* under the pen name Felicia Gallant.

3. Lisa Wilkinson's Pregnancy

Usually, an actress's pregnancy needs to be written into her character's storyline. In the case of Lisa Wilkinson (Nancy Grant, *All My Children*), it was after the writers had decided to make Nancy pregnant that Wilkinson discovered she was pregnant in real life as well. Blurring the line between fiction and reality even further, Wilkinson was pregnant by her then-husband John Danelle, who played Nancy's husband (and the father of her baby) Dr. Frank Grant on the show.

4. Infant CPR, *The Young and the Restless*

While he was a baby, Nicholas Newman on *The Young and the Restless* accidentally swallowed a dime and needed infant CPR performed on him. A few days after Melody Thomas Scott (who plays Nicholas's mother, Nikki) taped the scene, her own seven-month-old daughter, Elizabeth, choked on a piece of food and required similar medical attention. The day after the episode aired, the show received a call from a viewer who had copied the CPR technique used on Nicholas to save her own child.

5. Beverlee McKinsey's Departure from *Guiding Light*

To accommodate Beverlee McKinsey's annual month vacation in 1986, *Guiding Light* sent Alexandra Spaulding on a vacation as well. On her way out the door, Alexandra—fearful of a corporate coup by brother Alan (then Chris Bernau)—reminded the board members of a clause in her contract preventing them from voting her out as CEO while she was on vacation. McKinsey pulled a similar move in 1992 when she departed from her role as Alexandra. While the show was preparing to send Alexandra away for an eight-week vacation, McKinsey was planning on leaving the show altogether. On the last day of taping before her "vacation," McKinsey announced that the day would be her last and reminded the producers of a clause in her contract allowing her to leave the show at any time with an eight-week notice.

6. The Learning Robot, *Days of Our Lives*

In 1983, during daytime's fascination with science fiction, *Days of Our Lives* brought a robot onto the show as a comic foil for Eugene Bradford (John de Lancie). On the show, the robot SICO was created as a focusing point for learning-impaired children. The robot reached one such child in the audience, a six-year-old autistic boy. The boy laughed at a scene between Eugene and SICO, which was the first time he had ever responded in such a way to anything he saw on TV. Following that breakthrough, the boy's parents were able to enroll him in a school for students with special needs.

7. Candice Earley's "Arrest" for Prostitution

Candice Earley, who played teen prostitute Donna Beck on *All My Children*, was walking home from the studio one night when she was stopped by a police officer. The officer insisted that she was a prostitute with a warrant out on her and placed Earley under arrest. Earley managed to convince him that she was an actress before he actually dragged her down to the police station.

8. Falcon Crest Wine

Exterior scenes for *Falcon Crest* were filmed at The Spring Mountain Vineyards in St. Helena, California. In 1982, when the show moved into the Top Ten, Spring Mountain Vineyards decided to capitalize on its connection to the hit series and introduced two wines under the label "Falcon Crest."

9. Hope Brady's Wedding Dress

Days of Our Lives costume designer Lee Smith had traveled all the way to Paris looking for the right material for the wedding dress Hope Williams (Kristian Alfonso) wore when she married Bo Brady (Peter Reckell). The dress ended up costing somewhere in the area of $20,000. When Alfonso later married real estate executive Simon McCauley, she wore that exact same dress.

10. Debbi Morgan on *Generations*

In 1981, Debbi Morgan (who would go on to play Angie Hubbard on *All My Children*) played Lynette Porter on the late-night soap opera *Behind the Screen*. On the show, Lynette was an actress starring on a soap opera called *Generations*. Nine years later, Morgan herself left *All My Children* to star on the NBC soap opera *Generations*.

10 STORYLINES ACTORS OBJECTED TO PLAYING

1. Ruth Warrick (Phoebe Tyler, *All My Children*)

During *All My Children*'s early months, various characters were protesting against the Vietnam War. Warrick, who herself had been involved in peace marches, hated the fact that Phoebe had such disdain for them. So she made the choice to play Phoebe as a bit of a "bubblehead," as she put it. That didn't sit well with the directors, who told her to play Phoebe straight or they would have to replace her.

2. Leigh McCloskey (Zach Kelton, *Santa Barbara*)

McCloskey didn't like the twist that his character, the gynecologist who examined Eden Capwell (Marcy Walker) after her rape, would turn out to be the serial rapist. Women, he felt, had a hard enough time trusting their gynecologists without the soap planting any more fears in their minds.

3. Louise Sorel (Augusta Lockridge, *Santa Barbara*)

Sorel was quite vocal in her distaste for a storyline in which Augusta became fascinated with Dash Nichols (Timothy Gibbs), the man who raped her sister, Julia (Nancy Grahn). She found herself written off the show shortly thereafter.

Note: A few years previously, it should be noted, Nancy Grahn didn't think that Julia would get involved with Gina Timmons's (Robin Mattson) blue-collar brother, Mack Blake (Steve Bond), and the plot was shelved.

4. James Mitchell (Palmer Cortlandt, *All My Children*)

Mitchell thought that Palmer was too smart to be taken in as easily as he was by gold digger Cynthia Preston (Jane Elliot).

5. Bob Hastings (Bert Ramsey, *General Hospital*)

Hastings hated the way Bert Ramsey, the likeable, milk-drinking police commissioner was revealed to be the criminal mastermind Mr. Big. He considered it a betrayal of all Bert had stood for. Letters he received from police officers across the country agreed with him.

6. Donna Mills (Abby Ewing, *Knots Landing*)

Mills hated the fact that Abby was responsible for the kidnaping of Valene Ewing's (Joan Van Ark) twin babies. She thought it made Abby too evil. The show redeemed Abby by making her the one who told Valene where the children were.

7. Darnell Williams and Debbi Morgan (Jesse and Angie Hubbard, *All My Children*)

Playing the most prominent black couple in soaps at the time, Williams and Morgan recognized their position as role models. As such, they didn't like the decision to make Angie pregnant during her secret marriage to Jesse.

8. Beth Maitland (Traci Abbott, *Young and the Restless*)

Since so many teenaged viewers saw Traci as a role model, Maitland worried about the message that would be sent out by Traci's suicide attempt.

9. William Devane (Greg Sumner, *Knots Landing*)

Devane considered the strip croquet match between Greg and Paige (Nicollette Sheridan) the stupidest scene the writers had ever come up with. He has acknowledged, however, that it is also one of the most popular scenes that *Knots Landing* has ever aired.

10. Larry Hagman (J. R. Ewing, *Dallas*)

Hagman blamed the whole international intrigue plotline surrounding Angelica Nero (Barbara Carrera) for the show's declining ratings during the 1985–86 season.

10 ACCIDENTS THAT HAPPENED ON THE SET

1. A candlelit love scene between Gabrielle Medina (Fiona Hutchison) and Max Holden (Nicholas Walker) on *One Life to Live* was supposed to end with Max's bar going up in flames. Shooting the scene proved disastrous in and of itself. First, Hutchison's hair got too close to the candle and caught fire. That was quickly taken care of. Then Hutchison got too close to the smoke machine and suffered smoke inhalation. One of the extras playing firemen subsequently dropped Hutchison as he was carrying Gabrielle to safety.

2. Back when *General Hospital* was filmed live, few things used to bother John Beradino (Steve Hardy) more than actors arriving late and unprepared. Several times he took out his frustration by punching holes in the door to Steve's office. The third time the show had to replace the door, they replaced it with an oak one—before it had been plywood—but didn't tell Beradino. The next time he punched the door, he broke his hand.

3 During a storyline in which Lisa was suffering from pneumonia on *As the World Turns*, Eileen Fulton had to do her scenes in a makeshift oxygen tent. The main difference between the prop tent and a real one was that the prop one did not have oxygen being pumped into it. No one remembered to unzip the back of the tent, and Fulton, who had been playing the scene as unconscious, passed out and almost suffocated. Because the show taped live, the crew waited until the commercial to open the tent and revive her.

4. Although the annual *Dynasty* catfight between Alexis Colby (Joan Collins) and Krystle Carrington (Linda Evans) was a favorite with the fans, Collins preferred her battles verbal. During one of those catfights, Evans got a little too physical and Collins wound up in the hospital with a wrenched back.

5. *Search for Tomorrow's* Jerry Lanning once got a little too into his role as hit man Nick D'Antoni. During a scene between Nick and Liza Walton (Sherry Mathis), Lanning choked Mathis so hard that she turned blue. Lanning and Mathis, it should be noted, got married a week later.

6. Peter Brown took over the role of *Loving's* Roger Forbes from John Shearin just as Doug Donovan (Bryan Cranston) was learning that Roger had slept with his fiancée, Merrill Vochek (Patricia Kalember). In one of Brown's first scenes with Cranston, Doug was coming after Roger to settle things man to man. Cranston didn't pull his punch in time, and he knocked Brown out cold.

7. Brian Patrick Clarke and Sherilyn Wolter's first year as Grant Putnam and Celia Quartermaine on *General Hospital* was anything but congenial. Wolter had told one soap magazine that they had wanted to "punch each other's lights out" that first year. In one scene, she came pretty close. Celia slapped Grant across the face when she believed that he never loved her. Wolter slapped Clarke so hard that his ears were ringing. The two have subsequently become friends.

8. Jaime Lyn Bauer was coming down with a flu when she had to tape an ambulance scene for *Days of Our Lives*. She was strapped into a stretcher and the ambulance was jerked back and forth as if to simulate a rather tumultuous ride. Bauer began to hyperventilate, and by the time the scene was over, she was nearly unconscious. As soon as she stepped out of the ambulance, she collapsed onto the studio floor. Emergency medical technicians were brought in to revive her. They gave her oxygen and ice to cool down her fever until she was well enough to be sent home.

9. During a fight scene on *Days of Our Lives* between Bo Brady and some Russian agents, Peter Reckell broke his hand in two places. At first, he didn't even realize what he'd done, but the pain in his hand just wouldn't go away. His doctor fitted him with a removable cast so that he could take it off while taping his scenes.

10. All day *Santa Barbara*'s A Martinez and Marcy Walker (Cruz and Eden) had practiced a sensual but dangerous dance move called the death drop: the woman throws herself to the floor, and the man catches her by the hands as she's inches away from the floor. Martinez caught Walker every time during the rehearsals. Come tape time, he missed. Walker did a complete body drop against the cement studio floor. Although she wasn't any too happy with him, she did the scene again and he did catch her the second time.

10 INSIDE JOKES THAT WERE SLIPPED INTO SHOWS

1. Skeleton in the Attic

For years, a story about *All My Children*'s early days has circulated regarding Joe Martin's son Bobby. According to legend, Bobby went upstairs to polish his skis and was never heard from or referred to ever again. (While there was once a Bobby Martin who faded into oblivion, he did so at summer camp, not upstairs polishing his skis.) The *All My Children* writers decided to have a little fun with the legend during an episode in which Opal Gardner (Jill Larson) was accidentally locked in the attic of the Martin house. While rummaging around for something she could use to get herself out, she stumbled upon a skeleton sitting next to a pair of skis. Hanging above the skeleton's skull was a baseball cap with the name "Bobby" stitched across the front of it.

2. Erica Wishes for an Emmy

While in Budapest, *All My Children*'s Erica Kane (Susan Lucci) had been kidnaped by Edmund Grey (John Callahan), who wanted revenge on his half-brother, Dimitri Marrick (Michael Nader), who was Erica's lover. When Erica thought Dimitri was two-timing her with his wife, Angelique (Season Hubley), she decided to help Edmund with his quest for vengeance. She got on the phone and played the part of a tortured kidnap victim to the hilt. Edmund complimented her performance with the line, "You deserve an Oscar."—to which Erica responded, "I'd settle for an Emmy." It was a perfectly set up and executed stab at Lucci's famed losing streak at the Daytime Emmy awards.

3. Buzz Avoids the Press

When *Guiding Light*'s Buzz and Nadine Cooper (Justin Deas and Jean Carol) appeared on the romance-themed game show *Soulmates*, they became local celebrities in Springfield. While Nadine loved all the media attention, Buzz did whatever he could to avoid it. When finally confronted about the way he was acting, he commented simply, "I don't like publicity." Deas, who rarely grants interviews and has been known not to pick up an Emmy or two, couldn't help but enjoy a little smirk as he delivered the line.

4. David Hasselhoff's Face

Part of killer David Kimball's (Michael Corbett) plan to begin a new life on *The Young and the Restless* was to get himself a new face. To please his girlfriend, David held a plastic surgeon hostage and demanded that the doctor give him David Hasselhoff's face. Longtime fans of *The Young and the Restless* got a kick out of the scene because Hasselhoff had starred on the show for many years as Dr. Snapper Foster.

5. Henry Darrow's Emmy

During a scene with daughter-in-law Eden (Marcy Walker), *Santa Barbara*'s magician Rafael Castillo (Henry Darrow) opened his suitcase and started removing varied props. Among the things he pulled out was the Supporting Actor Emmy Darrow had recently won for playing the role of Rafael. Rafael regarded the award for a moment, wondering aloud how it had gotten in there, then quickly set it aside.

6. Macdonald Carey's Star

While Jack and Jennifer Deveraux (Matthew Ashford and Melissa Reeves) were honeymooning in Los Angeles, *Days of Our Lives* shot some scenes on location. In one of those scenes on Hollywood Boulevard, Jack and Jennifer came upon Macdonald Carey's (Dr. Tom Horton on the show) star on Hollywood's Walk of Fame.

7. Eden's Chauffeur

This was a joke very few people would have gotten without the press clueing them in ahead of time. Marcy Walker had decided to leave *Santa Barbara* to star in the new Stephen J. Cannell series *Palace Guard*. In her last scene, Eden was shown getting into a limousine and being driven away from Santa Barbara. For the role of the chauffeur, the producers hired Stephen J. Cannell himself, the joke being that he was literally taking her away from *Santa Barbara*.

Note: A year after Walker left *Santa Barbara* for prime-time, A Martinez (Cruz Castillo) followed in her footsteps, landing a role on *L.A. Law*. In Martinez's first scene on the show, Stuart Markowitz (Michael Tucker) was showing his character around the office. When Stuart asked where he had come from, Martinez replied, "Santa Barbara."

8. "The name is Margaret Elizabeth McLarty."

During an airport scene in which Eileen Fulton (Lisa Hughes) returned to *As the World Turns* in 1984, a woman walked up to Lisa and asked if her name was Eileen. Lisa snapped at the woman that her name was Margaret Elizabeth McLarty (which is Fulton's real name).

9. Miss Jones

During the 1985–86 season, *Falcon Crest* introduced the character of the homicidal Erin Jones (Jill Jacobson), whom Richard Channing always referred to as Miss Jones. When asked why he refused to call her by her first name, he replied: "I can never call you Erin. Sounds like one of the Waltons." The line not only worked in and of itself, it was a good-natured poke at *Falcon Crest* creator Earl Hamner, who had also created *The Waltons*.

10. Trevor and Shana Collide

During a crossover storyline between *Loving* and *All My Children*, Trevor Dillon (James Kiberd) chased a criminal from Pine Valley to Corinth. In Corinth, he got into a fender bender with Shana Alden (played by Kiberd's real-life wife, Susan Keith). During the course of the ensuing argument, Trevor expressed his sympathy for the jerk who was married to Shana—to which Shana replied, "And I feel sorry for the idiot who's married to you."

CURIOUS REASONS WHY 10 ACTORS LOST THEIR JOBS

1. Tom Selleck (Jed Andrews, *The Young and the Restless*)

Producer Bill Bell refused to sign Tom Selleck to a contract because he didn't like the sound of his voice—"too high and squeaky," Bell said.

2. Robyn Griggs (Maggie Cory, *Another World*)

Although the show says it released Griggs to take Maggie in a different direction, Griggs maintains that she was fired for being friends and being photographed with John Wayne Bobbitt, who made worldwide news when his wife severed his penis while he was sleeping. Previous to the firing, Griggs says, the show had told her to put an end to the friendship.

3. Billy Hufsey (Emilio Ramirez, *Days of Our Lives*)

Hufsey was told by the producers to cut his hair. He didn't, and the next thing he knew, he was out of a job. His popularity with the audience led to his almost immediate rehiring.

4. Patricia Kalember (Merrill Vochek, *Loving*)

Unlike Hufsey, Kalember wanted to cut her hair. She wanted a style that was more befitting the professional image of the television reporter she played. As soon as she did, however, she was written off the show.

5. Amy Gibson (Alana Anthony, *The Young and the Restless*)

The producers told her to lose weight. She didn't and was soon written off the show.

6. Ilene Kristen (Delia Reid, *Ryan's Hope*)

Like Gibson, Kristen attributes her being fired to the fact that she had gained weight. The weight gain was an unfortunate side effect of some medication she was taking at the time. She came back to the show in 1986.

7. Kathleen Turner (Nola Aldrich, *The Doctors*)

The producers didn't think Turner was "hot" enough as an actress.

Note: She was replaced with Kim Zimmer (later Reva Lewis, *Guiding Light*), whom movie producers didn't think was "hot" enough to play Kathleen Turner's role in *Body Heat*.

8. John Colenback (Dan Stewart, *As the World Turns*)

The producers didn't take too kindly to Colenback actually exercising an "out" clause in his contract which allowed him time off to do a play. Dan Stewart was therefore written off the show, and when he was brought back, the role was recast with John Reilly (later Sean Donnelly, *General Hospital*). Colenback, however, returned as Dan after Reilly left.

9. Dan Lauria (Gus, *One Life to Live*)

TV evangelist Jerry Falwell caught scenes of Lauria playing a pimp named Gus on *One Life to Live* and complained about it. Lauria's Gus was soon written off the show.

10. Gil Rogers (Ray Gardner, *All My Children*)

On *All My Children*, Rogers could be seen terrorizing the Martin family as rapist Ray Gardner. During the commercial breaks, he could be seen as a kindly grandfather teaching his grandson the wonders of nature and of Grape Nuts cereal. The cereal company, a major sponsor for the show, didn't exactly like the audience associating the grandfather in their ads with rapist Ray Gardner. Ray was soon blown up. Now that the ads no longer run, *All My Children* does occasionally bring Rogers back as Ray's ghost.

5

Casting Call

THE 10 ACTORS WHO HAVE BEEN WITH THEIR SHOWS THE LONGEST

1. Helen Wagner (Nancy Hughes McCloskey, *As the World Turns*)

   40 years and counting: 1956 to present. Wagner was originally fired after her first thirteen-week cycle ended, but was hired back almost immediately. In the early '80s, she left the show for a couple of years when she and co-star Don MacLaughlin (Chris Hughes) were reduced to mere walk-ons.

2. Don Hastings (Bob Hughes, *As the World Turns*)

   36 years and counting: 1960 to present. Bob Hughes had been introduced as a child when the show debuted. Prior to aging Bob into a college student, Hastings had been with *The Edge of Night* since its premiere, which took place the same day as *As the World Turns*.

3. Patricia Bruder (Ellen Lowell Stewart, *As the World Turns*)

   36 years and counting: 1960 to present. Bruder took over her role from Wendy Drew, who had been with the show since the beginning. In 1995, Bruder was reduced from contract player to recurring status.

4. Eileen Fulton (Lisa Grimaldi, *As the World Turns*)

36 years and counting: 1960 to present. Fulton left in the mid-'60s to star on the *As the World Turns* spin-off *Our Private World* and returned two years later. She left again in 1983, but returned the following year.

5. Mary Stuart (Joanne Gardner Barron, *Search for Tomorrow*)

35 years: 1951–1986. Stuart stayed with show for its entire run.

6. Larry Haines (Stu Bergman, *Search for Tomorrow*)

35 years: 1951–1986. Haines was introduced shortly into the show's run.

7. John Beradino (Steve Hardy, *General Hospital*)

33 years and counting: 1963 to present. Beradino has been with the show since its premiere.

8. Rachel Ames (Audrey Hardy, *General Hospital*)

32 years and counting: 1964 to present. Audrey was originally scheduled to die shortly after marrying Steve.

9. Charita Bauer (Bert Bauer, *Guiding Light*)

32 years: 1952–1984. Bauer joined the radio cast of *The Guiding Light* in 1950. On radio and television, she played Bert simultaneously from 1952 to 1956, when the series went off the radio.

10. Henderson Forsythe (Dr. David Stewart, *As the World Turns*)

31 years: 1960–1991. For the last few years, Forsythe appeared on the show sporadically.

FIRST CHOICES FOR 12 ROLES

1. Robert Foxworth for J. R. Ewing, *Dallas*

The role of J. R. Ewing was originally offered to Robert Foxworth, who would go on to star as Chase Gioberti in *Falcon Crest*. Foxworth had some trouble, however, with playing J. R. as totally wicked as the script called for. He thought the character should be softened at least a bit. Larry Hagman, on the other hand, liked J. R. just the way he was. His obvious enthusiasm for playing such an out-and-out villain won him the role.

2. Clu Gulagher for Chase Gioberti, *Falcon Crest*

Although Chase Gioberti was a character more to Robert Foxworth's liking, a strong man with a conscience, he was not the first choice to play him on the series. Clu Gulagher, who had starred in such TV westerns as *The Tall Man* and *The Virginian* as well as the short-lived prime-time soap *The Survivors*, had gone so far as to film the pilot episode. When critics found the pilot "too ordinary," Gulagher was replaced with Foxworth.

3. Samantha Eggar for Maggie Gioberti, *Falcon Crest* and for Pamela Capwell, *Santa Barbara*

Like Gulagher, British film actress Samantha Eggar had also filmed the *Falcon Crest* pilot. The producers ultimately decided she wasn't quite right for the part of Maggie and hired Susan Sullivan instead. When *Santa Barbara* was casting C. C. Capwell's long-lost wife, Pamela, the producers decided to hire a name actress and chose Eggar. Although she accepted the role, she backed out after she received her first script and realized how much work was involved. The part went to Shirley Ann Field, who was quickly replaced by Marj Dusay.

4. Lloyd Bochner for C. C. Capwell, *Santa Barbara*

Lloyd Bochner, who had played Cecil Colby on *Dynasty*, suffered a heart attack right before he was to begin playing the role of *Santa Barbara's* C.C. Capwell. In his place was cast another *Dynasty* alumnus, Peter Mark Richman (Andrew Laird), who was soon replaced by another *Dynasty* alumnus, Paul Burke (Neal McVane), who was soon replaced by Charles Bateman. In 1986 Jed Allan (Don Craig, *Days of Our Lives*) took over the role and kept it until the series was cancelled in 1993.

5. Jane Elliot for Augusta Lockridge, *Santa Barbara*

Jane Elliot turned down the role of Augusta Lockridge because she preferred not to leave New York. (*Santa Barbara* was not only set but also taped in California.) Instead, she took the role of Cynthia Preston on the New York–based *All My Children*. A couple of years later, however, she would head West to play Angelica Deveraux on *Days of Our Lives*.

6. Grant Show for Ben Shelby, *Ryan's Hope*

Grant Show (now Jake Hansen, *Melrose Place*) was originally hired to play the role of Ben Shelby, Maggie Shelby's (Calli Timmons) troubled brother on *Ryan's Hope*. Because of Show's resemblance to actor David Sederholm (who played police lieutenant Bill Hyde), the producers decided to revamp the role to be Bill Hyde's troubled brother, Rick. The role of Ben was shelved for a couple of years and then given to Jim Wlcek (who went on to play Linc Lafferty on *As the World Turns*).

7. Linda Evans for Pamela Ewing, *Dallas*

Before *Dallas* had an official title, it was referred to as the "Untitled Linda Evans Project." As the storylines developed, the role of Pam didn't look as though it was going to be big enough for Evans, so she opted out of the series. The role then came down to a choice between Victoria Principal, who got it, and Judith Chapman, who would go on to star on three daytime soap operas: *Ryan's Hope* as Charlotte Greer; *General Hospital* as Ginny Blake; and *Days of Our Lives* as Angelica Deveraux. Evans, of course, went on to play Krystle Carrington on *Dynasty*.

8. George Peppard for Blake Carrington, *Dynasty*

Peppard disagreed with the producers over the direction of the character and walked off the set. John Forsythe took over the role.

9. Mickey Rooney for Katherine Chancellor's kidnaper, *The Young and the Restless*

During the semi-comic storyline in which Katherine Chancellor (Jeanne Cooper) was kidnaped and replaced with a look-alike (also played by Cooper), *The Young and the Restless* wanted Mickey Rooney to play the part of the man who held her captive. The character would have been named Mick after Rooney. Both he and second choice Red Buttons turned the role down. Third choice Morey Amsterdam said yes, and the character was named Morey.

10. Sophia Loren for Francesca Gioberti, *Falcon Crest*

Sophia Loren was the first choice for the part of Angela Channing's (Jane Wyman) half-sister Francesca Gioberti on *Falcon Crest*. Loren's salary demands were too far beyond what the show was willing to pay, and the part went instead to another famed Italian screen star, Gina Lollobrigida.

11. Faye Dunaway for Sable Colby, *The Colbys*

In addition to moving John James and Emma Samms (Jeff and Fallon Colby) over from *Dynasty*, the producers wanted to cast *The Colbys* with movie stars like Charlton Heston (Jason Colby), Barbara Stanwyck (Constance Colby), and Katherine Ross (Francesca Langdon). For the role of Jason's wife, Sable, the producers wanted Faye Dunaway. Although Dunaway was interested, the show could not meet her salary demands. Angie Dickinson (*Police Woman*) was also considered for the part before it was offered to British actress Stephanie Beacham.

12. Cher for Ruby Ashford, *Search for Tomorrow*

In 1983, shortly before her film career took off, Cher agreed to appear on *Search for Tomorrow* as Ruby Ashford, newcomer Lloyd Kendall's (Peter Haskell) companion. At the last minute, Cher backed out of the deal. The part then went to another 1960s rock singer, Michelle Phillips of the Mamas and the Papas. (Phillips would go on to play Anne Matheson on *Knots Landing*.)

12 SOAP ROLES THAT GOT AWAY FROM NOW-FAMOUS ACTORS

1. *Dynasty*'s Krystle Carrington (played by Linda Evans)
   Who Else Auditioned: Deidre Hall (Marlena Evans, *Days of Our Lives*)

2. *All My Children*'s Linda Warner (played by Melissa Leo)
   Who Else Auditioned: Film star Julia Roberts (*Pretty Woman*)

3. *Santa Barbara*'s Kelly Capwell (played by Robin Wright)
   Who Else Auditioned: Julia Roberts, Lynn Herring (Lucy Coe, *General Hospital*), and Marcia Cross (Kimberly Shaw, *Melrose Place*)

4. *General Hospital*'s Frisco Jones (played by Jack Wagner)
   Who Else Auditioned: Grant Show (Jake Hansen, *Melrose Place*), Brad Maule (who was then cast as Frisco's brother Tony), Randall England (who became Frisco's enemy Jack Slater), and Kevin Bernhardt (who filled in for Jack Wagner when he was out with a back injury).

5. *Days of Our Lives'* Doug Williams (played by Bill Hayes)

    Who Else Auditioned: John Aniston (currently Victor Kiriakis on the show)

    Note: Bill Hayes ended up marrying his leading lady, Susan Seaforth Hayes, who played Julie. Aniston went on to do *Love of Life*, where he met his own future wife, Sherry Rooney.

6. *All My Children's* Tara Martin (played by Karen Lyn Gorney)

    Who Else Auditioned: Susan Lucci (who would be cast as Erica Kane instead)

    Note: Gorney had originally read for the part of Erica Kane.

7. *Guiding Light's* Morgan Richards (played by Kristen Vigard)

    Who Else Auditioned: Lisa Brown (who would be cast as Nola Reardon)

    Note: Doug Marland created the role of Nola for Brown as a spoiler in the Morgan/Kelly romance. He also created for her the role of Iva Snyder on *As the World Turns*.

8. *All My Children's* Brian Bodine (played by Matt Borlenghi)

    Who Else Auditioned: Movie actor Brendan Fraser (*School Ties* and *Encino Man*)

9. *General Hospital's* Frankie Greco (played by Robert Fontaine)

    Who Else Auditioned: Rick Hearst (currently Alan-Michael Spaulding, *Guiding Light*)

    Note: Fontaine also beat out Antonio Sabáto, Jr., for the role of Rafe on *Santa Barbara*.

10. *Loving's* Lorna Forbes (played by O'Hara Parker)

    Who Else Auditioned: Marla Maples

    Note: Years later, Maples guest-starred as herself on the show.

11. *General Hospital's* A. J. Quartermaine (played now by Sean Kanan)

    Who Else Auditioned: Steve Burton (who now plays A. J.'s half-brother Jason)

    Note: Even Kanan didn't get the role the first time he went up for it. He lost out to Gerald Hopkins. When the show let Hopkins go to take the character in a new direction, Kanan auditioned again and won the role.

12. *Beverly Hills 90210's* Brenda Walsh (played by Shannen Doherty)

    Who Else Auditioned: Gabrielle Carteris (Andrea Zuckerman on the show)

10 ACTORS WHO PLAYED TWO UNRELATED ROLES ON THE SAME SOAP

While many characters eventually discover a long-lost twin or are kidnaped by a look-alike impostor at some point during their years with a soap, sometimes an actor who played one role on a soap will play another, totally unrelated role with no word of explanation as to the physical resemblance between the two characters.

1. Quinn Redeker

In 1979, *The Young and the Restless'* Nikki Reed (Melody Thomas Scott) killed her father, Nick (played by Quinn Redeker), when he tried to rape her. After a few years as the villainous Alex Marshall on *Days of Our Lives*, Redeker returned to *The Young and the Restless* as Danny Romalotti's (Michael Damian) father, Rex Sterling. He was killed on the show yet again, this time while trying to stop a burglary.

2. Beverlee McKinsey

It was *Another World*'s rags-to-riches stories. Beverlee McKinsey started off on *Another World* as a have-not, originating the role of Emma Frame Ordway. Barely had she left the show, when she turned around and returned as the wealthy Iris Carrington, the role that made her famous.

3. Leigh McCloskey

Leigh McCloskey made little impression on *General Hospital* as Dr. Michael Baranski. As Mafia prince Damian Smith, however, he was the catalyst for more than half the show's storylines in 1994. McCloskey had also played two roles on *Santa Barbara*: rapist Zach Kelton and District Attorney Ethan Asher. While the two men were not related, the resemblance between them was noted—often with a look of pure horror on someone's face.

4. Christine Jones

In 1975, Christine Jones played Sheila Rafferty on *One Life to Live*. Ten years later, she was Pamela Stuart, one of Asa Buchanan's spare wives. In between, she filled in as Victoria Lord while Erika Slezak was on maternity leave.

5. Gary Pillar/Gary Carpenter

As Mike Bauer, Gary Pillar spent a year on *Another World* before bringing the character back to *Guiding Light.* Ten years and two Mike Bauers later, Pillar (now using the name Gary Carpenter) returned to *Another World* to play Raymond Gordon.

6. Roy Thinnes

Roy Thinnes played two of Cassie Callison's fathers-in-law on *One Life to Live,* Alex Crown and General Sloan Carpenter.

7. Nicholas Coster

Nicholas Coster originated the role of John Eldridge, Lisa Hughes's (Eileen Fulton) second husband, which he played on *As the World Turns* and its prime-time spin-off *Our Private World.* Almost thirty years later, Coster returned to *As the World Turns* not as John Eldridge—that part had been revived and buried by Michael Levin—but as European businessman Eduardo Grimaldi, who would become Lisa's seventh husband.

8. Louise Shaffer

Louise Shaffer was both *Search for Tomorrow*'s second Emily Rogers Hunter (in 1967) and its second Stephanie Wilkins Wyatt (in 1984).

9. John Considine

While most actors who have played two characters on the same show usually play something short term the first time around, John Considine had been on *Another World* for eight years (1974–1982) as Vic Hastings before returning four years later to play Donna Love's (Anna Stuart) evil father, Reginald.

10. Velekka Gray

Velekka Gray not only played two separate roles on *The Young and the Restless*—Sharon Reaves, a doctor, and Ruby, a manicurist—she played them during the same period of time in 1983.

THE 13 MOST RECAST ROLES ON DAYTIME

1–2. Patti Barron Whiting (*Search for Tomorrow*) and Tom Hughes (*As the World Turns*)

11 recasts

3–5. Jamie Frame (*Another World*), Michael Powers (*The Doctors*), and Mike Horton (*Days of Our Lives*)

> 9 recasts

6–7. Marianne Randolph and Michael Randolph (both *Another World*)

> 8 recasts

8–9. Annie Stewart Ward (*As the World Turns*), and Kevin Buchanan (*One Life to Live*)

> 7 recasts

10–13. Mary Anderson (*Days of Our Lives*), Paul Stewart (*As the World Turns*), Hope Bauer Spaulding (*Guiding Light*), and Dee Stewart Dixon (*As the World Turns*)

> 6 recasts

8 DIFFICULT RECASTS THAT WORKED OUT SUCCESSFULLY

1. Robert Kelker-Kelly as Bo Brady, *Days of Our Lives*

As Bo Brady, Peter Reckell hit superstar status on daytime. When he and Kristian Alfonso left *Days of Our Lives* in the late '80s, they were both written out. They returned in 1990, but Alfonso left again six weeks later, and her character was "killed off." When Reckell left, the part was recast—a move Reckell himself has voiced dismay over. But Robert Kelker-Kelly picked up several *Soap Opera Digest* awards (a combination of editors' choices and fans voting) proving that he had won over fans and critics alike. Despite Kelker-Kelly's immense popularity, he was fired in 1995 and replaced with Reckell himself.

2–3. Anne Heche and Jensen Buchanan as Victoria and Marley Hudson, *Another World*

What's most amazing is that these roles have been recast successfully twice. Ellen Wheeler won an Emmy for playing the twins as did her replacement, Anne Heche. Although *Soap Opera Digest* initially picked Jensen Buchanan as the Worst Recast of the Year when she took over the roles, the editors nominated her as Best

Heroine for their *Soap Opera Digest* Awards a few years down the line. When Buchanan left the role, the producers couldn't find anyone to replace her. Eventually, the show coaxed Buchanan back, promising her that she only had to play Victoria and not Marley as well.

4. Jill Larson as Opal Gardner, *All My Children*

Dorothy Lyman picked up back-to-back Emmys for playing off-the-wall Opal Gardner. Surprisingly, she was not contacted when the show was bringing the character back some five years after she left. (Lyman has gone on to do several other daytime soaps since then.) Her replacement, Jill Larson, has managed to pick up an Emmy nomination of her own for playing Opal.

5. Peter Bergman as Jack Abbott, *The Young and the Restless*

Terry Lester was immensely popular as Jack Abbott on *The Young and the Restless* and picked up four Emmy nominations for his work. Many doubted that Peter Bergman, who played *All My Children*'s good-guy Dr. Cliff Warner on and off for a decade, could do justice to the part. But Bergman proved them wrong, picking up not only nominations but a pair of back-to-back Emmys.

6. Marj Dusay as Alexandra Spaulding, *Guiding Light*

Beverlee McKinsey is considered by many to be the finest soap actress out there. The search for her replacement took *Guiding Light* a long time. Marj Dusay has proven to be a wise choice. In 1995, she was nominated as Best Actress, an honor that McKinsey never received for her work on *Guiding Light*.

7. Jess Walton as Jill Abbott, *The Young and the Restless*

Brenda Dickson, an original *The Young and the Restless* castmember, was immensely popular in the role of Jill Abbott. While the part had been recast before, no one really clicked in the part the way that Dickson did—until Jess Walton came along. She has an Emmy to show just how well she's made the part her own.

8. Drake Hogestyn as Roman Brady, *Days of Our Lives*

In the early '80s, Wayne Northrop was the leading man on *Days of Our Lives*. When he left, the show "killed off" the character and went through the whole plastic surgery cliché to bring in another actor, that being Drake Hogestyn. Despite how popular Northrop was, the show wasn't about to fire Hogestyn when Northrop agreed to come back. A convoluted plot was set up to allow both actors to be on the show at the same time. Interestingly, the writers didn't know what to do with Northrop's Roman after a couple of years and wrote him off the show while Hogestyn's fake Roman (now known as John Black) continues to thrive on the front burner.

12 ODD RECASTING CHOICES

1–2. Sabrina Fullerton and Frannie Hughes, *As the World Turns*

In 1986, while in London, Frannie Hughes (played at the time by Julianne Moore) saw a woman who could have been her identical twin. For the next few months, Frannie chased around Europe looking for the woman she'd seen. While not a twin, Sabrina Fullerton (also played by Moore) turned out to be Frannie's long-lost half-sister/first cousin. (They shared the same father, Bob Hughes, while their mothers were sisters, Kim Reynolds and Jennifer Hughes.) The physical resemblance between the two characters was so great that Frannie's fiancé, Seth Snyder (Steve Bassett), once slept with Sabrina by accident. When Moore left the show, both characters were written off as well. Mary Ellen Stuart revived the role of Frannie but not of Sabrina. Despite the major role the characters' resemblance to each other had played in their storylines, the producers hired not only a different actress to play Sabrina (Claire Beckman) but an actress who bore not even a passing resemblance to Stuart.

3. Blair Daimler, *One Life to Live*

This has to win the award for least politically correct recasting. The role of Blair Daimler, Dorian Lord's blackmailing, gold-digging niece, was originally played by Mia Korf, an Amerasian actor. At one point, reference had even been made to Blair's father being Asian. Two years after Korf left the show, the producers decided to revive the character. Although they auditioned Asian and Amerasian actresses, they ultimately gave the part to the very Caucasian Kassie Wesley.

4. Duke Lavery, *General Hospital*

When Ian Buchanan left the role of Duke Lavery, the character was presumed dead, killed by the mob—but no body was ever found. In 1989, Buchanan came back to *General Hospital* for a few days to facilitate a plastic surgery storyline that would allow the role of Duke to be recast. When the bandages came off, the audience saw the face of Gregory Beecroft, who had just recently been killed off as Brock Lombard on *As the World Turns*. With his new face and without his trademark Scottish accent, Duke became Jonathan Paget, a mystery man in Port Charles. Despite all the effort the show had put into recasting the part, Duke was killed off within a matter of months, this time for good.

5. Dr. Dan Walton, *Search for Tomorrow*

Martin E. Brooks originated the role of Dan Walton in 1960. When he left a year later to do a play, Philip Abbott took over the part. While fans of the show were used to the recasting of roles, more than a few were left a little confused when Brooks returned to the show in 1962, not to resume his role as Dan but to play Dan's best friend, Dr. Everett Moore.

6. Marley and Victoria Hudson, *Another World*

Ellen Wheeler had originated the roles of twins Marley and Victoria Love on *Another World* and won an Emmy award for playing both parts. After she left the show, her replacement Anne Heche won herself an Emmy for playing the dual roles. When Heche left, Wheeler (who had won a second Emmy for playing AIDS patient Cindy Chandler on *All My Children*) approached the show about returning. Despite the fact that Wheeler had originated the roles and had won an Emmy for her work, *Another World* didn't feel that she was right for the part anymore. The show instead hired Jensen Buchanan, who had played Sarah Gordon on *One Life to Live*.

7. Grace Forrester, *Days of Our Lives*

Camilla Moore played the evil Gillian Forrester while her real-life twin sister, Carey Moore, played Gillian's good twin, Grace. After Gillian was killed off, Camilla took over the role of Grace, and Carey Moore ended up being the one to leave the show.

8–9. Mason Capwell, *Santa Barbara* and Mike Roy, *All My Children*

Recasts are always a bit jarring on the audience, especially when they involve high-profile characters being replaced by well-known actors. Usually, the show tries to make the change-over less jarring by sending the characters away for a week, a month or even a year and then reintroducing them played by the new actor. Unfortunately, storyline restraints didn't allow the producers of *Santa*

Barbara and *All My Children* such luxury when it came to replacing Terry Lester as Mason Capwell and Nicholas Surovy as Mike Roy. Both recasts took place midway during an episode. *Santa Barbara* cut away to a commercial with the blond Lester playing Mason and returned to find in his place the dark-haired Gordon Thomson, who had played Adam Carrington on *Dynasty*. Similarly, *All My Children* fans had come back from a commercial to find the gritty Surovy replaced by the aristocratic Hugo Napier, who had played Gunnar Stenbeck on *As the World Turns*.

10. Dr. James Grainger, *The Young and the Restless*

While John O'Hurley did bear a closer physical resemblance than his predecessor John Phillip Law to Peter Barton, who played Grainger's son Scott, O'Hurley is only one year older than Barton, which is a bit of stretch even by soap's casting standards.

11–12. Fallon and Amanda Carrington, *Dynasty*

American-born Pamela Sue Martin and Briton Catherine Oxenberg originated the roles of Fallon and Amanda Carrington respectively on *Dynasty*. Yet, when the roles were recast, Fallon picked up a British accent being played by British-born Emma Samms and Amanda lost her accent being played by American Karen Cellini.

2 CURIOUS RECASTS PRODUCERS CONSIDERED

1. Alan Spaulding, *Guiding Light*

Although Michael Zaslow had created the most distinctive villain in *Guiding Light* history, Roger Thorpe, the show approached him about taking over the role of Alan Spaulding when Chris Bernau fell ill. Zaslow suggested instead that the show resurrect the presumed dead Roger Thorpe, which it did.

2. Marlena Evans, *Days of Our Lives*

Back in the late '80s when it looked as though Deidre Hall was never coming back to *Days of Our Lives*, the producers thought about recasting the part. Hall would be more than a little difficult to replace, but the show knew of one actress the audience might accept as Marlena: Deidre Hall's twin sister, Andrea Hall-Lovell, who had played Marlena's twin sister Samantha on the show. The resemblance was so

Photographer: Michael Goldman

LINDA DANO
(Felicia Gallant, *Another World*)

Boy, has this Daytime Emmy Award–winner changed her look through the years. Linda Dano has long been a favorite of *Soap Opera Update*, always so accommodating and accessible that it simply made sense to include one of our favorite photos of this multitalented star.

Note: All photographs were taken exclusively for *Soap Opera Update*.

Photographer: E. J. Carr

SUSAN LUCCI AND MICHAEL NADER
(Erica Kane and Dimitri Marrick, *All My Children*)

This photo was used on the cover of our June 27, 1995 issue, which marked a new focus for the magazine as we expanded our news coverage and reader participation. How apropos that the reigning queen of daytime, Susan Lucci, graced this cover, having had the distinction of appearing on the very first *Soap Opera Update* cover seven years ago.

KRISTIAN ALFONSO AND PETER RECKELL
(Hope and Bo Brady, *Days of Our Lives*)

Talk about timing! *Soap Opera Update* was set to shoot a Bo and Hope cover for our August 8, 1995 issue the week that Robert Kelker-Kelly was fired from the show. Bo originator Peter Reckell stepped in with a moment's notice and agreed to grace the cover in the midst of a hectic schedule—and before his signature beard had fully grown in. How great it is to have this supercouple of the '80s together again and to have them on our cover reunited for the very first time.

Photographer: Bill Morris

MARTHA BYRNE
(Lily Walsh Grimaldi,
As the World Turns)

Martha Byrne's return to *As the World Turns* in 1993 was met with great fanfare. Her Daytime Emmy Award–winning turn as Lily Walsh was sorely missed when the actress chose to leave the show to pursue greener pastures in Hollywood. We love this photo because it shows a sultrier side to this talented lady who virtually grew up before our eyes.

KATHERINE KELLY LANG
AND RONN MOSS
(Brooke Logan and
Ridge Forrester,
The Bold and the Beautiful)

Photographer: Greg Henry

This LA-based show, despite being a half hour, has seen a multitude of stars and characters set port in town. Through all of the storyline trials and tribulations, however, one thing has remained constant: the star power and onscreen romance of Katherine Kelly Lang and Ronn Moss as Brooke and Ridge. Many a photo has been taken of this smouldering duo, but we felt this shot epitomized their beauty and chemistry.

NOELLE BECK AND ROBERT TYLER
(Trisha Alden and Trucker MacKenzie, *Loving*)

The truth of the matter is that *Loving* was always the lowest rated soap on the air. *Soap Opera Update* hardly ever—almost never, to be quite honest—put it on our cover. But when it came to the appeal of Noelle Beck and Robert Tyler, who as Trisha and Trucker received the majority of viewer mail that came to the office, we figured, why not? When you look like this couple, how can you lose?

Photographer: E. J. Carr

Photographer: Danny Sanchez

BETH EHLERS, MARK DERWIN, MELINA KANAKAREDES, RICK HEARST, KIMBERLY SIMMS, AND VINCENT IRIZARRY
(Harley Cooper, A. C. Mallett, Eleni Cooper, Alan-Michael Spaulding, Mindy Lewis, and Nick McHenry, *Guiding Light*)

Imagine the scheduling to get six top stars of the highly popular *Guiding Light* together for one shoot. We were thrilled when it all came together because at the time of this March 3, 1992 cover, these three romances were heating up the screen.

RENA SOFER AND WALLY KURTH

(Lois Cerullo and Ned Quartermaine, *General Hospital*)

This was the second marriage for Port Charles lovebirds Ned and Lois, mainly because lovebird Ned was chirping in Katherine's birdcage as well. Nevertheless, the wedding went off without a hitch, and so did this June 13, 1995 cover, which ranks as one of our favorite wedding covers ever.

DOUG DAVIDSON, LAURALEE BELL, AND MICHAEL DAMIAN
(Paul Williams, Christine "Cricket" Blair, and Danny Romalotti,
***The Young and the Restless*)**

Would she or wouldn't she? That was the question as Christine prepared to marry Paul only two weeks after her ex-husband—and the great love of her life—Danny re-entered her life. This January 10, 1995 cover showed the threesome in happy moments. (As fans will remember, only hours before the nuptials, Danny's jealous and maniacal wife Phyllis ran the bride and groom-to-be over with her car!)

Photographer: E. J. Carr

ROGER HOWARTH
(Todd Manning, *One Life to Live*)

We have to admit that we went into this October 4, 1994 cover with a little trepidation. After all, we'd be showcasing a rapist with the cover line: "Has Todd Raped Again?" Apparently, our readers wanted to know. Roger Howarth's popularity as the redeemed Todd Manning and the intrigue of the storyline had them tuning in. Good sport Howarth even donned a mask for the dual image cover.

close that the audience had once mistook Samantha for Marlena when Samantha was killed by the Salem Strangler. Andrea Hall-Lovell, who has gotten out of show business, had no interest in taking over her sister's role, and the show abandoned its plans to recast.

5 CASES WHERE ACTORS RETURNED TO THEIR ROLES AFTER THEIR CHARACTERS HAD GONE THROUGH MAJOR RECONSTRUCTIVE PLASTIC SURGERY

1. Lily Walsh, *As the World Turns*

Heather Rattray took over the role of heroine Lily Walsh a few months after Martha Byrne vacated the role. According to the story, her face, damaged in an explosion, had been redone. (She was also significantly taller.) Lily's new look was meant to signify some major internal changes that had taken place within the character. For a while, she was developing into a ruthless business person not unlike her adoptive mother, Lucinda (Elizabeth Hubbard). When Rattray left the role in 1994, Byrne returned to it.

2. Steven Carrington, *Dynasty*

The plastic surgery storyline that transformed Al Corley into Jack Coleman served no plot purposes. It was employed ostensibly because *Dynasty* had never recast a role before. Blake recognized Steven right away in the street because of his eyes. When Coleman was not available to do the *Dynasty* reunion movie, Corley was hired to play Steven, probably so as not to jar the audience too much readjusting to a third Steven.

3. Joe Novak, *Ryan's Hope*

When Roscoe Born left *Ryan's Hope*, the part of Joe Novak was recast with Michael Hennessy with no explanations. The character was presumed dead for two years until Walt Willey (now Jackson Montgomery, *All My Children*) took over the role of Joe with a physically altered face. Few viewers caught on to the fact that Willey was really Joe since he also stood almost a foot taller than Born and was blonde. When Joe and his wife, Siobhan, left and came back, Born resumed the role long enough for Joe to be killed off.

4. Max Holden, *One Life to Live*

When James De Paiva left the show, Max's car hit a tree and exploded. The plastic surgeon molded him into Nicholas Walker, who didn't prove popular enough with the audiences. Fan favorite De Paiva returned shortly thereafter. His first day back in the role, De Paiva looked straight into the camera and said, "I feel like the old Max again."

5. Roman Brady, *Days of Our Lives*

This may be the oddest case of an actor returning to a role. In 1986, Drake Hogestyn took over the role of Roman Brady from the immensely popular Wayne Northrop, who had left the show two years earlier. When Hogestyn joined the show, Roman had a new face but no memory. For a while, he worried that he might actually be Roman's archenemy, Stefano DiMera. Eventually he regained his memory—or so the story went for six years. When Northrop expressed interest in returning to the role of Roman in 1992, *Days* jumped at the chance to get him back especially since it involved reteaming him with Deidre Hall, who was also returning to the show. Hogestyn, however, had proven himself too popular with the fans to simply fire him. So, a convoluted plot unfolded about the Hogestyn Roman only having been brainwashed into thinking he was the real Roman for the past six years. Beyond the confusing plotlines that have resulted from the search for Hogestyn's real identity, the placement of Hogestyn and Northrop in the same scenes together, revealing how unalike their builds are, makes everyone on the show look a little foolish for having been tricked by this impostor. In the end, Northrop's return lasted only two years; the character of Roman was written out for lack of storyline while Hogestyn, who now calls himself John Black, remains front and center.

6

The Celebrity Columns

25 FAMOUS FANS OF THE DAYTIME SOAPS

1. Roy Rogers, cowboy star: *Guiding Light*

2. Dale Evans, cowgirl star: *As the World Turns* and *Guiding Light*

3. Liza Minnelli, singer/actress: *One Life to Live*

4. Michael Keaton, actor: *The Bold and the Beautiful*

5. Stevie Nicks, singer: *General Hospital*

6. Russell Baker, *New York Times* columnist: *All My Children*

7. Aretha Franklin, The Queen of Soul: *The Young and the Restless*, *As the World Turns*, and *Guiding Light*

8. John Malkovich, actor: *The Bold and the Beautiful*

9. Luther Vandross, singer: *All My Children, One Life to Live,* and *General Hospital*

10. Marlee Matlin, Oscar-winning actress: *Loving*

11. Kate Pierson, singer with the B-52s: *All My Children*

12. Janet Dailey, romance novelist: *Days of Our Lives*

13. Shelby Foote, Civil War historian: *As the World Turns*

14. Camille Paglia, social critic: *The Young and the Restless*

15. Gladys Knight, singer: *All My Children*

16. Ron Palillo, *Welcome Back, Kotter's* Horshack: *Another World*

17. Toni Braxton, singer: *The Young and the Restless*

18. Loni Anderson, actress: *Days of Our Lives*

19. Barry Gibb, 1/3 of the Bee Gees: *The Young and the Restless*

20. Renata Tebaldi, opera singer: *As the World Turns*

21. Van Cliburn, pianist: *All My Children* and *As the World Turns*

22. Catherine O'Hara, actress: *As the World Turns*

23. Nichelle Nichols, *Star Trek's* Lt. Uhura: *All My Children* and *The Young and the Restless*

24. The Artist Formerly Known as Prince, singer/musician: *General Hospital*

25. Prince Albert of Monaco: *The Young and the Restless*

10 LEGENDARY FIGURES WHO WATCHED THE DAYTIME SOAPS

1. Bette Davis, actress: *As the World Turns* and *Guiding Light*

2. Andy Warhol, pop artist: *As the World Turns*

3. Judy Garland, actress/singer: *Another World* and *Search for Tomorrow*

4. Thurgood Marshall, Supreme Court Justice: *Days of Our Lives*

5. Fritz Lang, movie director: *Dark Shadows*

6. Cole Porter, songwriter: *The Edge of Night*

7. P. G. Wodehouse, writer: *The Edge of Night*

8. Tallulah Bankhead, actress: *The Edge of Night* and *The Secret Storm*

9. Vincent Price, horror movie actor: *Dark Shadows*

10. Tennessee Williams, playwright: *Another World* and *From These Roots*

12 PROFESSIONAL ATHLETES WHO WATCH THE SOAPS

1. Wayne Gretzky, Los Angeles Kings

Gretzky appeared as himself in a barroom scene with Melody Thomas Scott on *The Young and the Restless*, which he watches. Although Gretzky also follows *One Life to Live* and *General Hospital*, he has turned down offers to appear on any other soaps.

2. Cal Ripken, Jr., Baltimore Orioles

While traveling on the road, Ripken signs in under the name Brad Carlton, Don Diamont's character on *The Young and the Restless*.

3. Sugar Ray Leonard, boxer (retired)

Leonard is a fan of *The Young and the Restless* and a personal friend of Eric Braeden, who plays Victor Newman on the show and who himself boxes onscreen and off for exercise.

4. Danny Sullivan, racing car driver

Sullivan chatted with *All My Children*'s Erica Kane during the Montgomery Cup Ball in 1987. Three years later, he filmed a promotional spot celebrating the show's twentieth anniversary.

5. Dave Justice, Atlanta Braves

Justice played a business acquaintance of Victor Newman on *The Young and the Restless.*

6. Isiah Thomas, formerly of the Detroit Pistons; currently Vice-President of the Toronto Raptors

Thomas watches *All My Children, One Life to Live,* and *Guiding Light.* In college, he would not take courses that met in the afternoon. Thomas appeared on the 1993 Daytime Emmy Awards in a segment highlighting celebrity soap fans.

7. Dave Cone, Toronto Blue Jays

A longtime fan of *All My Children,* Cone can remember back to Erica's first husband.

8. Warren Moon, Minnesota Vikings

Moon watches both *The Young and the Restless* and *All My Children.* When he quarterbacked for the Houston Oilers, he said that half the team watched *The Young and the Restless* in the training room.

9. Barry Bonds, San Francisco Giants

A fan of Fiona Hutchison, Bonds followed her from *One Life to Live* (where she played Gabrielle Medina) to *Guiding Light* (where she played Jenna Bradshaw).

10. Flipper Anderson, L.A. Rams

Anderson pushed a wheelchair down a corridor in a hospital scene on *The Young and the Restless.*

11. Tommy Hearns, boxer

Hearns one time pulled up beside Eric Braeden's car in his limousine to give him tips on how Victor should handle his women on *The Young and the Restless.*

12. Charles Barkley, Phoenix Suns

When Charles Barkley was on the Philadelphia 76ers, he showed up late for a day game because he didn't want to miss the end of *All My Children.*

6 SOAP FANS IN THE WHITE HOUSE

1. President George Bush: *All My Children*

2. Jacqueline Kennedy Onassis: *Dark Shadows*

3. Eleanor Roosevelt: *The Edge of Night*

4. Ladybird Johnson: *General Hospital*

5. Rosalyn Carter: *Ryan's Hope*

6. Miss Lillian (Jimmy Carter's mother): *All My Children*

Note: When Augusta Lockridge (Louise Sorel's character on *Santa Barbara*) went blind, she received a note from President Reagan, who promised that he and First Lady Nancy would be praying for her recovery.

10 CELEBRITIES WHO GOT TO APPEAR ON THEIR FAVORITE SOAPS

1. Carol Burnett

A longtime *All My Children* fan, Carol Burnett occasionally incorporated the show's plotlines into the opening segments of her variety show, where she chatted with the studio audience. In 1976, she made her first appearance on the soap as Mrs. Johnson, a patient at Pine Valley Hospital. In 1983, she came back for a week, playing Verla Grubbs, a friend of Myrtle Fargate's who discovered during the course of her stay in Pine Valley that Langley Wallingford was her biological father. During *All My Children*'s twenty-fifth anniversary in 1995, Burnett reprised her role as Verla, coming back to tell her father she was engaged to be married. Burnett also hosted a prime-time special commemorating the show's anniversary.

2. Elizabeth Taylor

Elizabeth Taylor earned a place in daytime history and on the cover of *People* magazine when she guest-starred on *General Hospital* in the fall of 1981. Taylor had contacted the show about appearing on it, and producer Gloria Monty created for her the role of Helena Cassadine, widow of Mikos Cassadine, the mad scientist Luke Spencer had accidentally killed. Helena crashed Luke and Laura's wedding to place her curse on them. Because the outdoor wedding had already been filmed, Taylor's scenes had to be edited in. Taylor did, however, get to tape a confrontation scene between her favorite character, Luke, and Helena. Two years later, Taylor popped up on *All My Children* during Carol Burnett's week on the show. Taylor played a charwoman in a scene with Burnett, a spoof on the character from Burnett's variety series.

3. Sammy Davis, Jr.

Like Carol Burnett, Sammy Davis, Jr., was one of the first major celebrities to go public with their love for the daytime soaps. In the 1980s, Davis got to appear on three of the shows he loved, *Love of Life*, *One Life to Live*, and *General Hospital*. He sang on *Love of Life*, and his first *One Life to Live* stint as con man Chip Warren earned him a 1980 Emmy nomination for Outstanding Cameo. He returned to the show twice more, in 1981 and 1983. On *General Hospital*, Davis played Eddie Phillips, Bryan's estranged father who wanted to make peace with his son before he died.

4. Joan Crawford

Joan Crawford's adopted daughter, Christina Crawford, had landed the role of gold digger Joan Borman Kane on *The Secret Storm*. When Christina was hospitalized, Joan, who watched the show, offered to fill in for her. Despite the forty-year age difference between Joan and Christina, the producers saw Crawford's appearance on the show as a potential ratings booster.

5. Crystal Gayle

Another World fan Crystal Gayle came onto the show as herself to debut the song "Another World (You Take Me Away To)," which would become the new theme song. On the show, she was introduced as a friend of Felicia Gallant (Linda Dano). Gayle performed the song with country singer/Broadway star Gary Morris, who had played Wayne Masterson on *The Colbys.* The song was included on an album they recorded together. During her stint on *Another World,* Gayle was almost attacked by the Sin Stalker, the serial killer who had been terrorizing Bay City at the time.

6. Liberace

Like Crystal Gayle, *Another World* fan Liberace was also brought on as himself and introduced as a friend of Felicia Gallant. One of Liberace's stipulations for appearing on the show was that he get to work with Linda Dano. Liberace not only got an invitation to Felicia's wedding to Zane Lindquist, he also got preferential seating up front. During his few days on the show, Liberace and Dano managed to squeeze in a piano duet. The show filmed a subsequent guest shot at Liberace's apartment in the Trump Tower during which he sang his trademark theme song "I'll Be Seeing You" to Felicia.

7. Reba McEntire

Once *One Life to Live* approved Susan Batten's (Luna Moody) request to bring country star Reba McEntire on the show, Batten herself flew to a McEntire concert to extend the invitation. McEntire, who has been watching the show since the early '70s, immediately accepted. McEntire played herself, an old friend of Luna's who used to have a crush on Bo Buchanan back when he owned his record company. During her two-day stint on the show, McEntire sang two songs: "The Greatest Man I Never Knew" and "Is There Life Out There?"

8. Imogene Coca

A devoted fan of the CBS line-up, comedienne Imogene Coca did a short but by her own admission none-too-memorable stint on *As the World Turns.* "All I remember is that the character [I played] was dull," Coca told one magazine. She had a far better time when she guest-starred as a cleaning woman-turned-model on rival soap *One Life to Live.*

9. Carol Channing

Carol Channing was one of the celebrities—along with Steve Allen, Jayne Meadows, and Charlton Heston—who guested on *The Bold and the Beautiful* during a fashion show benefit for The American Film Institute. During the filming, Channing ad-libbed a few lines to show everyone there how big a fan she was of the show. When Stephanie Forrester invited the celebrities to a party following the fashion show, Channing replied, "Only if Maria [Stephanie's maid] makes her famous enchiladas."

10. Roseanne

Both Roseanne and her TV persona are fans of the ABC soap line-up. She named Llanford, the setting for her show, after Llanview, the setting for *One Life to Live.* In a bit of cross-promotion between ABC prime-time and daytime, Tony Geary and Genie Francis guested as Luke and Laura on an episode of *Roseanne,* and two months later, Roseanne showed up on *General Hospital* as Jennifer Smith, the Mafia princess Luke had almost married. Roseanne's then-husband, Tom Arnold, played Jennifer's husband, Billy "Bags" Bollman. There was talk that Roseanne would also be playing a one- or two-day role on *One Life to Live.* While Clint Ritchie (Clint Buchanan), Bob Woods (Bo Buchanan), and John Loprieno (Cord Roberts) played their *One Life to Live* roles on *Roseanne,* Roseanne did not end up in Llanview.

15 NON-ACTORS WHO HAVE APPEARED AS THEMSELVES ON THE DAYTIME SOAPS

1. Barbara Bush, First Lady

All My Children: During a bone-marrow transplant story, *All My Children* closed one episode with a plea from then–First Lady Barbara Bush urging viewers to sign up for the National Registration.

2. Fabio, male model

The Bold and the Beautiful: Fabio showed up at Sally Spectra's bachelorette party.

Note: Fabio and Darlene Conley, who plays Sally, had been presenters together at the *Soap Opera Digest* Awards.

3. Rich Little, impressionist

The Young and the Restless: Little was hired by Brad Carlton's ex-wife Lisa Mansfield to mimic Brad's voice on a tape, saying good-bye to Traci, as part of her scheme to kidnap him.

4. Bob Eubanks, *Newlywed Game* host

Days of Our Lives: Eugene and Calliope Bradford appeared as contestants on *The Newlywed Game*.

5–6. Pat Sajak and Vanna White, *Wheel of Fortune* hosts

Santa Barbara: Gina Capwell competed on *Wheel of Fortune* to earn enough money for her and Keith Timmons to buy a house.

Note: Sajak had once done a one-day spot on *Days of Our Lives* as a news reporter.

7. Ed Koch, former Mayor of New York City

All My Children: Koch ran into Erica in a restaurant in New York City.

8. Donald Trump, business mogul

All My Children: Like Mayor Koch, Trump also ran into "old friend" Erica Kane in a New York restaurant.

9. Ivana Trump, businesswoman/novelist

One Life to Live: To commemorate the show's 6000th episode, Ivana Trump walked through the lobby of Ivana's, a fictitious hotel/casino in Atlantic City where some of the characters were staying.

10. Robin Leach, *Lifestyles of the Rich and Famous* host

Guiding Light: Leach appeared in one of Harley Cooper's fantasies of being rich.
One Life to Live: Leach hosted the Daisy Awards, a parody of the Daytime Emmys.

11. Nicole Miller, fashion designer

As the World Turns: Miller visited with fellow fashion designer Barbara Ryan.

12. José Eber, Hollywood hairstylist

The Bold and the Beautiful: A friend of model Ivana, Eber made over Jessica Forrester.

13. Cheryl Tiegs, supermodel

All My Children: Tiegs won a beauty contest that fellow model Erica was expecting to win.

14–15. Warren Buffet, financial investor, and Tom Murphy, CEO of ABC

All My Children: Buffet and Murphy gave financial advice to Erica Kane on several occasions. Buffet was also used in a scheme by Opal to make Palmer jealous.

3 REAL-LIFE PSYCHIATRISTS/THERAPISTS WHO HAVE TREATED SOAP CHARACTERS

1. Dr. Joyce Brothers

One Life to Live: Brothers counselled Meredith Lord, who was suffering from postpartum depression after one of her twins died.

2. Dr. Ruth Westheimer

One Life to Live: Westheimer, a sex therapist, helped Alex Hesser mold Mortimer Bern into the sexual equal of her late husband, Carlo.

3. Irene Kassorla

General Hospital: Kassorla worked with Lesley Webber while she was having troubles with her husband, Rick, in 1979. She returned to the show in 1991 to counsel Dominique Taub, who had been abused by her millionaire husband.

10 TALK-SHOW HOSTS WHO HAVE PLAYED THEMSELVES ON THE SOAPS

1. Oprah Winfrey

All My Children: While still a news anchor in Baltimore, Winfrey introduced herself to Mark Dalton and Pamela Kingsley while they were dining at Nexus.

2–3. Regis Philbin and Kathie Lee Gifford

All My Children: Philbin and Gifford attended a charity ball sponsored by Phoebe Tyler Wallingford to save the environment.

4. Sally Jessy Raphael

All My Children: Raphael met Stuart and Cindy at the Goalpost. On *Another World*, she dropped by Bay City to visit fellow talk-show host Felicia Gallant.

5. Geraldo Rivera

The Young and the Restless: Rivera introduced himself to author Traci Abbott in a restaurant scene and invited her to come on to his show.

6. Dinah Shore

Mary Hartman, Mary Hartman: Country singer Loretta Haggers appeared on *Dinah's Place*, where she got in trouble for making an anti-Semitic comment.

7. Dick Cavett

All My Children: Erica Kane ripped her mother and most of Pine Valley apart on Cavett's talk show. Cavett later showed up to help her open her nightclub.

Note: Cavett has acted in character on *The Edge of Night* and *One Life to Live*.

8. Mike Douglas

Knots Landing: Douglas interviewed Valene Ewing about her book *Capricorn Crude* and tried to get her to admit that it was about the Ewings.

9. David Susskind

Mary Hartman, Mary Hartman: Mary Hartman suffered a nervous breakdown on air while being interviewed by Susskind on his show.

10. Johnny Carson

The Doctors: Carson appeared on *The Doctors* to promote The National Association for Mental Health.

7

Actor's Choice

LINDA DANO'S 12 FAVORITE STORYLINES AND EPISODES FROM ANOTHER WORLD

In 1993, Linda Dano won the Emmy as Outstanding Actress for her role as Felicia Gallant on Another World. *During her past thirteen years on the show, Felicia's plotlines have run the gamut from madcap comedy to heavy drama. Each genre holds some special memories for Dano. They are listed in no particular order.*

Dramatic Storylines and Moments

1. "I loved the chemistry . . . between Lucas and Felicia. John Aprea, who played Lucas, was an old friend [of mine]. As he started to leave the show . . . Lucas was shot as a story point. [Those last scenes between Lucas and Felicia were] painful because not only was Felicia losing the love of her life, Linda Dano was losing a really great friend. Both made it doubly sad. So the work was quite easy to do. The whole of Lucas's death was very poignant stuff for me to play [and] brilliantly done by the writing team."

2. "Lucas's death catapulted [Felicia into the alcoholism story]. The only thing she

could do at that point, she felt, was turn to something that took the pain away. She chose alcohol. It wasn't difficult for me to play because what I played was not alcoholism. I played the pain. By playing the pain, alcohol was just a cover. The writers ... didn't miss a beat. They really hit every level, so it was quite easy for me to play. It was like I jumped on the car and we took a ride together."

3. "Another favorite scene was the day that Felicia threw Cass Winthrop (Stephen Schnetzer) out of her apartment. Early in my run on the show, they had been lovers. Felicia found out [that Cass] had cheated on her with Cecile (Nancy Frangione). It was one of those scenes ... you hope and pray for, one of those moments that starts to take on a life of its own. You're no longer just saying words and doing a part."

4. "When Brent Collins died, Wallingford died on the show. That is a day I will always remember. Brent died in real life, and within a couple of weeks we played his character's death on television. It was such a painful time for Stephen and me that we needed to play it almost simultaneously. We needed to share it with his fans. That way we could all hold hands and cry together. Somehow, it became a very big family funeral."

5. "Lorna's rape was a very poignant, very personal storyline for me. In those days, Alicia Coppola played the role. It's funny because both Alicia and Robin Christopher (the current Lorna) have become very close, very dear friends of mine. Both girls feel like my daughters. Because of my love for both of them, when something dreadful happens like a rape, you take it personally. Because their work was so superb, it was easy to be supportive of that. I felt that the writers did give the opportunity for Felicia as the mother to play out all the emotions of anger and protection and support. To be so helpless, to try to help and not be able to was great ... 'gray' stuff to play."

6. "When John Aprea entered the show as Felicia's great love Lucas, [it] was like going home again. We were able to [act like] kids. We were able to capture [their past together]. The other part of that story was when Lucas told Felicia that the daughter she [gave birth to had actually] lived. Felicia always believed that her daughter died at childbirth. They're two different pieces of the same story, [and both were] absolutely memorable to me."

Comic Scenes and Fond Memories

7. "About two or three years into my playing Felicia, Stephen, Brent, and I became . . . involved in a lot of crazy capers. My favorite was the day [Wallingford and Felicia] ended up in a gorilla cage. [The two of them] eventually got out of the cage and got the gorilla into the back of a truck. Then [they] lost the brakes on the truck and ended up crashing into a restaurant and burning the place down. It was insanity. Yet it was so good-natured and so much fun that the audience to this day asks me about it."

8. "When Liberace came on the show, he became a great friend of mine because of his love affair with *Another World* and his love affair with Felicia Gallant. Two things happened during the Liberace visits. He and I played 'Chopsticks' together on television, which was a great moment for Felicia and for [me]. The second time he came on, we went to his apartment . . . at the Trump Tower. He played 'I'll Be Seeing You' [on the piano] and sang it to me."

9. "All the stuff I got to do with Nancy was fun, but the one [scene] I remember best [was when] Felicia and Cecile were dressed up as nuns for another caper. [They] got stopped by a cop and . . . had to sing to him, 'The hills are alive with the sound of music.' "

10. "When Felicia married Mitch, we did it at a track in New Jersey. The whole company was [there]. A dress was made for me. [It was] one of a kind and very Felicia Gallant. It was just a glorious, fun, beautiful day. Doug Watson walked [Felicia] down the aisle. It's a [very fond] memory that I have of Doug. In fact, in my home I have a photograph of me on his arm."

11. "When Felicia was still involved with Cass Winthrop, she tried to seduce Jamie Frame. He wanted to write a book, so he came over to her house. [As] he was sitting on her couch, she tried to undress him. One of the soap opera magazines picked it as the funniest scene of the year."

12. "My real-life husband, Frank Attardi, always comes to Felicia's weddings. He's also been a waiter and a reporter. When he came on [the show] as Beau Wexler, I wasn't there to help him. I was off doing a Perry Mason movie. Frank [had come] on the show . . . to tell everyone why Felicia didn't come back to

town, that she was off doing this movie for Perry Mason. Then he came back again as Beau Wexler. [That second time Beau was on the show] he tried to kiss [Felicia, but she] stopped him."

ROBIN MATTSON CONFESSES THE 10 WORST SINS SHE'S COMMITTED IN HER SOAP CAREER

In her twenty-year career on the soaps, Robin Mattson has gotten to play some of the most devious villains daytime has ever seen: Heather Webber on General Hospital, *Gina Capwell Timmons on* Santa Barbara *and Janet "From Another Planet" Green on* All My Children. *As Heather, Gina, and Janet, she has gotten to break almost every commandment and most laws. She reveals here what she considers the worst sins she's committed on daytime.*

On *Santa Barbara*

1. Pulling the plug on a comatose C. C. Capwell

2. Poisoning Mason's Chinese food

3. Stealing C. C.'s art collection and replacing it with forgeries

4. Crashing Cruz and Eden's wedding

On *General Hospital*

5. Impersonating a nurse to slip in and out of the mental hospital

6. Intending to kill Diana Taylor

7. Sleeping with Scotty Baldwin while engaged to Joe Kelly

On *All My Children*

8. Coming to Pine Valley under an assumed name

9. Fixing the brakes on Laurel Montgomery's car, causing a near-fatal accident

10. Building a bomb to set off at Trevor and Laurel's wedding
Note: Because of the 1995 Oklahoma bombing incident, *All My Children*'s writers had Janet change her mind about actually detonating the bomb.

JEANNE COOPER'S 10 FAVORITE STORYLINES AND SCENES FROM *THE YOUNG AND THE RESTLESS*

Jeanne Cooper has been playing Katherine Chancellor Sterling on The Young and the Restless *since the show's debut in March of 1973. She is the only original castmember still with the show. She shares here her favorite storylines and scenes.*

1. "Katherine's alcoholism is the basis of the character. The highlight of that story-line [came] when she went to her first AA meeting. We had gotten permission from AA to do the scene, and [representatives] were there observing to make sure we didn't do anything out of line. Katherine was just totally, totally terrified to be there. When she said, 'My name is Katherine. I'm an alcoholic,' it was an incredible moment. It remains a highlight moment of the entire series because it was so universal and it hit with such impact."

The rest of the entries, Cooper says, are in no particular order.

2. "Katherine's whole future started on a windy, thunderous night. She looked through the tack-room door and saw her husband (Phillip) and Jill making passionate love. It changed the course of her life even to this day."

3. "A lot of people remember the scene where Phillip wanted a divorce so he could marry Jill who was pregnant with his child. Katherine and he had this fight where he said there was nothing left. He was empty and void of all caring for her. Katherine got up and threw her drink across the room. She said, 'To hell with it. I don't want to be with someone who doesn't want to be with me.' It was a very poignant turn in the story because it was the resignation of two people."

4. "The one scene that I totally, totally resisted the whole way was one between Phillip and Katherine where they were both lying in bed. She asked him in such a pitiful tone, 'Please make love to me.' He tried to, but he just couldn't do it. So she turned over on her side and said the Lord's Prayer. When I saw that in the script, I thought I would die. I said, 'I'm asking God to give him an erection? Give me a break.' Doing that scene was like pulling teeth. The director said, 'Jeanne, just try it. Don't fight it.' Of course, Donnelly Rhodes was shaking with laughter on the other side of the bed, which the audience couldn't see. I did the scene, and a couple of tears slid down to the pillow—not out of sympathy for the scene, but because it was so painful to do. I thought, God, please don't ever let them write a scene like that again or I will bolt. Then I watched it on the screen. The lighting and the tenderness of that scene and the desperation were simply beautiful. I got mail the likes of which you have never seen."

5. "One of the stories from the beginning that the people who were watching then all remember is the stableboys. Katherine would call the stable, and one of the boys would come up to the house. Jill (who was Katherine's assistant at the time) didn't know what was going on. She really thought they were there to discuss horse racing. One time she walked in on Katherine in bed with one of the stableboys. Jill just backed out of the room horrified."

6. "One of my very, very favorite storylines started when Katherine decided to kill herself. She was on a cruise ship, dead drunk, and she jumped overboard. She woke up in some little shack in the jungle. A rebel (Felipe Ramirez) had picked her up and saved her life, which disturbed her greatly because she had been planning on dying. There she was in the jungle with all the banana leaves and her jewels and Felipe, who spoke very little English. They developed a wonderful relationship. She became as hotheaded as he was. She would be yelling at him in English and then switch to Spanish. It was beautifully written and beautifully developed.

When they decided to end the story, Katherine had a leg wound and needed to see a doctor. Because Felipe was wanted by the government for being a rebel, he would have been taking his life into his hands, taking her to a hospital. But he did—with her protesting all the way. He did manage to escape, so he is still out there."

7. "Katherine has had the greatest barrage of husbands. Her marriage to Derek Thurston was totally delightful because he was such a sly fox. It was a cat-and-mouse kind of marriage. Katherine got him dead drunk, and he woke up the next morning and found out he was married to her."

8. In 1984, Cooper underwent a facelift and allowed film footage of the actual surgery to be incorporated into Katherine's storyline. "That was a highlight of highlights because I didn't know it would have the international reaction it did. There was an incredible reaction, which was a positive one. It made people feel better about having cosmetic surgery. It also brought people in for reconstructive surgery. So much good was done from that, it was just unreal."

9. "The gentlest and most loving romance Katherine had was the one she had with Rex Sterling. He made her laugh. He gave her hope. It was a bonding kind of love that she never thought she could ever have. There was one episode where he really decided to loosen Katherine up. She was standing at the window, and she saw him coming up on his motorcycle. She was totally terrified, but he talked her into getting on and going for a ride with him. She realized right then that that was what loving somebody was all about, taking big chances. That was the change in Katherine's way of thinking about a lot of things. That was when she decided she would marry him. Quinn Redeker (who played Rex) is the most compatible human being I've ever been with as a person and as an actor. I really felt like I was married to him."

10. "Jill and Katherine have had the longest-running fight in soap opera history. A woman who should have been like a daughter to Katherine became her enemy. It really is a love-hate situation. The absolute topper came in 1995 when Jill thought that Katherine was going to testify for [her] at Billy's custody hearing. At the courthouse, Katherine told Jill, 'I'm not here to testify for you. I'm here to testify against you.' Jill had had her hopes built up that Katherine would be her key witness. Instead, Katherine said to Jill, 'See, when you really want something and somebody takes it away from you—that's how you feel.'

[An outraged Jill lunged at Katherine.] It was the first time in twenty years that the fight became violent."

PETER BERGMAN'S LIST OF DAYTIME'S 12 BEST WORKHORSES— ACTORS WHO CAN MAKE ANY SCENE WORK

Peter Bergman is one of the most respected actors in daytime. He has won two Best Actor Emmys, playing Jack Abbott on The Young and the Restless, *and was also nominated for an Emmy for his work as Dr. Cliff Warner on* All My Children. *So who does he most admire? "When I think of the really good actors in daytime television, I think of the ones who have the hardest work to do," Bergman says. "By that, I mean the ones who don't have the big storylines, the ones who don't have the witty, acerbic, clever dialogue to carry them. The people who just get in there and do real, honest, solid work—those are the people I admire."*

In no particular order, twelve who come to mind for Bergman are:

1. Brad Maule (Dr. Tony Jones, *General Hospital*)

2. Julia Barr (Brooke English, *All My Children*)
   At one point, when Bergman was on *All My Children*, the show hinted at a romance between Cliff and Brooke. "I would have gone for it in a minute," Bergman says.

3. Richard Shoberg (Tom Cudahy, *All My Children*)

4. Lauren-Marie Taylor (Stacey Forbes, *Loving*)

5. Robert S. Woods (Bo Buchanan, *One Life to Live*)
   "He's had a lot of big storylines, but he's still sort of an Everyman."

6. Scott Holmes (Tom Hughes, *As the World Turns*)

7. Maureen Garrett (Holly Lindsey, *Guiding Light*)

8. Jerry ver Dorn (Ross Marler, *Guiding Light*)

9. Scott Reeves (Ryan McNeil, *The Young and the Restless*)

10. Kristoff St. John (Neil Winters, *The Young and the Restless*)

11–12. John McCook and Susan Flannery (Eric and Stephanie Forrester, *The Bold and the Beautiful*)
   "The people doing the crazy things are all around them. They are the reactors."

BILL HAYES AND SUSAN SEAFORTH HAYES'S 12 FAVORITE DOUG-AND-JULIE STORYLINES FROM *DAYS OF OUR LIVES*

In the early 1970s, Bill Hayes and Susan Seaforth Hayes became daytime's first supercouple. Not only were Doug Williams and Julie Olson the star couple on Days of Our Lives, *the actors had fallen in love in real life as well. When* Time *magazine did an article on the daytime soaps, it was Bill Hayes and Susan Seaforth Hayes who wound up on the cover. In 1984, they left the show together. Each has come back for a few years separately, and they still drop by for the occasional visit.*

"We have many favorite Doug-and-Julie storylines," they say. "Here are the first ones that come to mind."

1. Doug stages and produces The Cat Scanner Revue, in which he plays Chico to Julie's Harpo. Alice Horton is Groucho. Doug plays a violin while Julie strips in the background.

2. Lee Dumonde has a stroke while trying to bash Julie's head in.

3. Julie goes into labor while Susan Martin has a heart attack.

4. Doug marries Julie's mother, Addie, and Julie is *surprised*.

5. Julie and Doug honeymoon in Italy following five years of thwarted love.

6. Julie burns her face off and then hides out, eventually divorcing Doug.

7. Doug plays the clown at Doug's Place, then pantomimes the "Carousel Waltz" to a drugged Julie.

8. Doug sings "My Boy Bill" to Addie; she delivers Hope, then dies.

9. Kim, Doug's Polynesian Princess ex-wife, walks on Doug's back.

10. Julie gets raped, shoots the perpetrator (Larry Atwood), goes to court for murder . . . and is acquitted!

11. Doug has a Southern twin—Byron Carmichael—who expires, leaving him . . . Lee Dumonde.

12. At Julie and Doug's second wedding, he sings "Till There Was You," locks his ex-wife Lee in a closet and marches down the aisle.

KATHRYN LEIGH SCOTT'S 10 FAVORITE MEMORIES OF *DARK SHADOWS*

Kathryn Leigh Scott starred on Dark Shadows *when it debuted in 1966 and stayed until 1970, one year before the show went off the air. During those five years, as the show shifted settings to past times and parallel dimensions, Scott played a number of roles: Maggie Evans, Josette DuPrès, Rachel Drummond, and Lady Kitty Hampshire. Scott also played Maggie in the feature-film adaptation of the show,* House of Dark Shadows. *In the past decade she has published three books about the series:* My Scrapbook Memories of Dark Shadows, The Dark Shadows Companion, *and* The Dark Shadows Almanac.

She shares here her 10 favorite moments from her years on *Dark Shadows*.

1. "June 27, 1966. The first *Dark Shadows* episode. Victoria Winters (Alexandra Moltke) arrives in Collinsport to work as a governess and meets Maggie Evans in the local diner. I tell her, 'You're a jerk,' and advise her to leave town."

2. "During the 1795 storyline, in my role as Josette DuPrès, the episode in which I leap off Widows' Hill to escape from vampire Barnabas Collins (Jonathan Frid). Because the makeup man had no time to fit me with proper dentures, we used false fingernails for my vampire fangs."

3. "Also during the 1795 storyline, the episode in which Josette returns from the dead as a vampire. This time the makeup man used half a ping-pong ball to create the effect of an eye fallen out of its socket. Lovely."

4. "In 1966, the episode in which I first played Josette's ghost. On a day I was not scheduled to work, I offered to step in and replace a clothes dummy dressed in Josette's ghostly finery. The effect was so dramatic that I permanently inherited the role and brought Josette to life."

5. "In 1967, the episode in which Barnabas met Maggie in the diner for the first time. The chemistry evident between us that day inspired the writers to develop the legendary storyline involving the vampire's recreation of his long-lost love Josette DuPrès through his romance with Maggie Evans."

6. "During the 1795 storyline, the first time Lara Parker (Angelique) and I worked together. She played my maid from the island of Martinique, and we spoke in French to one another."

7. "In 1969, the episode in which I played two characters: Maggie Evans in the present time and Lady Kitty Hampshire, an English aristocrat, in 1897."

8. "In 1966, I played my first scene with Joan Bennett. Maggie Evans visits Collinwood for the first time and meets Elizabeth Collins Stoddard."

9. "In 1969, Maggie, now a governess at Collinwood, is terrorized by the ghost of Quentin Collins (David Selby) in a plot derived from Henry James's *Turn of the Screw.*"

10. "My final episode in 1970 when Sebastian Shaw (Chris Pennock) delivers Maggie to Windcliff Sanitarium. When I told producer Dan Curtis that I wanted to move to Paris and marry my fiancé, he said I was out of my mind. Dan didn't want me to leave the show, and although I had already been 'killed' a few

times on *Dark Shadows* and returned as a ghost, this was Dan's way of telling me I was crazy."

JACKLYN ZEMAN'S 10 MOST MEMORABLE STORYLINES FROM GENERAL HOSPITAL

Jacklyn Zeman has been playing General Hospital*'s Nurse Bobbie Jones since 1977. During that time she has picked up two Emmy nominations. As Bobbie, Zeman has gotten to tackle some socially relevant issues and play more than a few painful scenes.*

1. "The storyline where we did the heart transplant has to be up at the top. Tony and Bobbie's daughter, B. J., was brain dead, and they gave her heart to her cousin Maxie. It was so real, and it affected so many people."

2. "When they took Lucas (Bobbie's adopted son) away from her, that was also terribly heartwrenching to play. The thought of getting your child taken away is your worst fear as a parent."

3. "The whole Scotty/Laura/Bobbie love triangle was fabulous. It was when I first started on the show. I loved when I switched the pregnancy tests to show that I was pregnant by Scotty to get him."

4. "We did a wife-abuse story with David Groh, who played Bobbie's husband, Brock. When we began shooting those scenes, I started getting letters from women in that situation. People I worked with for many years told me they had things they wanted to talk about. This was before the days when people would really talk about a subject like that. I think we did a good thing by putting it on the air and telling people they could talk about it and get help."

5. "I loved the surrogate-mother storyline that we did with Sam Behrens, who played Jake. That came about because my mother lives in New Jersey, and the Baby M case was going on in the Hackensack courthouse. My mother sent clippings to me from all the local papers. I remember showing them to [our producer] Gloria Monty, and she came up with the idea to do a surrogate-mother story using Bobbie and Jake."

6. "We did a location shoot at the Bonaventure Hotel. [Bobbie's gangster boyfriend, Roy DeLuca, had gone there to assassinate the newly elected Senator Mitch Williams. Roy himself was shot in the process.] When he died in my arms, it was like doing *West Side Story*."

7. "I loved working with Rick Springfield (who played Noah Drake). I liked the romance and the courtship. All the problems with Noah's wealthy family not accepting Bobbie were very true to life. The audience really liked that story. A few years ago, Rick's fan club voted me their favorite leading lady."

8. "I remember the days when Tony Geary (as Luke Spencer) first came on the show. It was very exciting, planting the seeds for the Spencer clan and what was to happen over the next eighteen years."

9. "During the Disco Era, we had all that crazy pandemonium at the disco with the music and people dancing. It was very '70s, very reflective of what was going on."

10. "The Lhasa Fever epidemic brought the storyline back to the hospital. The show was called *General Hospital*—but you would forget that a lot of times because we didn't have medical stories. The Lhasa Fever story brought the focus back to the hospital and back to the core people."

JEAN LeCLERC PICKS 20 HIGHLIGHTS FROM HIS STORYLINES ON *ALL MY CHILDREN* AND *LOVING*

Jean LeClerc began playing the mercenary-turned-monk-turned-artist Jeremy Hunter on All My Children *in 1985. In 1992, ABC moved Jean LeClerc as Jeremy Hunter from* All My Children *over to* Loving *where he stayed until 1995. Both shows have given him some memorable moments.*

From *All My Children*

1. Jeremy and Erica's celibate affair. "It was hard to wear that celibacy on my shoulder, but when we did it, it was a relief for America."

2. Jeremy and Erica are marooned on an island together. "There came the first kiss. A great remote and a beautiful story."

3. The Jeremy/Erica/Natalie/Alex love quadrangle. "I loved every minute of it."

4. Jeremy is accused of murdering his own father at the fox hunt. "Great pitchfork fight."

5. Natalie blackmails Jeremy into marriage by claiming she is pregnant by him; Erica arranges a fake minister to "marry" them. "Girls! Girls! Girls!"

6. Jeremy rescues Brooke and Erica, whose plane has been hijacked by kidnapers and crashed into the jungle. "My Rambo days."

7. In prison (falsely accused of another murder), Jeremy almost marries Erica. Erica, however, has arranged a jailbreak. When Jeremy won't flee with her, Erica breaks things off between them. "No one believed that Erica would be that stupid, but the two of them had to be separated. They had to move on to new stories."

8. Jeremy gets involved with a mystery woman he has *seen* in his paintings. The woman turns out to be Erica's sister, Silver Kane, who has been programmed to kill Erica. He has to rescue both women from the evil Dr. Damon Lazarre. "So much fog, and the search for Silver went on and on and on."

9. Jeremy falls in love with Natalie for real while she is still married to Palmer Cortlandt. "They said we could have read the phone book and made it equally as interesting. That's the chemistry Kate Collins and I had."

10. Immediately after marrying Natalie, Jeremy discovers that his ex-lover Marissa is still alive, and that he has a son with her. "Jeremy had about three minutes of peace."

11. Jeremy and Marissa go on a last mission together. "It was great fun to work with Nancy Addison Altman."

12. After Natalie, Jeremy gets involved with the alcoholic Skye Chandler. "There goes Jeremy's co-dependency again."

13. Jeremy has to romance gold digger Ceara Connor away from his son David but falls in love with her himself. "A very clever storyline. In my first meeting with Genie Francis, we became instant friends."

14. Jeremy helps Ceara deal with her past as an incest victim; Ceara murders her abusive father. "A great storyline, so great that it scared a lot of people. Instead of enhancing Genie as an actress, it killed Ceara. Even though people recognized how good she was, people didn't want to watch that storyline. It was too painful."

15. Ceara and Jeremy marry. "Very fast."

On *Loving*

16. Jeremy copes with Ceara's death. "It was three days of crying nonstop."

17. College professor Jeremy is accused of sexual harassment by lovestruck Hannah Mayberry. "It was a very interesting story because these things happen a lot on college campuses. It could have gone much further than it did."

18. Jeremy falls in love with Ava Rescott while she is using him to make Leo jealous. "Very strange from Jeremy's point of view to fall in love with an Ava Rescott. Maybe he was reminiscing about Erica Kane."

19. Jeremy rescues Ava from Cesar Faison and King Kong. "I think we went seventy-two hours without sleeping. It was exhausting but what fun."

20. In a dual role, Jeremy is kidnaped by his presumed-dead twin brother, Gilbert, who takes his place. "At last, someone to work with."

JULIA BARR PICKS HER 10 MOST MEMORABLE STORYLINES

Julia Barr has played Brooke English on All My Children *for close to twenty years. (She left the show for a little over a year in the early '80s.) In 1990 she won the Daytime Emmy for Outstanding Supporting Actress. Her most memorable storylines, she says, are the ones in which Brooke takes a different turn from what she normally does and the ones that require more of an emotional investment as well as those that require a comedic touch.*

1. "The most meaningful storyline was definitely the one when [Brooke's young daughter] Laura was killed by a drunk driver. I think it was hard emotionally for everybody directly involved in the story because we all had children. In a bizarre way, that made it easy too. Once you are a parent, there are things you have a feeling for. To constantly bring those feelings up and to engage them in a storyline was not easy. I had known that this particular storyline was coming up. As a courtesy, which I'm glad they did, they told me about it two weeks before the script was actually in my hands. I was shocked, but they said it would be a catalyst for a number of stories. I remember the day I finally got the script. I felt this horrible pall come over me. It didn't last after the day, but reading the script, I kept thinking, How am I going to do this?"

2. "I really didn't want Brooke to remain childless after Laura's death. I said to one of the writers that I wanted my character to have a child again. Since Dixie had Adam's son, I thought it would be interesting if Brooke and Tad were put together for a brief time and that a child came out of that. I am glad the writers agreed."

3. "I liked playing the custody battle between Brooke and Tad and then the ectopic pregnancy. It was very draining and very demanding, but from an acting point of view, it brought into play a different aspect of my character. Brooke is usually reasonable and rational and stable, but because of all the things brought to bear on her, I was able to play her in a different manner."

4. "Through the years, my favorite times have been with David Canary as Adam when the writers have put us together either combatively or romantically. I remember one show that was submitted for an Emmy the year I won. It had a lot of stuff in it in terms of me confronting Adam about him sleeping with Dixie and that she was pregnant with his child."

5. "There was a great scene way back when where Phoebe caught Brooke in the poolhouse fooling around with Dan Kennicott. It was so much fun because Phoebe is a character given to outrage, and that was the most outraged Phoebe could become."

6. "I think what led to a maturation in Brooke was the Eddie Dorrance story. Brooke was young and foolish; she was going to sow her wild oats and take up with the most unlikable character she could find. That was Eddie. She treated him like dirt, and he was smitten with her. While they were on a date, Eddie raped her. Then she had an abortion. After that, she began to take stock of different things."

7. "I loved the Brooke and Tom story because Dick Shoberg (who plays Tom) and I have always had a working chemistry without even thinking about it. Dick was this solid rock as a person and as an actor. I feel we really developed a married quality."

8. "I'm sorry they don't engage Erica and Brooke a little more often. There was one story where they were on a private plane together that was hijacked. The two of them had to become unwilling allies because they were in such a dangerous position. It was funny, our characters having to come together for a common goal."

9. "The show did an interesting story when Brooke was a reporter for the local TV station. There was one viewer who became obsessed with her. It culminated with her being brought together with him by force. She had to figure out where he was at if she was going to come out of there alive and intact. I found that part of the story really interesting to play."

10. "A lot of people enjoyed the retirement home scam. The story had a lot of little sidebars. The character of Edmund was pretending to be a gigolo who was involved with Phoebe, and I played the outraged niece. The fact that Edmund and Brooke were working together brought out this tremendous romantic aspect to the story. There was also humor in it, which you don't always get a chance to play."

LOUISE SHAFFER PICKS 10 SCENES AND STORYLINES THAT SET RYAN'S HOPE APART FROM OTHER SOAPS

Louise Shaffer has had the opportunity to view Ryan's Hope *from two different perspectives. From 1977–1984, she played Rae Woodard, a role for which she was named 1983's Outstanding Supporting Actress. A few years after leaving the show, she returned as one of its writers. She has also written two murder mystery novels:* All My Suspects, *which takes place on the set of a daytime soap, and* Talked to Death.

1. "Frank Ryan's first political campaign was very fresh, very young. The whole family and community were involved. It's what you like to dream American politics and the immigrant experience are like."

2. "A hospital strike took place very early on in the series. The show presented both sides extremely fairly."

3. "The Mary Ryan/Jack Fenelli romance was a wonderful story. He was kind of the untamable, undomesticated guy, and she managed to tame and domesticate him."

4. "The St. Patrick's Day shows were very special. They were very New York, and very ethnic, very Irish. A favorite of those shows was one in which all the guys got down on their knees and serenaded Mary with the song, 'It was Mary, it was Mary, what a grand old name.'"

5. "Maeve and Jill had a wonderful relationship when Jill was in love with Frank and Frank was married to Delia. There were some wonderful scenes with the two women, Maeve and Jill. One in particular comes to mind. Maeve, who was obviously very religious, said to Jill, 'It's easier to find a lover than it is a friend.'"

6. "Nell Carter did a brief turn as the leader of a tenants' strike in her building. It was a minor story about this wonderful, feisty woman who was running her tenants' union. It was one of those nuggets of New York realism that *Ryan's Hope* used to do that I never saw another soap do back then."

7. "Toward the end of the series, Keith Charles came on the show as Roger's valet. It was Jeeves cubed. It was one of the best character turns I've ever seen in daytime because it wasn't too much. It wasn't over the top. It wasn't fake British. Ron [Hale, who played Roger,] and Keith played it beautifully together."

8. "There was a wonderful love scene between Jill and Seneca in which she had a cold and he brought her breakfast in bed. It was such an unromantic setup—her nose was running, there was Kleenex all over the place—but it turned into this wonderful, giggly romantic scene. Back then when they did romantic scenes, the woman had her mascara on, and if she was in bed, she was wearing a sexy nightgown. But this was a woman with a cold wearing her flannels."

9. "I'd never seen anybody deal with the stock market on daytime before Delia. Somehow, she'd get a feeling and she'd play it. For quite a while, she was winning. There was flaky Delia doping the commodities market and making one killing after another. It was funny, and it was charming. Of all the characters on any show that you would think would be able to play the stock market, Delia?"

10. "On the last show that was ever going to happen for *Ryan's Hope*, Maeve was sitting in the bar, and of course, she had to sing 'Danny Boy' one last time. Helen figured she wasn't going to be able to get through it. Sure enough, her eyes started to fill up about halfway through. Her voice didn't crack, but she knew she was starting to go a little bit. So she turned to all of us as Maeve and said, 'Sing with me.' So everybody tried to sing along, helping Helen get through it. There were all these great voices singing this really emotional song that meant the show to many of us."

EILEEN FULTON PICKS HER 10 FAVORITE STORYLINES

Eileen Fulton started on As the World Turns *back in 1960 in what was supposed to be a short-term role as Bob Hughes's (Don Hastings) girlfriend, Lisa Miller. Despite quitting three times "forever," she is with the show 36 years later and still one of daytime's strongest presences.*

1. "My favorite storyline is the Eduardo Grimaldi story that I played recently. I got to play everything with him. I got to play the romantic passion, then the sorrow and grief of losing him. I got to be the hysterical widow, throwing myself into the grave. Then I got to be vindictive and horrible to John Dixon because Lisa blamed him for Eduardo's death. Lisa turned back into her old horrible self. It was everything I started to do when I first came on the show except that there was more reason to it, more depth. I loved working with Larry Bryggman. He's such a wonderful actor. I loved having all those horrible fights with him."

2. "When I first came on the show, Lisa was hideously spoiled. Bob's whole family catered to her because she was so willful. That was fun to play because it's not at all like Eileen Fulton."

3. "When Lisa was unfaithful to Bob, that was just despicable and wonderful. I got to lie and cheat and plot and plan."

4. "I liked the Michael Shea storyline a lot. Lisa had an affair with Michael, who was another doctor at the hospital. When she was pregnant by him, he wouldn't marry her for the baby's sake. So Lisa was horrible to him, and he deserved to be treated horribly. When their little boy got to be two years old, Michael saw him and thought, that's an extension of myself. In order to get the child, Michael tried to court Lisa, but she wouldn't have anything to do with him. Then he caught her son Tom in his office stealing drugs, and he blackmailed her into marrying him. Lisa got back at him in just awful, underhanded little ways. It was a wonderful storyline with a great twist."

5. "When Michael Shea was murdered, the audience didn't know whether Lisa did it or not. The producers wouldn't tell anybody who did it. I said, 'I don't care who did it, but you let me know if *I* did or did not do it.' I had to know my inner monologue. The producer at the time said, 'Actors are such children. You can't keep it to yourself.' So I threatened him. I said, 'If you don't tell me, I will tip it in such a way to make up your mind for you.' The producer got a little scared because the show was live. He told me that Lisa didn't do it. I was the only one who was let in like that."

6. "I enjoyed the whole storyline with Farley Granger (as Earl Mitchell) because that included some intrigue. I had always liked Farley. When I was a teenager and he was in the movies, I used to have a crush on him."

7. "I loved working with James Douglas (who played Grant Colman). Lisa got paranoid that Grant was flirting around even though he really wasn't. Women thought he was handsome and went after him, but Grant didn't see it. Lisa got fed up with it, and Grant got fed up with her being so jealous all the time. But the audience could see she had good reason. I had some great, bitchy scenes with the different women."

8. "I enjoyed doing the menopause storyline. Before I went through it myself, I wanted to act it. I didn't have anything else going on at the time, so I told [headwriter] Doug Marland, here's something I can do, and he wrote it in."

9. "I can't say I enjoyed doing the racial prejudice story because I think that prejudice is hateful. But I felt it was important to do. I was surprised at the turn in my character, but they asked me first if I would do it."

10. "'The Willows' was the first gothic story that we did. It was fascinating—especially because a very similar story was happening to me in my own life. Lisa ran away from Grant, changed her name, and went on a trip. She was driving into the mountains during a big storm, and her car ran out of gas. She came upon this inn, where she met this man, Bennett Hadley. Lisa became almost a prisoner of his. In my own life, preceding this story and unbeknownst to anyone but my lawyer and my parents, I had left my own husband, changed my name, and gone on vacation. My brother and I had driven up to the mountain, and when we got there, there was a huge storm. In the show, Lisa looked like Bennett's dead wife, who was named Ruth. That was the name I had used, Ruth Stern. I hadn't talked to anybody about what happened. Then I came and got my script, and there it was. It was eerie."

8
Critical Decisions

Chosen by Mimi Torchin
Soap Opera Weekly *Editor-in-Chief Mimi Torchin could easily have come up with at least fifty "Best Storylines," but pressed to limit herself to ten, these are the ones that leapt to mind. They are listed in no particular order.*

1. The Romantic Triangle of Liza, Tad, and Liza's mother, Marian, *All My Children.*
   This was a particularly interesting story because it helped define Tad as a cad, which he truly was in those days. It also provided a little sympathy for Liza, which the character sorely needed. But most important, Jennifer Bassey (Marian) had the best chemistry with Michael Knight (Tad) that he's ever had with a woman before or since. It was a highly charged and sexy story. Funny too.

2. Domestic Abuse, *All My Children.*
   Domestic abuse is a story explored too seldom on daytime considering the extent of the problem in this country. *All My Children* created a terrifying story for Leora heartbreakingly played by the wonderful Lizabeth MacKay Sanders, a patient and friend of Joe Martin. Both emotionally and physically abused by her

disturbed husband, Kurt, Leora sought comfort from Joe, which made Ruth increasingly jealous and put a strain on their usually rock-solid marriage. The story was realistically played out and resolved *without* Leora killing Kurt, the standard cop-out used in more recent soap (and TV movie) abuse plotlines.

3. The Doug Cummings Story, *As the World Turns.*

At his best, no one could touch writer Doug Marland for involving, gut-wrenching, human drama. And he was at the top of his form when he created the story of Douglas Cummings, a fan obsessed with ex-chanteuse Kim Reynolds Hughes. John Wesley Shipp won an Emmy for his chilling portrayal of the psychotic but charming Cummings, who wormed his way into Kim's life and eventually became engaged to her daughter Frannie. The story ended with Cummings being murdered and Kim on trial for the crime. Thinking Frannie had killed Cummings, Kim took the rap. But the killer was someone else, and both women were eventually exonerated. The moment when Kim discovered the shrine to her in a room in Cummings's house with her recording of "Someone to Watch Over Me" (Marland's favorite song) cued up on the stereo was one of the most arresting and horrifying in the soap's history. The story was a high point in Kathryn Hays's then thirteen-year portrayal of Kim.

4. Holly Unravels When Blake and Ross Betray Her, *Guiding Light.*

Poor Holly, one of daytime's unhappiest women, thought loneliness was in the past when she fell for attorney Ross Marler. But when her daughter, Blake, seduced Ross to bug Holly and that seduction turned to love, Holly fell apart in a big way. She drank too much, lashed out in rage and pain at anyone who got in her way, lost her job, and ultimately almost lost her life when she took a painkiller (she suffered from migraines) with liquor. The show dropped the ball by not showing us Holly's rehabilitation, but her unraveling—in the hands of the wonderful Maureen Garrett—was magnificent soap opera, haunting and riveting on a daily basis for months.

5. Reva and Josh's Love Story, *Guiding Light.*

Nobody writes big stories like Pam Long, and nobody plays big characters with as much panache as Kim Zimmer. The two of them together are like the Macy's Fourth of July fireworks display to the tenth power. The love affair between Zimmer's Reva and Joshua Lewis (played by the handsome Robert Newman) was as enduring as it was tortured. Will fans ever forget Reva in the fountain, stripped to her teddy, crying to the wheelchair-bound Josh, "See my shame, Joshua?"

Although Reva married both Josh's brother, Billy, and their father, H. B., Josh and Reva finally tied the knot and had two children. Although their romance ended tragically in 1990 as Reva, in the midst of a postpartum depression, drove her car off a bridge in the Florida Keys, Zimmer returned to the show as Reva last summer.

6. The Salem Strangler, *Days of Our Lives*.

This story featured not only a fascinating mystery but the introduction of the Roman Brady/Marlena Evans romance, which has been a mainstay of the show for many years. This story might even have marked the show's transition from the rather traditional, family/romance soap opera it was to the gothic potboiler it has turned into. Notable also was the incredible stunt the show pulled making fans think that Marlena had been killed by the Strangler when it was actually Marlena's twin sister, Samantha, who was murdered.

7. The Revelation of Lily's Parentage, *As the World Turns*.

Once again, Doug Marland's genius for family drama was demonstrated when, over an ample period of time, we learned that Iva Snyder had been raped at age thirteen by her cousin Josh and that the child conceived during that rape was Lucinda Walsh's adopted daughter, Lily. The moment when Lily learned the truth was one of the most dramatic moments ever on that show: Iva in the barn, holding a pitchfork aloft, shouted at a surprised Josh and Lily, "Take your hands off her. She's your daughter!" The revelation set into motion many other stories including Lily and Holden on the run. The story as a whole also explained a great deal of Snyder family history. It was another example of classic soap opera of the highest order.

8. The Christmas Miracle, *Texas*.

As is almost always the ironic case, as a cancelled soap gets closer to the end, it just gets better and better. This was certainly true of NBC's ill-fated *Texas*, which became an enthralling soap in its last months, the high point of which was the return "from the dead" of Ashley and her newborn child on Christmas Day. A pregnant Ashley was thought to have perished in a flood, but she was rescued by an angel named Seth. Ashley was played by Pam Long who had also assumed the reins as headwriter and vastly improved the show during her brief tenure—alas too late to rescue it. Long's penchant for schmaltzy family drama and big characters (she created *Guiding Light*'s Reva) seldom left a dry eye in the house when she turned on the sentiment. The Christmas miracle was a thrilling introduction to the great storytelling talents of the then-fledgling writer.

9. B. J.'s Heart, *General Hospital*

One of the most finely wrought and heartrending stories in recent memory. *General Hospital* took a big risk when it killed off Tony and Bobbie's young daughter, B. J., in a school-bus accident. But her death was not in vain because her heart was transplanted into the body of her dying cousin Maxie, Frisco and Felicia's little girl. I can hardly remember a more painful moment than seeing Tony Jones put his head on the chest of his niece Maxie and listen to the transplanted heart of his dead child beating so strongly. Every actor was at peak performance, and the writing was impeccable. The story is certain to go down in soap history as one of the premiere examples of the genre at its best.

10. The Alice/Steve/Rachel Triangle, *Another World.*

Perhaps the classic romantic triangle, this long-running story provided everything great soap opera should be: romance, angst, lies, love, and conflict. Agnes Nixon created this triangle, pitting the sweet Alice Matthews against the wily girl from the wrong side of the tracks, Rachel Davis, for the affections of handsome, ambitious Steve Frame. Jacquie Courtney (Alice), George Reinholt (Steve), and Robin Strasser (Rachel) created such a firestorm of passion and drama that *Another World*, which had been near cancellation, rose to the number-two spot in record time. When Nixon was lured away by ABC, Harding Lemay was brought in to write *Another World*, and he was so inspired by this triangle that he kept it on the front burner for another four years, with Victoria Wyndham successfully replacing the seemingly irreplaceable Strasser as Rachel. Wyndham has remained on the show for more than two decades and has become *Another World*'s number one heroine.

10 OF THE DUMBEST MOMENTS IN SOAP HISTORY

Chosen by Alan Carter
Alan Carter, who has worked at People *and* TV Guide, *currently writes for* Entertainment Weekly, *where he does the magazine's "Soap Box" column.*

1. Marlena is possessed by Satan, *Days of Our Lives*

Great special effects couldn't save this overdone and overwrought plot.

2. The underground city of Eterna, *One Life to Live*

This deserved the all-time dumbest plot award until Marlena's possession came along. An underground city with track lighting? And no dust?

3. Pigeon puffs, *Santa Barbara*

Louise Sorel was rightfully outraged during the premiere week of this show when the writers asked her character to feed her daughter's carrier pigeon to the family as hors d'oeuvres. The most tasteless plot ever—no pun intended.

4. Brooke's mother is Cobra, *All My Children*

One of those amazing, out-of-left-field plot developments, it was revealed that Brooke's mother was a major international drug dealer. A plot that had everyone scratching their heads.

5. Erica Kane chases Nazis, *All My Children*

TV's most socially relevant and responsible program blew it bigtime with this storyline. Erica tried to prove her lover's father (evil Lars Bogard) was a former Nazi, but giving her intentionally humorous lines like "I don't have the right shoes to chase Nazis" was insulting.

6. Delia's kidnaping, *Ryan's Hope*

For a show known for its reliance on reality, when Delia got kidnaped by King Kong (no kidding), it signaled the beginning of the end for the acclaimed show.

7. The freezing of Port Charles, *General Hospital*

Long since surpassed as the dumbest all-time plot, the townsfolk of the once sci-fi mad *General Hospital* slogged through one plot in which an evil and power-mad scientist (aren't they always?) threatened to freeze the world—and he started with Port Charles until being thwarted by (who else?) Luke and Laura.

8. Casey the Alien, *General Hospital*

If mad scientists weren't enough for the out-of-this-world fantasy of *General Hospital*, the show's writers literally went all out with the introduction of Casey the Alien. And was it just me, or was there always some strange sexual subtext going on there between Casey and young Robin?

9. A house "crashes" into the Reardon house, *Guiding Light*

Soap writers are always looking for inventive ways to get their male characters shirtless. This was not one of them. The audience was told that a house on wheels had crashed into the Reardon home, rendering their air conditioning useless—all summer long—and all the men in the Reardon home had to walk around sans tops.

10. "Eric, I have a surprise for you," *The Bold and the Beautiful*

For twenty-plus years, the audience was told, Stephanie left the house on Wednesdays and disappeared. We soon discovered she was visiting a secret hide-away. For an affair? Nah, too easy. She was visiting a daughter, supposedly who had water on the brain, that she never told her husband about. Huh? What was even *dumber* was the discovery that the supposedly impaired woman was actually running a scam on Stephanie. Double huh?

ALL MY CHILDREN'S TOP 11 STORYLINES

Chosen by Gary Warner
When it comes to All My Children, *Gary Warner literally wrote the book. He is the author of the best-selling* All My Children: The Complete Family Scrapbook *and, most recently,* General Hospital: The Complete Scrapbook. *He also serves as the producer, writer, and host of* Soap Talk, *provides questions for radio's "ABC Soap Quiz" and co-produced the videos* ABC Daytime's Greatest Weddings *and* All about Erica.

1. Stuart and Cindy's Love Story

The tender courtship of a simple man and his AIDS-afflicted wife proved to be one of daytime TV's most uplifting tales. Multiple-Emmy winners David Canary and Ellen Wheeler made us laugh and cry in a poignant, human story of courage in the face of death.

2. Tad "the Cad's" Madcap Mother-Daughter Affair

Pine Valley's loverboy tried to juggle relationships with Liza Colby and her oversexed, middle-aged mother, Marian—often with hilarious results. A tribute to raging hormones!

3. Will Cortlandt's Descent into Hell

Wild Will Cortlandt gave everyone in town ample reason to kill him. This story, with its twists, turns, and subplots, kept viewers guessing whodunit for months. (It was Janet Green!)

4. Adam, Brooke, and Dixie's Love/Hate Triangle

Adam Chandler was at his no-good best when, while married to Brooke, he impregnated Dixie, then tried to drive her crazy to gain custody of the child!

5. Phil and Tara's Star-Crossed Romance

Two innocent kids driven apart by a scandalous secret from the past—and a teenage terror by the name of Erica Kane! The original "young love" storyline. Often copied, but never duplicated.

6. Jesse and Jenny's Summer in New York

After running away to New York, two kids struggled to survive in the big, bad city. Their special friendship was one of soap's most endearing relationships.

7. Janet Steals Her Sister's Life

After throwing Natalie down a well, Janet "From Another Planet" assumed her own sister's identity—and slept with her fiancé! A wonderful balance of humor and suspense. Actress Kate Collins deserved two Emmys for her dual role—but she wasn't even nominated for one. Go figure.

8. Adam's Pursuit of Erica

Adam loved Erica, but what he loved even more was making Erica miserable! Schemes, scams—and a twin brother in the attic!

9. Mark's Drug Addiction

A brutally realistic tale of a man's personal and professional downfall and how the love and concern of his friends and family saved his life.

10. Palmer's Endless Schemes to Keep Nina and Cliff Apart

Domineering Palmer Cortlandt thought he could keep his shy daughter sheltered from the outside world—until she met handsome Cliff Warner. Palmer tried every trick in the book to keep them apart—he even told Nina she was going blind.

11. Daisy and Palmer Find Love Again

Never have two characters complemented each other as well as Daisy and her ex-husband Palmer. This was a love-hate-love relationship that made us laugh cry and want more, more, more!

DAYTIME'S 10 MOST SOCIALLY PROGRESSIVE STORYLINES

Chosen by Karen Lindsey
Author, teacher, and social critic Karen Lindsey wrote a soap opera column for The Middlesex News *from 1989 to 1990 and has written on the soaps for a number of other publications. Her essay "Race, Sexuality and Class in Soapland" appears in the book* Gender, Race and Class: A Text Reader *(ed. Dines and Humez; Sage Publications, 1995). She teaches sections on soap opera in courses on television history and women in media at Emerson College and the University of Massachusetts. Her list is based on the importance of the issues and the complexity and sensitivity of their treatment.*

From the '60s

1. Carla's Attempt to Pass as White, *One Life to Live*

One Life to Live was the first show to put a black character with a black issue in the forefront. The confrontations between light-skinned Carla Gray and her dark-skinned, working-class mother, Sadie, looked at the complexity of black identity in a racist society. Ellen Holly's magnificent acting job as Carla brought out all the nuances of the wrenching story.

From the '70s

2. Wife Abuse, *One Life to Live*

When the women's movement identified wife abuse as a serious issue in the early 1970s, *One Life to Live* was a groundbreaker in dramatizing the problem. Jenny, the sweet ex-nun, was beaten by her husband, Brad, who went through the classical abuse/repent/abuse cycle. Her evolution from forgiving victim to self-defending survivor was powerful and important.

From the '80s

3. Hank's Homosexuality, *As the World Turns*

Soapland is relentlessly heterosexual. A lesbian character wandered briefly into *All My Children*'s Pine Valley in 1983 but left shortly thereafter with no sign that she'd had a lover. Hank did have a lover, though we only met him in Hank's last episode on the show. The show explored homophobia through Hank's troubled teenaged friend Paul and Paul's caring but misguided stepfather, Hal. We need more Hanks on more shows and as permanent residents.

4. White Supremacy, *Days of Our Lives*

Here we had a black character in the forefront of a story, clearly addressing racism at its grimmest. Dr. Marcus Hunter was a danger to a corrupt government official because, as a boy, Marcus had witnessed the bombing of a black church in which three little girls were killed. Both the black character's centrality and the history lesson (the story was clearly based on the 1950s bombing of a black church in Alabama) were a refreshing relief from black marginality in soaps.

5. Natalie's Rape, *All My Children*

I picked this out of all the rape stories because it's easy to depict the evil of rape when the victim is nice and the rapist a villain. But Natalie was an adulteress and a fortune hunter who'd had an affair with Ross while involved with his father. Ross was a troubled nice guy with an alcohol problem. This scenario might invite an audience to dismiss the rape. Instead, we saw it in all its ugliness as Natalie's fight to be believed culminated in Ross's loss of his family, imprisonment, and ultimate redemption through accepting his guilt and its consequences.

From the '90s

6. Casey's Right to Die, *As the World Turns*

Possibly the single most riveting story in the history of soaps. Casey, paralyzed and dying, begged his friend/stepdaughter Margo to promise she would pull the plug when he was brain-dead. Margo's agonized agreement and the reactions of her family and community in the aftermath created a painful exploration of a hard topic while honoring Margo's and Casey's decisions.

7. Jessica and Duncan's Interracial Marriage, *As the World Turns*

They weren't the first—*General Hospital's* Tom and Simone were—but in a genre defined by sexiness, Tom and Simone had as much chemistry as the Bobsie Twins. Jessica and Duncan were believably steamy. Opposition to them came not from nasty rednecks, but from likeable, established characters, who were forced to confront their unconscious racism.

8. Native American Sacred Ground, *As the World Turns*

This was the first time the soaps acknowledged the existence of Native Americans. Lyla Peretti's friendship with her young Indian boarder gave her and the viewers a lesson in Native American culture and white insensitivity. Again, *As the World Turns* didn't cop out by having racism represented by a bigoted outsider. Rather, good guy Cal Stricklyn's capitalistic acquisitiveness blinded him to the rights of native people. As a result, he lost Lyla and we won a fine if all-too-brief storyline.

9. Ellie's Abortion, *As the World Turns*

Most "good girls" in Soapland don't even consider abortion unless the conception is the result of rape or incest. Ellie Snyder's abortion, though based on the possibility that the child would be born deformed, was set against the background of her own ambivalence about having children and her husband's proven lack of responsibility as a father. The issue was explored fully with the focus on Ellie's right to make the decision on her own.

10. Mac's Battle with Alzheimer's Disease, *As the World Turns*

If this list seems a little top-heavy with *As the World Turns*, there's a reason. In its quiet, homey way, *As the World Turns* has taken on more social issues than any other soap including *All My Children*. Alzheimer's is a particularly unglamorous disease. Its victims are elderly, and there is no cure. *As the World Turns* was the first show that had the courage to take it on and with a beloved regular character.

DAYTIME'S 5 MOST SOCIALLY REGRESSIVE STORYLINES

Also chosen by Karen Lindsey

From the '70s

1. Laura's Rape, *General Hospital*

Luke shoved Laura to the floor; she screamed, "No!" Afterward, they were a great couple. But a romance begun with boy rapes girl? Both Tony Geary and Genie Francis later had the sense to repudiate the origins of the Luke/Laura romance. Had the rape been confronted, had Luke been forced to face what he'd done to Laura, some of the damage may have been undone. In 1995, the writers added insult to injury. Laura had kicked Luke out of the house because his involvement with the mob endangered their children. Luke came to the house to attempt a reconciliation. She rebuffed him; he followed her to the bedroom, broke down the door, and smothered her with kisses as her cries of "No" melted into a passionate "Yes." This echo of the rape, transmuted into the coyness of a woman whose "no" is really "yes," nullified Laura's earlier experience, her seriousness about her own decisions—and the seriousness of rape itself.

From the '80s

2. Ashley's Abortion, *The Young and the Restless*

Ellie of *As the World Turns* had her abortion because she didn't want to have a baby. Ashley Abbott of *The Young and the Restless* had hers because she thought the pregnancy might upset her lover, whose wife was believed terminally ill. So, "choice" became subverted into stand-by-your-man. Even so, Ashley was punished with a nervous breakdown. She deserved it.

3. The Asian Quarter, *General Hospital*

Asians, as we all know, are inscrutable and sinister or cutely inarticulate. *General Hospital*'s Asian Quarter story gave us both. Our nice, white heroes battled a Fu Manchu–like crime ring and were helped by an assimilated Chinese man cutely named Yank and an even cuter Chinese grandmother who spoke pidgin English laced with hippie slang. In the middle of it all was a mysterious elder known only as the Ancient One, appropriately played by *Charlie Chan* veteran Keye Luke.

From the '90s

4. Drucilla's Reformation, *The Young and the Restless*

Drucilla Barber showed up in Genoa City as a rebellious, streetwise black teenager, angry at white America. Her Aunt Mamie was a maid in the Abbott home, and Drucilla challenged the dichotomous upstairs-downstairs positions of the white and black characters. She was "cured" of her anger by an assimilated black man who forced her to learn to read and cook. Racism was denied and African-American anger reduced to the misguided rantings of a scared kid. (Ironically, by 1995 John Abbott was romancing Mamie—but by then Drucilla was safely demilitarized.)

5. Susan's Pregnancy, *As the World Turns*

This was a huge disappointment, especially in the context of a rare and sensitively done older woman/younger man romance. Susan was a distinctly unmaternal woman, whose relationship with her grown daughter was troubled. She was one of Soapland's few characters who had been allowed not to want children. But she decided to give her young husband a child and did so with infinite trouble, technological and emotional—proving once again that all Real Women want kids.

12 OF THE BEST CHARACTERS IN SOAP HISTORY

Chosen by Lynn Leahy
Soap Opera Digest *editor-in-chief Lynn Leahy describes a truly memorable character as the marriage of a charismatic performer and a marvelous story—the more tragic, the better. Here are twelve of her all-time favorites.*

1. Roger Thorpe, *Guiding Light*

A character works when the audience knows what he wants. And Springfield pariah Roger Thorpe is desperately needy: for power, for money, for love. The perennial outsider looking in, Roger is so consumed with envy he's never happy. He doesn't want something unless it belongs to someone else, and when he does get what he's after (often Holly), it's never enough. As soon as Roger grabs that brass ring, it turns to rust. As vicious and self-obsessed as Roger can be, we can't help feeling compassion for someone who sees enemies around every corner, but whose worst enemy is himself.

2. Jill Abbott, *The Young and the Restless*

Watching Jill Abbott's frantic attempts to claw her way to respectability (and inevitably falling on her face) has been a daytime sport since *The Young and the Restless* premiered in 1973. So far, money hasn't bought it, and neither has marriage. Overdressed and oversexed, this drama queen catapults from one crisis to another. Jill just can't help herself—can't help sleeping with her boss's husband, with her husband's son, with her contractor. And since Jill is forever blaming other people for her problems, she never walks away a whit wiser.

3. Betsy Stewart, *As the World Turns*

That trembling lip, those brimming blue eyes—as played by Meg Ryan, Betsy Stewart was the quintessential enchanting heroine. Sweet without being saccharine, Betsy could renounce the man she loved for an ambitious social climber and not look like a sap. Though buffeted by circumstance, Betsy wouldn't let herself be victimized. With an inner strength and a core of goodness that made us respect her as well as adore her, Betsy belongs in the heroine hall of fame.

4–5. Luke and Laura Spencer, *General Hospital*

Speaking of heroines, the all-time fave must be the innocent child-woman Laura Webber Spencer. She married Scotty while in her teens but soon fell for anti-hero Luke Spencer. Luke paved the way for a different genre on daytime. He wasn't classically handsome, he didn't have money or a job, and he forced himself on Laura the first time they made love. That said, they were the most popular soap couple ever, and their 1981 wedding remains the most-watched event in daytime history. When young Laura looked up at Luke with all that love shining in her eyes, viewers fell for him too. And they're still tuning in.

6. Mona Kane, *All My Children*

Put-upon Mona Kane was a selfless mother who wanted little more than happiness for her daughter. Unfortunately, her daughter was Erica Kane. An exasperated Mona nursed the spoiled, insecure Erica through one scrape after another. As entertaining as it was watching Erica get herself in trouble with men, it was even more fun watching her explain herself to her mother. As Mona rolled her eyes through Erica's wild tales and lame self-justifications, you got the feeling that beneath Mona's groans of "Erica, how could you!" she was thinking, where did I go wrong? A supporting character who sometimes stole the show, Mona was warm, funny, and hopelessly devoted to her impossible daughter.

7. Rita Stapleton, *Guiding Light*

Earthy Rita Stapleton drew men like flies, and she didn't turn away quite as many of them as she should have. Sure, she adored the solid-as-a-rock doc Ed Bauer, but she just couldn't resist men who were hazardous to her health like Alan Spaulding (and his private plane). Rita wanted to be good—really, she did—but domesticity wasn't her natural state. She had a wild side she never could conquer. That prim nurse's uniform didn't fool anyone; Rita was one of daytime's all-time sexiest women.

8. Anna Devane, *General Hospital*

A grown-up—how refreshing! Smart and sophisticated, self-sufficient Anna Devane never needed a man to take care of her. Anna was a woman in charge of her life, too confident to settle for less than she deserved. Not that she'd send a man packing at the first sign he wasn't perfect. Anna had made mistakes too and paid for them. She didn't demand perfection, just honesty. But as forthright as she was, Anna came to Port Charles as a woman of mystery and never lost her enigmatic edge.

9. Jake McKinnon, *Another World*

Jake McKinnon is a land mine: take one unguarded step, and he'll knock you off your feet. In a genre littered with antiheroes, Jake has a fiery passion that sets him apart from the pack of the muscular misguided. His unrestrained displays of rage, love, and revenge are the work of a little boy who never gained command of his emotions or got a firm grasp on the difference between right and wrong. This growling, howling id would do anything for the people he loves (Paulina and Vicky) and anything to the people he hates (the rest of Bay City).

10–11. Asa Buchanan, *One Life to Live* and John Dixon, *As the World Turns*

Meet the crankiest characters on soaps. Asa Buchanan and John Dixon, with their checkered pasts, are more likely to be ornery than evil, but don't cross them. They're overprotective of their families and possessive of their wives (not that they can hang on to them for very long—they keep marrying women who don't really love them). They don't give a fig about what anyone thinks. Everyone else in town may tiptoe around the truth, but you can count on Asa and John to tell it like it is. Which is why what they say is always worth listening to.

12. Victor Newman, *The Young and the Restless*

Hands down, the best role on daytime. Victor Newman is a complex, dark charmer, an autocrat who is as likely to surprise us with a burst of generosity as with an act of unspeakable cruelty. The revenge-mad control freak can't stand being crossed. Victor punished his first wife's lover by torturing him in the basement; years later, he yanked the Abbott family's company out from under them after Jack Abbott dallied with Victor's second wife, Nikki. Of course, Victor has a tender side too, but that has a limited reach. He loves his children but wants to govern their lives. When his most recent wife Hope became pregnant with a child who might become blind, Victor couldn't bear the thought of an imperfect heir. You'd have to be a masochist to be attracted to a despot like Victor. Apparently, there are a lot of masochists out there.

THE 10 SOAP OPERA CHARACTERS MOST SIGNIFICANT FOR FEMINISM

Chosen by Martha Nochimson
Dr. Martha Nochimson teaches in the English Department at Mercy College in Dobbs Ferry, New York, and in the Department of Film and Television at the Tisch School of the Arts at New York University. She has written for five soap operas: Ryan's Hope, Search for Tomorrow, Guiding Light, Loving, *and* Santa Barbara. *She is the author of* No End to Her: Soap Opera and the Female Subject *(University of California Press) and a study of the films of David Lynch that will be released by the University of California Press in 1996.*

1. Victoria Lord, *One Life to Live*
   (played by Gillian Spencer, later by Erika Slezak)
   The quintessential soap opera heroine. Her multiple identities began the hard-core discussion in daytime about the problems women experience trying to be both sexual and successful.

2. Laura Webber, *General Hospital*
   (played by Genie Francis)
   The break-up of her marriage to Prince Charming (Scotty Baldwin) and her adventures with the Frog (Luke Spencer) asked all the right questions about where female sexuality fits into the fairy tale.

3. Dorian Lord, *One Life to Live*
   (played longest by Robin Strasser)
   An honest, complex portrait of a woman who, though often self-serving in her

grab for power, frequently exposes her own emotional underbelly and the dark realities of the superficially better-behaved characters.

4. Kimberly Brady, *Days of Our Lives*
    (played by Patsy Pease)
    A heroine with a precedent-setting story about battling the consequences of childhood sexual abuse, particularly the way that her lover, Shane Donovan, inadvertently continued the abuse.

5. Julia Wainwright, *Santa Barbara*
    (played by Nancy Lee Grahn)
    The first and best consciously feminist heroine on daytime showed us a non-stereotypical picture of the sexual, capable, witty woman. Where are you now when we need you?

6. Calliope Jones, *Days of Our Lives*
    (played by Arleen Sorkin)
    The only successful representation of a non–gold digger, tender/tough cookie who marches hilariously to the beat of her own drummer. She gave female eccentricity an endearing place in daytime. Come back!

7. Marty Saybrooke, *One Life to Live*
    (played by Susan Haskell)
    Her rape story bypasses chic sensationalism and really explores the nexus of promiscuity, cruelty, low self-esteem, and rape; also the possibility of redemption through feminine courage.

8. Lucinda Walsh, *As the World Turns*
    (played by Elizabeth Hubbard)
    At her best, she gives us an unsentimental look at the desire for sexual love, daughterly love, and economic power in strong women.

9. Eden Capwell, *Santa Barbara*
    (played by Marcy Walker)
    She destroys the ideal of the mewing, blue-eyed, blonde sex object (i.e. Nikki Newman and Cricket Romalotti on *The Young and the Restless*)—such an insult to women. An American icon is reborn with spunk, brains, and sexual initiative.

10. Carla Gray, *One Life to Live*
    (played by Ellen Holly)
    The first and best daytime contract role for an African-American woman. She gave us incandescent revelations of what it is to be a talented, ambitious black woman in a white society.

And 2 Might-Have-Beens

1. Erica Kane, *All My Children*
   (played by Susan Lucci)
   Pinocchio almost became a real woman dealing with the traumatic reappearance of her illegitimate daughter (by rape), Kendall Hart. Who demonized Kendall and turned the story into a validation of Erica's ego?

2. Jenna Bradshaw, *Guiding Light*
   (played by Fiona Hutchison)
   Almost a great story about a guttersnipe with a classy act who makes big waves and inspires big dreams in Buzz Cooper, the extraordinary ordinary man. Who pulled the plug on this potentially heartstopping heroine?

THE 10 BEST ACTORS CURRENTLY ON DAYTIME

Chosen by the Author
Note: In order to be impartial, I eliminated from consideration performers who participated in the book.

1. Charles Keating (Carl Hutchins, *Another World*)
   Nature blessed Charles Keating with two incredible props: a Shakespearean-timbred voice that delivers lines gift-wrapped and a pair of eyebrows that double-accent every emotion that crosses his face.

2. David Canary (Adam and Stuart Chandler, *All My Children*)
   Adam, Stuart, Adam posing as Stuart, Stuart posing as Adam—David Canary's gift for nuance almost makes you forget that he's only one man.

3. Peter Simon (Ed Bauer, *Guiding Light*)

Subtle but consistently solid, Peter Simon is the classic soap actor. His work is a tribute to the days when soap operas took place over kitchen and operating tables.

4. Larry Bryggman (John Dixon, *As the World Turns*)

Daytime's equivalent to a marathon runner, Larry Bryggman has rarely slowed down during his twenty-six years and counting on *As the World Turns*. Part of his secret appears to be pacing. He doesn't waste energy pushing himself ahead of the crowd in every scene. But once he does kick into high gear, few actors can keep up with him.

5. Tony Geary (Luke Spencer, *General Hospital*)

Now that the height of Tony Geary's popularity has passed, it's time to admire the depth of his acting. Although his work as Bill Eckert proved his range, his return to the role of Luke showed just how much Geary has grown as an actor.

6. Michael Zaslow (Roger Thorpe, *Guiding Light*)

Despicable, sympathetic, frightening, charming, romantic, vengeful . . . Roger Thorpe has given Michael Zaslow the chance to play everything, and Zaslow in turn has made Roger everything the character could be.

7. Darnell Williams (Jacob Johnson, *Loving/The City*)

One of the most important African-American actors in the history of daytime, Darnell Williams has never whitewashed his performance or resorted to easy stereotypes.

8. Phil Carey (Asa Buchanan, *One Life to Live*)

Asa Buchanan is larger than life, larger than Texas, and Carey fills every inch.

9. Keith Hamilton Cobb (Noah Keefer, *All My Children*)

It's not common for an unknown actor to receive an Emmy nomination less than a year into his first soap role. But Keith Hamilton Cobb has made the most impressive soap debut in recent memory. And it looks like he's only just getting started.

10. Jonathan Jackson (Lucky Spencer, *General Hospital*)

In a medium where children rarely bear more than a passing resemblance to either of their onscreen parents, *General Hospital*'s casting director found in

Jonathan Jackson the perfect cross between Tony Geary (Luke) and Genie Francis (Laura). What made the casting a real coup was Jackson's immense talent, which appears to be "genetic." He is the best child actor to hit daytime since his onscreen mother first showed up in Port Charles twenty years ago.

THE 10 BEST ACTRESSES CURRENTLY ON DAYTIME

Chosen by the Author

1. Erika Slezak (Victoria Lord, *One Life to Live*)

Three more Emmys and Erika Slezak will have one for each of Vicki's personalities. And she deserves every single one of them. Slezak has made some of the alters like Nikki and Tori so appealing as characters in and of themselves that it would be a shame for Vicki to ever be completely cured.

2. Ellen Dolan (Margo Hughes, *As the World Turns*)

There is a reason why Doug Marland trusted Ellen Dolan with the two most powerful storylines he ever wrote for daytime, Casey's right to die and Margo's rape/AIDS scare. Dolan is tough enough to tackle the really difficult scenes, and she's generous enough to share the experience with her castmates and the audience.

3. Susan Lucci (Erica Kane, *All My Children*)

At this point, a Trustees Award would look to some like a consolation prize because Susan Lucci couldn't win a regular Emmy. The truth is, a regular Emmy isn't a big enough award for Lucci. A regular Emmy honors an actor for one year's worth of work. Lucci has kept Erica Kane fresh and vibrant for more than twenty-five years, and her scenes dealing with her childhood rape and subsequent pregnancy prove that Lucci can handle the heaviest of drama.

4. Lynn Herring (Lucy Coe, *General Hospital*)

Lynn Herring would have been a great silent film star. She acts with eyes, with her face, with her whole body. Even with the sound turned all the way down, you can tell if Lucy's cozying up to a man because she wants him or if she's merely toying with his libido for fun and profit.

5. Robin Strasser (Dorian Lord, *One Life to Live*)

An actress who can hold her own with giants like Erika Slezak and Phil Carey, Robin Strasser could have dwarfed newcomers like Nathan Fillion (Joey Buchanan) and Tuc Watkins (David Vickers). Instead, she chose to lift them up, and in the process brought their scenes together to even greater heights.

6. Susan Haskell (Marty Saybrooke, *One Life to Live*)

One Life to Live waited many years for an actress to fill the void left by Judith Light (who had played Karen Wolek). If Susan Haskell stays with the show long enough, she could very easily inherit Erika Slezak's crown as anchor heroine.

7. Leslie Charleson (Monica Quartermaine, *General Hospital*)

During Monica's recent battle with breast cancer, there were moments when Leslie Charleson's performance felt more lived than acted. But that's the way Charleson has always played Monica, opting for real rather than noble.

8. Maeve Kinkead (Vanessa Chamberlain, *Guiding Light*)

It's easy for an actress to be elegant and dignified wearing a ballroom gown and diamonds. Maeve Kinkead, though, doesn't lose one iota of that elegance or dignity when Vanessa changes into a pair of jeans and a sweatshirt. She brings to daytime the same type of quiet strength that her sister-in-law Meryl Streep brings to the big screen.

9. Darlene Conley (Sally Spectra, *The Bold and the Beautiful*)

From drag to pratfalls, Darlene Conley is completely unafraid to do whatever it takes to make a scene work. She dives into her scenes the same way Sally dives into pools, headfirst.

10. Louise Sorel (Vivian Alamain, *Days of Our Lives*)

Picture Vivian rolling around on Carly Manning's grave after she had the poor woman buried alive. Or picture Vivian with her head shaved, laid out for a midnight lobotomy. Louise Sorel is one of the few actresses a writer can trust to take a plotline all the way over the top.

CRITICAL DECISIONS

DAYTIME'S 10 MOST SORELY MISSED ACTORS

Chosen by R. Scott Reedy
For the past four years, R. Scott Reedy has been tracking down and interviewing daytime alumni for Soap Opera Weekly's Star Track *column. In compiling his list of the ten actors he'd most like to see back on daytime, he avoided stars like Judith Light (Karen Wolek,* One Life to Live*) and Demi Moore (Jackie Templeton,* General Hospital*) who have made a name for themselves in prime-time and movies; instead, he concentrated on actors who could conceivably return to daytime.*

1. Maeve McGuire (Kate McCleary, *Search for Tomorrow*; Elena de Poulignac, *Another World*; Nicole Travis, *The Edge of Night*)
   McGuire's recent short-term stints on *Guiding Light* and *One Life to Live* were wonderful but left us wanting more.

2. Beverlee McKinsey (Alexandra Spaulding, *Guiding Light*; Iris Carrington, *Another World* and *Texas*)
   Admittedly a daytime diva of the first order, McKinsey is nonetheless sorely missed.

3. Judith Chapman (Angelica Deveraux, *Days of Our Lives*; Ginny Blake, *General Hospital*; Charlotte Greer, *Ryan's Hope*; Natalie Bannon Hughes, *As the World Turns*)
   Chapman combines strength and control with an intriguing dash of vulnerability.

4. Larkin Malloy (Clay Alden, *Loving*; Travis Montgomery, *All My Children*; Kyle Sampson, *Guiding Light*; Sky Whitney, *The Edge of Night*)
   Malloy's commanding small-screen presence would enhance any show.

5. Sharon Gabet (Melinda Cramer, *One Life to Live*; Brittany Peterson, *Another World*; Raven Alexander, *The Edge of Night*)
   Daytime needs more actresses who are so masterful at playing vixens and women on the edge.

6. Anthony Herrera (Dane Hammond, *Loving*; James Stenbeck, *As the World Turns*; Jack Curtis, *The Young and the Restless*)
   Known for his suave villains, Herrera has enough style to breathe life into any part.

7. Lane Davies (Mason Capwell, *Santa Barbara*; Evan Whyland, *Days of Our Lives*; a temporary Ridge Forrester, *The Bold and the Beautiful*)

Two actors may have succeeded him on *Santa Barbara*, but few would argue that it was Davies who owned the role. It's time he took possession of another one.

8. Susan Pratt (Barbara Montgomery, *All My Children*; Dr. Claire Ramsey, *Guiding Light*; Annie Logan, *General Hospital*)

Whether portraying a nurse, doctor, or corporate executive, Pratt is always a true professional.

9. William Gray Espy (Mitch Blake, *Another World*; Snapper Foster, *The Young and the Restless*)

Expert as Espy is at playing the antihero, his return would no doubt earn him a hero's welcome.

10. Jada Rowland (Carolee Aldrich, *The Doctors*; Amy Ames, *The Secret Storm*)

A veteran actress whose combined soap services exceed twenty-five years. Forget the gold watch. Give this woman a job.

THE 20 BEST-LOOKING MEN AND WOMEN ON DAYTIME

Chosen by Freeman Günter
Managing Editor of Features Freeman Günter writes the text for Soap Opera Weekly's *"Dressed for Success" section, critiquing the fashion triumphs and disasters of actors and actresses off the screen. He shares with us his choices for the best-looking men and women whose photos have crossed his desk. They are listed in no particular order.*

The 10 Best-Looking Women

1. Robin Strasser (Dorian Lord, *One Life to Live*)

A fascinating-looking woman. She can look old and haggard from certain angles; then she can smile or turn her head into the light, and she will become radiant and young and lovely. Robin's beauty comes and goes, and that makes it all the more fabulous to look at.

2. Wendy Moniz (Dinah Chamberlain Marler, *Guiding Light*)
    So contemporary looking. It's such a no-nonsense, no-fussing kind of beauty.

3. Mari Morrow (Rachel Gannon, *One Life to Live*)
    Her skin has a glow that makes her even more beautiful in person than on the screen.

4. Anna Lee (Lila Quartermaine, *General Hospital*)
    People may question this choice, but Anna Lee is so pretty, every time I see her on the screen I feel good.

5. Katherine Kelly Lang (Brooke Logan Forrester, *The Bold and the Beautiful*)
    She's just so refreshing to look at.

6. Hunter Tylo (Taylor Hayes Forrester, *The Bold and the Beautiful*)
    Such a face, like one of the great faces of Old Hollywood.

7. Krista Tesreau (Tina Lord, *One Life to Live*)
    A wonderful-looking woman on *and* off the screen.

8. Eva La Rue (Maria Santos Grey, *All My Children*)
    She has a kind of porcelain perfection that is amazing.

9. Melina Kanakaredes (Eleni Cooper, *Guiding Light*)
    A spectacular, timeless beauty which has nothing to do with styles or fads.

10. Susan Lucci (Erica Kane, *All My Children*)
    I thought about not choosing Susan because it's so cliché by now. But she is quite wonderful-looking. And she's even more wonderful-looking now than she used to be.

The 10 Best-Looking Men

1. Dylan Neal (Dylan Shaw, *The Bold and the Beautiful*)
    He has that All-American look.

2. Tuc Watkins (David Vickers, *One Life to Live*)

Tuc has a lot of dimensions in his acting, which makes his looks more interesting. And the most beautiful arms in daytime.

3. Shemar Moore (Malcolm Winters, *The Young and the Restless*)
   Such a magnificent work of art. How could I not put him on the list?

4. John McCook (Eric Forrester, *The Bold and the Beautiful*)
   So debonair. So handsome. So suave.

5. Randolph Mantooth (Alex Masters, *The City*)
   He's got a slightly lived-in face that's so craggy and handsome. Maybe the sexiest man on TV.

6. Jon Lindstrom (Kevin Collins and Ryan Chamberlain, *General Hospital*)
   He's got an intelligent forehead and eyes and a soft mouth. He looks like a sensitive man you would enjoy knowing.

7. Nathan Fillion (Joey Buchanan, *One Life to Live*)
   Not the typical hunk mold, but he has a wonderful humanity that shows in his looks and makes him exceptional.

8. Rick Hearst (Alan-Michael Spaulding, *Guiding Light*)
   Classically handsome like an old-time movie star.

9. Sean Kanan (A. J. Quartermaine, *General Hospital*)
   Sean looks like an intelligent, well brought-up young man from a good family.

10. Bryan Buffinton (Bill Lewis, *Guiding Light*)
    He's the perfect example of a good-looking kid who's growing into himself as a man without going through an awkward stage.

9
Background Music

12 SOAP OPERA SOUNDTRACKS THAT HAVE BEEN RELEASED

1. *The Young and the Restless* (MCA, 1987)

The Young and the Restless cast has long boasted a number of singers, many of whose musical talents were exhibited on the show in concert scenes. In 1987, MCA capitalized on that talent by releasing an album of songs by the show's stars: Michael Damian (Danny Romalotti), Tracey E. Bregman (Lauren Fenmore), Beth Maitland (Traci Abbott), Patty Weaver (Gina Roma), and Colleen Casey (Faren Connor).

2. *Dallas: The Music Story* (Warner Bros., 1985)

Like the *The Young and the Restless* soundtrack, *Dallas: The Music Story* features the musical talents of castmembers Steve Kanaly (Ray Krebbs), Howard Keel (Clayton Farlow), and Jennilee Harrison (Jamie Ewing). Their tracks were intermixed with those from country artists such as Gary Morris (Wayne Masterson, *The Colbys*) and Crystal Gayle.

3-4. *Beverly Hills 90210* (Giant, 1992) and *Beverly Hills 90210: The College Years* (Giant, 1994)

In addition to the theme song, the *Beverly Hills 90210* soundtrack included a collection of material from artists like Paula Abdul, Jody Watley, and Chaka Khan. Songs from the soundtrack were then incorporated into the TV series and videos were run during the closing credits. (A couple of the videos featured castmembers from the show.) The soundtrack put two songs into the top ten: Shanice's "Saving Forever for You" and the Vanessa Williams/Brian McKnight duet "Love Is." Two years later, Giant released a second soundtrack, *Beverly Hills 90210: The College Years.*

5. *Melrose Place: The Music* (Giant, 1994)

Like *Beverly Hills 90210, Melrose Place* ran videos to the songs from its soundtrack during its closing credits. The music from the *Melrose Place* album was far more alternative than that on the *90210* soundtrack, featuring artists such as Aimee Mann, Urge Overkill, Annie Lennox, and The Divynils.

6. *One Life to Live* (SBK Records/ERG, 1994)

Some of the artists who cut tracks for the *One Life to Live* soundtrack came on the show to perform their songs: Darlene Love and Bill Medley performed their version of "You're My Soul and My Inspiration" at Tina Lord's (then Karen Witter) bridal shower, while Billy Dean sang "Here We Are My Friend" on Luna Moody's (Susan Batten) radio show. Another song, "Teach Me How to Dream," was incorporated into Marty and Suede's love story; on the show, they wrote the song together. Music from the soundtrack was highlighted during a special Valentine's Day all-music episode of the show.

7. *The Heights: Music from the Television Show* (Capitol, 1992)

The Commitments, an Irish film about the birth of a blue-collar band, launched not one but two soundtracks. The producers of the Fox serial *The Heights* were no doubt hoping for similar success from their TV series about a struggling rock band. Because the show was cancelled midway through its first season, only one soundtrack was ever released. Castmembers from the series not only sang on it, they played their own instruments and a few wrote their own songs.

8. *Twin Peaks* (Warner Bros., 1990)

The *Twin Peaks* soundtrack was co-produced by David Lynch, who had co-created and co-produced the television series.

9–12. *Original Music from Dark Shadows* (Philips, 1969), Volume 2 (Media Sound, 1986), Volume 3 (Media Sound, 1987) and Volume 4 (Media Sound, 1988).

BACKGROUND MUSIC

In 1969, the immense popularity of *Dark Shadows* launched a soundtrack album that included the incredibly popular "Quentin's Theme" (but not the same version that was climbing the pop charts—that was released on another album). In 1986, approximately fifteen years after *Dark Shadows*'s last airdate, a second volume of music from the show was released followed by a third and fourth released in 1987 and 1988. In 1990, Media Sound rereleased the original soundtrack on CD.

6 SOAP OPERA THEME SONGS RELEASED AS SINGLES

1. "Nadia's Theme" by Barry DeVorzon and Perry Botkin, Jr. (The Theme to *The Young and the Restless*)

The song that has opened *The Young and the Restless* for more than twenty years was originally titled "Cotton's Theme" and was written for the 1972 movie *Bless the Beasts and the Children*. The piece got worldwide exposure during the 1976 summer Olympics when Romanian gymnast Nadia Comaneci performed her gold medal–winning routine to it. After the song was retitled "Nadia's Theme" and picked up by radio stations, it became a Top 10 single.

2. "Another World (You Take Me Away To)" by Crystal Gayle and Gary Morris

Another World's current theme song was debuted on the show by Gayle, who is a fan of the show, and Morris, who had starred on *The Colbys* as blind country singer Wayne Masterson. The song was included on an album of duets by Gayle and Morris and hit the Top Ten on the country music charts.

3. "How Do You Talk to an Angel?" by the cast from *The Heights*

While it is not uncommon for an unsuccessful movie to launch a #1 theme song, it was unheard of for a low-rated TV show to do so. Only three TV shows ever had their theme songs hit #1—*Welcome Back, Kotter*, *Miami Vice*, and *S.W.A.T.*—and they had all been Top 20 shows. *The Heights*, on the other hand, usually ranked in the bottom 20, which didn't seem to matter to radio listeners.

4. "Faces of the Heart" by Dave Koz

Dave Koz's instrumental piece "Faces of the Heart" literally jazzed up *General Hospital*'s opening credits. When Koz decided to release the song as a single, he filmed a video that starred *General Hospital* alumna Emma Samms (Holly Sutton Scorpio).

5. "Falling" by Julie Cruise

In the two-hour movie that premiered *Twin Peaks*, Julie Cruise performed "Falling," a version of the show's theme song with lyrics. Her version became a modest hit on college and alternative rock radio stations.

6. "Dynasty"

Performed by Bill Conti, the instrumental theme to *Dynasty* hit the charts but fell short of the Top 40.

10 SOAP ACTORS WHO RECORDED TOP 10 SINGLES

1. Rick Springfield (Noah Drake, *General Hospital*)

Rick Springfield recorded the Top 20 hit "Speak to the Sky" in 1972, but scored a string of Top 10 hits after landing a role on *General Hospital*: "Jessie's Girl" (a #1 single), "Don't Talk to Strangers," "I've Done Everything For You," and "Affair of the Heart." Springfield only had one more Top Ten single after leaving *General Hospital*: "Love Somebody" from his feature-film debut, *Hard to Hold*.

2. Michelle Phillips (Ruby Ashford, *Search for Tomorrow*; Anne Matheson, *Knots Landing*)

As one-fourth of the 1960s quartet The Mamas & the Papas, Michelle Phillips scored half a dozen Top 10 hits, the biggest of which was the #1 single "Monday, Monday." Other Mamas & the Papas hits included: "California Dreamin'," "I Saw Her Again," "Words of Love," "Creeque Alley," and "Dedicated to the One I Love," which was used on *Knots Landing* during a scene in which Phillips's character, Anne, was dancing around the living room with her old flame Mack MacKenzie (Kevin Dobson).

3. Ronn Moss (Ridge Forrester, *The Bold and the Beautiful*)

In the late '70s, some ten years before his soap career began, Ronn Moss played bass for the rock group Player who recorded the #1 single "Baby Come

Back" and the Top 10 hit "This Time I'm in It for Love." "Baby Come Back" was used in a scene during the summer of 1994 in which Ridge pursued his ex-fiancée, Brooke Logan (Katherine Kelly Lang).

4. Bill Hayes (Doug Williams, *Days of Our Lives*)

In 1955, Bill Hayes, who had been a regular on Sid Caesar's *Your Show of Shows*, released the single "The Ballad of Davy Crockett." The song spent five weeks at the top of the charts. Hayes's only other Top 40 hit was also Western-themed, "Wringle Wrangle" from the movie *Westward Ho, The Wagons*.

5. Jamie Walters (Ray Pruitt, *Beverly Hills 90210*)

Jamie Walters, a castmember of *The Heights*, sang lead vocals on the show's theme song "How Do You Talk to an Angel?" which became a #1 hit. While playing rising rock star Ray Pruitt on *Beverly Hills 90210*, Walters landed his second Top Ten single, "Hold On."

6. Shaun Cassidy (Dusty Walker, *General Hospital*)

While starring on *The Hardy Boys* in 1977, Shaun Cassidy landed three Top 10 singles: "Hey Deanie," "That's Rock 'n' Roll," and the #1 hit "Da Doo Ron Ron." Ten years later, Cassidy joined the cast of *General Hospital* as Dusty Walker, an up-and-coming singer who'd been brainwashed into becoming an assassin whenever he heard a certain song.

7. Michael Damian (Danny Romalotti, *The Young and the Restless*)

Michael Damian's only Top 10 hit, the #1 single "Rock On," was a remake of a David Essex hit from the mid-'70s. Damian's version had been used in the movie *Dream a Little Dream* and was performed on *The Young and the Restless* as a hit song of Danny's.

8. Gloria Loring (Liz Curtis, *Days of Our Lives*)

Gloria Loring's duet with Carl Anderson "Friends and Lovers" climbed to #2 on the music charts and was among the twenty biggest hits of 1986. The song had been introduced on *Days of Our Lives* as a love theme for Shane Donovan (Charles Shaughnessy) and Kimberly Brady (Patsy Pease).

9. Jack Wagner (Frisco Jones, *General Hospital*)

"All I Need" was sung by Frisco Jones to his pre-Felicia (Kristina Wagner) love interest Tanya Roskov (Hillary Edson). It became a hit single for Jack Wagner himself. Frisco's love song to Felicia, "Lady of My Heart," was released in 1985 as the flip side to "Premonition."

10. Rex Smith (Darryl Crawford, *As the World Turns*)

In the late '70s, Smith landed a Top 10 hit with "You Take My Breath Away," a song he performed in *Sooner or Later*, a TV movie about teen sex. When Darryl married Frannie Hughes (Mary Ellen Stuart), he looked at his bride and said, "You take my breath away." Smith's only other Top 40 hit was a duet with Rachel Sweet, a remake of Robert Knight's "Everlasting Love."

Note: Kylie Minogue, an actress on the Australian soap *Neighbours*, landed a Top 10 hit on the American charts with her remake of Little Eva's "The Loco-Motion."

10 SONGS WRITTEN ABOUT SOAP OPERAS

1. "Erica Kane"

The alternative rock group Urge Overkill, who recorded songs for the *Melrose Place* and *Pulp Fiction* soundtracks, are big fans of *All My Children*. On their debut album *Saturation*, they included a song about Erica Kane titled "Erica Kane."

2. "Who Shot J. R.?"

During the summer of 1980, Gary Burbank with Band McNally released the novelty single "Who Shot J. R.?" which put to music the question *Dallas* had the whole world asking. The song climbed up to #67 on the *Billboard* charts.

3. "Penny"

The song "Penny" was written about *As the World Turns*'s Penny Hughes by Mark Rydell, who played Penny's boyfriend Jeff Baker. Rosemary Prinz, who played Penny, released the song as a single in 1966 and included it on her album *Penny Sings*.

4. "Nobody Cares About Langley"

Louis Edmonds (Langley Wallingford, *All My Children*) wrote the song "Nobody Cares About Langley" in protest of his declining storyline on the show. He included the song in his cabaret act and on the CD *Nobody Cares About Langley. All My Children* once built a fantasy sequence around the song.

5 "Jillian's Theme"
John Gabriel (Seneca Beaulac, *Ryan's Hope*) included on his album the song "Jillian's Theme," which was written about Seneca's wife Jillian Coleridge (played by Nancy Addison).

6. "Barnabas"
In 1969, the group Vampire State Building recorded the song "Barnabas," a tribute to *Dark Shadows*'s resident vampire Barnabas Collins (played by Jonathan Frid). On the flip side of the single was the song "I'm Bats About You."

7. "Julie's Theme"
Susan Marie Snyder, who played Julie Wendall on *As the World Turns*, released a dance version of "Julie's Theme" (written about her character) on her own three-song cassette *Anchor the Light*.

8. "General Hospital"
In 1980, a new-wave band named Planet Street put to music plotlines from *General Hospital* to create a song of the same title. Although the band released the single locally around Boston, a lawsuit with ABC over use of the title "General Hospital" killed plans to release the song nationally.

9. "General Hospi-tale"
Also in 1980, Boston radio personality Lisa Lipps put her *General Hospital* updates to music and created the novelty rap song "General Hospi-tale." (Lipps had learned from Planet Street's mistake and altered the song's title.) Although the plotlines recounted in the song were a year out of date by the time the single was released nationwide in 1981, "General Hospi-tale" by the Afternoon Delights managed to crack the Top 40. It is considered to be one of the first rap songs to do so.

10. "Quentin's Theme"
As "Quentin's Theme (Shadows of the Night)" was climbing up the singles chart, twenty versions of the song—both instrumental and vocal—were collected onto one album, titled *Quentin's Theme*. Artists who covered the song on the album included Andy Williams, Lawrence Welk, the Ray Conniff Singers, and Mantovani.

It was The Charles Randolph Grean Sounde who recorded the version that made it, appropriately enough, to #13 on *Billboard*'s pop chart.

5 SONGS HELPED UP THE CHARTS BY *GENERAL HOSPITAL*

1. "Baby Come to Me" by Patti Austin and James Ingram

"Baby Come to Me" had peaked at #73 on *Billboard*'s Hot 100 in the spring of 1982 and fell off the charts completely two weeks later. That summer, it was revived as the theme song for *General Hospital*'s Luke Spencer (Tony Geary) and Holly Sutton (Emma Samms), who was just being introduced on the show. By early fall, the song was back on the charts; by February, it was a #1 single. The song's twenty-three-week climb to the top (including the five weeks it charted in early 1982) make it one of the slowest-climbing #1 hits in music history.

2. "Rise" by Herb Alpert

Unlike "Baby Come to Me," "Rise" was already rising up the charts when it was used as the background music during the now infamous scene in which Luke raped newlywed Laura Baldwin (Genie Francis) on the floor of his disco. The song was in fact a Top 5 hit the week it premiered on the show. Exposure on the soap did, however, help "Rise" knock Michael Jackson's "Don't Stop till You Get Enough" out of the top spot and become a gold record. It should be noted that it was Tony Geary himself who brought the song to the attention of Jill Phelps, then music director for the show.

3. "Think of Laura" by Christopher Cross

Although perfectly named, "Think of Laura" was not written specifically to herald Genie Francis's six-week return to *General Hospital* in the fall of 1983. Like "Baby Come to Me," the song had peaked well below the Top 40 before being discovered by *General Hospital*. As with "Rise," the song had been brought to the show's attention by Tony Geary. The whole fever surrounding Genie Francis's return to *General Hospital* pushed Cross's song into the Top 10.

4. "Jessie's Girl" by Rick Springfield

Although Springfield, who played Dr. Noah Drake, never performed on

General Hospital, the show did use his songs like "Jessie's Girl" during disco scenes as a sort of in-joke. (In some ways a stab at Springfield for refusing to sing on the show, characters occasionally made reference to hating one of his songs when it started playing in the background.) Beyond that, Springfield's role on *General Hospital* during its peak of popularity landed him on talk shows as well as music programs like *Solid Gold.* As a result, "Jessie's Girl" went all the way to the top of the charts during the summer of 1981.

5. "All I Need" by Jack Wagner

When Frisco Jones (Jack Wagner) was introduced on *General Hospital* in the spring of 1984, the character was a rock star, not a spy. That fall, Wagner released a five-track EP that included some of the songs he had performed on the show. Among them was "All I Need," which had become the love theme for Frisco and Tanya Roskov (Hillary Edson). It made it all the way to #2 on the charts, kept out of the top spot by Madonna's megahit "Like a Virgin."

10 ALBUMS RECORDED BY SOAP ACTORS

1. *At Doug's Place* by Bill Hayes (Doug Williams, *Days of Our Lives*)

Note: Hayes's wife, Susan Seaforth Hayes (Julie Williams, *Days of Our Lives*), sings two duets on the album.

2. *Phoebe Tyler Regrets* by Ruth Warrick (Phoebe Tyler, *All My Children*)

3. *Joanne Sings* by Mary Stuart (Joanne Gardner, *Search for Tomorrow*)

4. *TV's Penny Sings* by Rosemary Prinz (Penny Hughes, *As the World Turns*)

5. *Love of Life* by Gene Bua (Bill Prentiss, *Love of Life*)

6. *One Life to Live* by Wayne Massey (Johnny Drummond, *One Life to Live*)

Note: Massey's leading lady, Mary Gordon Murray (Becky Lee Abbott) recorded two duets with Massey on the album.

7. *Same Old World* by Eileen Fulton (Lisa Hughes, *As the World Turns*)

8. *Tonight at the Capri Lounge Starring Loretta Haggers* by Mary Kay Place (Loretta Haggers, *Mary Hartman, Mary Hartman*)

9. *Love in the Afternoon*
    Note: Featured a compilation of actors from the ABC soaps including: Susan Lucci (Erica Kane, *All My Children*), Stuart Damon (Alan Quartermaine, *General Hospital*), Helen Gallagher (Maeve Ryan, *Ryan's Hope*), James Mitchell (Palmer Cortlandt, *All My Children*), and Michael Storm (Larry Wolek, *One Life to Live*).

10. *With Love from the Soaps*
    Note: Featured a compilation of actors from different shows including: Matthew Ashford (Jack Deveraux, *Days of Our Lives*), Ricky Paull Goldin (Dean Frame, *Another World*), Brad Maule (Tony Jones, *General Hospital*), Scott Reeves (Ryan McNeil, *The Young and the Restless*), and Jeff Trachta (Thorne Forrester, *The Bold and the Beautiful*).

12 POPULAR SINGERS WHO HAVE PERFORMED ON THE DAYTIME SOAPS

1–2. Whitney Houston and Jermaine Jackson
    On *As the World Turns*: Houston and Jackson sang a duet at the Cinderella Ball.

3. Stevie Wonder
    On *All My Children*: Erica Kane (Susan Lucci) performed an impromptu duet with Wonder on "I Just Called to Say I Love You," after which he agreed to perform at the opening of the nightclub Panache.

4. Jeffrey Osborne
    On *Santa Barbara*: Osborne performed at Kelly Capwell's (Robin Wright) wedding to Joe Perkins (Mark Arnold).

5. Al Jarreau
    On *Days of Our Lives*: Jarreau performed at a fund-raiser where Stefano DiMera (Joseph Mascolo) had planted a bomb.

BACKGROUND MUSIC

6. Melissa Manchester

On *General Hospital*: Manchester was introduced as an old friend of Mac Scorpio (John J. York) and stopped by to perform at his club, the Outback.

7. Johnny Mathis

On *Ryan's Hope*: Katie Ryan (Julia Campbell) crashed Mathis's recording session to get him to listen to a song written by Dave Greenberg (Scott Holmes). The song was, in fact, the title track from Mathis's *Straight from the Heart* album.

On *As the World Turns*: He also stopped by the Mona Lisa on *As the World Turns* to sing a duet with Patti Austin.

8. B. B. King

On *General Hospital*: Blues legend B. B. King played at the opening of Luke's (Tony Geary) blues club.

9. Engelbert Humperdinck

On *Loving*: Engelbert Humperdinck performed a benefit concert for Alden University.

10. Ronnie Milsap

On *Another World*: Milsap played a singer at a country-western bar that record company executive Matt Cory (Matt Crane) went to check out.

11. Roberta Flack

On *Guiding Light*: Flack performed at Hamp (Vince Williams) and Gilly's (Amelia Marshall) wedding. She also sings a version of the show's theme song that is occasionally used during the show.

12. Julio Iglesias

General Hospital: Iglesias sang his remake of Patsy Cline's "Crazy" and was revealed to be an acquaintance of Miguel Mores (Ricky Martin).

10 MUSIC VIDEOS FEATURING SOAP STARS

1–2. "The Most Beautiful Girl in the World" and "The Undertaker," both by The Artist Formerly Known as Prince

Prince, a fan of *General Hospital*, called Vanessa Marcil (Brenda Barrett) personally and asked her to appear in his video for "The Undertaker." In it, she plays a drug addict who overdoses in Prince's recording studio. Prince was so impressed with her work and her beauty that he asked her to be in a second video, "The Most Beautiful Girl in the World." In that one, she plays an actress receiving an Academy Award. Prince subsequently declared Marcil the Most Beautiful Girl in the World.

3. "Everyday People" by Aretha Franklin

Aretha Franklin, a fan of the CBS soaps, sent a notice to the *As the World Turns* cast inviting them to be part of her "Everyday People" video. Lisa Brown (Iva Snyder) was the only castmember to respond. She gave up her lunch break to appear in the video. Spoofing on her job as a soap actress, Brown can be seen in a couple of shots blowing bubbles.

4. "She Drives Me Crazy" by Kermit the Frog

A comic remake of the Fine Young Cannibals hit, Kermit the Frog's video features an array of celebrity cameos dancing to and singing along with the song. Among those celebrities are: Tracey E. Bregman (Lauren Fenmore, *The Young and the Restless*), Martha Byrne (Lily Grimaldi, *As the World Turns*), and Tamara Tunie (Jessica Griffin, *As the World Turns*).

5. "How Many Ways" by Toni Braxton

Toni Braxton, a fan of *The Young and the Restless*, requested that Shemar Moore (Malcolm Winters) play her leading man in the video "How Many Ways." The video was filmed in Miami and in the Florida Keys. A rumor circulated shortly thereafter that the two were dating.

6. "On Bended Knee" by Boys II Men

Victoria Rowell (Drucilla Winters, *The Young and the Restless)*, Renee Jones, and Lark Voorhies (Lexie Carver and Wendy Reardon, *Days of Our Lives*), and *Facts of Life* alumna Kim Fields play girlfriends to the group's four members, who break up and make up during the course of the video.

7. "Hello" by Lionel Richie

Laura Carrington was cast as Lisa Baron on *One Life to Live* shortly after the show's casting director saw her in Lionel Richie's 1984 video "Hello." Carrington starred in the video as Richie's object of affection, a blind actress and sculptor. Carrington, who would go on to create the role of Simone Ravelle Hardy on *General Hospital*, also appeared in the video for Clarence Clemons's "Woman's Got the Power."

8. "He's My Weakness" by Rona Reeves

Rona Reeves's country ballad "He's My Weakness" was used as a theme song for Dorian Lord's (Robin Strasser) doomed relationship with Jason Webb (Mark Brettschneider). When Reeves filmed the video for the song, Brettschneider was hired as the male lead as a cross-promotion of sorts between *One Life to Live* and the country music video stations.

9. "Crying" by Roy Orbison and k. d. lang

When *One Life to Live* executive producer Linda Gottlieb approached Virgin Records about releasing a *One Life to Live* soundtrack, Co-Chairman Jeff Ayeroff countered with an offer of his own. He wanted to use soap actors in a video for a re-release of the Roy Orbison/k. d. lang duet "Crying." (Although not a soap opera fan himself, Ayeroff had long recognized the role soap operas played in popularizing songs.) Gottlieb immediately thought of the Max/Luna/Suede love triangle and recruited James De Paiva, Susan Batten, and David Leddingham into filming a video for the song. Footage from the video (minus the music) was subsequently used on *One Life to Live*.

10. "Heaven Bound, I'm Ready," by Shenandoah

In 1994, Teresa Blake (Gloria Marsh, *All My Children*) married Mike McGuire, drummer for the country group Shenandoah. In 1995, she played a factory worker in the video for their song "Heaven Bound, I'm Ready."

Note: Vincent Irizarry's last storyline as Lujack on *Guiding Light* revolved around taping a video for his cover of Bruce Springsteen's "Out in the Street." Before returning to *Guiding Light* as Nick McHenry, he popped up in one of those don't-blink-you'll-miss-it cameos in an actual Springsteen video, "Tougher Than the Rest."

10

The Bigger Screen

25 MOVIE STARS WHO STARTED OUT ON DAYTIME

1. Alec Baldwin (Billy Aldrich, *The Doctors*)

2. Meg Ryan (Betsy Stewart, *As the World Turns*)

3. Ray Liotta (Joey Perrini, *Another World*)

4. Kathleen Turner (Nola Dancy Aldrich, *The Doctors*)

5. Demi Moore (Jackie Templeton, *General Hospital*)

6. Janine Turner (Laura Templeton, *General Hospital*)

7. Tom Berenger (Tim Siegel, *One Life to Live*)

8. Kevin Bacon (Tod Adamson, *Search for Tomorrow*; Tim Werner, *Guiding Light*)

9. Susan Sarandon (Patrice Kahlman, *A World Apart*; Sarah Fairbanks, *Search for Tomorrow*)

THE BIGGER SCREEN

10. Laurence Fishburne (Josh Hall, *One Life to Live*)

11. Tia Carrere (Jade Soong, *General Hospital*)

12. Martin Sheen (Roy Sanders, *The Edge of Night*)

13. Armand Assante (Johnny McGee, *How to Survive a Marriage*; Mike Powers, *The Doctors*)

14. Christopher Reeve (Ben Harper, *Love of Life*)

15. Eric Roberts (Ted Bancroft, *Another World*)

16. Julianne Moore (Sabrina and Frannie Hughes, *As the World Turns*)

17. Raul Julia (Miguel Garcia, *Love of Life*)

18. JoBeth Williams (Carrie Wheeler, *Somerset*; Brandy Shellooe, *Guiding Light*)

19. Mark Hamill (Kent Murray, *General Hospital*)

20. Sigourney Weaver (Avis Ryan, *Somerset*)

21. Morgan Freeman (Roy Bingham, *Another World*)

22. Roy Scheider (Bob Hill, *The Secret Storm*; Jonas Falk and Dr. Wheeler, *Search for Tomorrow*)

23. Kate Capshaw (Jinx Avery, *The Edge of Night*)

24. Robin Wright (Kelly Capwell, *Santa Barbara*)

25. Christian Slater (D. J. LaSalle, *Ryan's Hope*)

8 FEATURE FILMS ADAPTED INTO SOAP OPERAS

All eight movies, it should be noted, were adapted from books.

1. Peyton Place

Just as the film *Peyton Place* was followed by the sequel *Return to Peyton Place*, the prime-time serial *Peyton Place* was followed by a daytime soap *Return to Peyton Place*.

2. Kitty Foyle

Kitty Foyle spawned a two-year radio soap and an even shorter lived television one. Curiously for a soap titled *Kitty Foyle*, the character of Kitty did not appear on the TV show until more than a month into its run.

3. Valley of the Dolls

Jacqueline Susann's *Valley of the Dolls*, one of the best-selling novels of all time, has been adapted into a feature film, a TV movie, and, most recently, a late-night soap that aired during the summer of 1994.

4. The Egg and I

Ma and Pa Kettle proved so popular in the comedy *The Egg and I*, they were spun off into their own film series during the 1950s. The characters, played by different actors, were also used in the 1951–52 soap opera version of the film.

5. Executive Suite

Cameron Hawley wrote the book *Executive Suite* on which the 1954 film and 1976 prime-time soap were based. Cash McCall—the title character from another Hawley book that was turned into a movie—served as the inspiration for *Another World*'s Steve Frame.

6. Best of Everything

When ABC adapted the 1954 film *Best of Everything* into a daytime soap, two movie actresses were cast in leading roles: Gale Sondergaard and Geraldine Fitzgerald.

7. Flamingo Road

The 1949 film of corruption in a small town focused on Lane Ballou (played by

Joan Crawford), a former carnival worker. In the prime-time soap version, Constance Carlyle (played by Morgan Fairchild) took center stage.

8. *Love Is a Many Splendored Thing*

The soap opera picked up years after the movie ended. Lead heroine Mia Elliott (played by Nancy Hsueh) was the daughter of the lovers in the movie. As in the movie, the soap dealt with an interracial relationship, this one between Mia and Vietnam vet Paul Bradley. Daytime was not ready, however, for an interracial storyline. Not only was the premise dropped six months into the show's run, Mia Elliott was written out of the show.

AND 2 SOAPS ON WHICH FEATURE FILMS WERE BASED

1. *Dark Shadows*

Dark Shadows inspired two horror films: *House of Dark Shadows* (1970) and *Night of Dark Shadows* (1971).

2. *Twin Peaks*

Twin Peaks: Fire Walk with Me detailed events leading up to Laura Palmer's murder.

10 MOVIES THAT INSPIRED SOAP STORYLINES

1. *Back to the Future*

Michael J. Fox travels back in time to the 1950s when his parents first fell in love. While there, he inadvertently comes between the two of them, which puts his very existence in jeopardy. The only way he can make sure that he'll be born is to bring his mother and father together.

On *Santa Barbara*: A honeymooning Cruz and Eden (A Martinez and Marcy Walker) discovered an enchanted mirror that transported them back to 1962, where they met Eden's parents, a newlywed C. C. and Sophia Capwell (Jed Allan and Judith McConnell). C. C. and Sophia were discussing the idea of having a baby that would be Eden. Talk of starting of family was cut short by C. C.'s jealousy over Sophia's attention to Cruz. Before Cruz and Eden could return to the present, they had to reconcile Sophia and C. C. to ensure that Eden would be born.

2. The Bedroom Window

Steve Guttenberg brings his boss's wife back to his apartment for a romantic encounter. While looking out the window in Guttenberg's bedroom, the woman witnesses an attempted murder. Rather than reveal their affair, Guttenberg and the woman agree that he should pretend to be the witness.

On *Days of Our Lives*: During the Riverfront Knifer plotline, Frankie Brady (Billy Warlock) had begun an affair with his college professor. While at her apartment one night, he witnessed a murder being committed. Rather than reveal why he was there, Frankie coached Paula so that she could pretend to be the witness.

3. Misery

Kathy Bates won an Oscar for playing the obsessed fan of romance novelist James Caan. Crazed over the fact that Caan has killed off her favorite heroine in order to concentrate on serious fiction, Bates holds him prisoner in her home and forces him to write a new romance novel for her.

On *Another World:* When Felicia Gallant (Linda Dano) decided to stop writing romance novels, obsessed fan Walter (Reed Birney) kidnaped Felicia and brought her to his house, where he kept her prisoner in his attic and forced her to write a new romance novel.

4. Wait until Dark

Blind housewife Audrey Hepburn, alone in her apartment, is tormented and almost raped by madman Alan Arkin.

On *One Life to Live*: Shortly after going blind, Nora Gannon (Hillary B. Smith) was stalked by escaped rapist Todd Manning (Roger Howarth). He tracked her down to a deserted beach house she had rented for the Christmas holiday. Boyfriend Bo Buchanan (Robert S. Woods) arrived, but Todd, pretending he had a gun, made Nora get rid of him. A movie buff, Nora tipped Bo off to the fact she was in danger by slipping the words "Don't wait until dark" into their brief conversation.

5. Witness for the Prosecution

Marlene Dietrich takes the witness stand with damaging testimony against husband (Tyrone Powers), who is on trial for murder. Powers's lawyer (Charles Laughton) cross-examines Dietrich with evidence that contradicts her entire testimony, leading her to break down and admit that she lied, and that her husband is innocent. At the end of the movie, it is revealed that the entire testimony had been an elaborate hoax.

The only way the jury would have believed Dietrich's claims of her husband's innocence would be if they had been pulled "unwillingly" from her. Her husband, she admits to Laughton, was indeed guilty of the murder with which he was charged.

On *General Hospital*: Dr. Kevin O'Connor (Kevin Bernhardt) was charged with two murders. During his trial, librarian Lucy Coe (Lynn Herring) took the stand to dispute his alibi that he was in the library at the time of one of the murders. During cross-examination, Lucy broke down and admitted that she lied because she was infatuated with him and he didn't return her affections. He was indeed in the library, she testified. In truth, Kevin had not been in the library. He and Lucy, who was his secret lover, hatched the plan to get him off. Kevin was, it turned out, very much guilty of the murders he had been charged with.

6. Dangerous Liaisons

Glenn Close and John Malkovich, members of the 18th-century French aristocracy, are bragging about their sexual conquests when Close proposes a bet. If Malkovich can seduce a woman of her choosing, then she (Close) will sleep with him. Confident of his victory, Malkovich takes the bet, and Close chooses the happily married Michelle Pfeiffer. Malkovich pursues Pfeiffer until she gives in to his charms and in the process falls in love with him. Close, however, reneges on her end of the bet.

On *General Hospital*: When Lucy Coe (Lynn Herring) suggested that Damian Smith (Leigh McCloskey) was not so irresistible to the opposite sex as he would like to believe, he proposed a bet. If he could seduce any woman of Lucy's choosing, Lucy would sell him her shares of ELQ stock and, as a bonus, she would go to bed with him. Lucy sicced Damian on her longtime rival, the happily married Bobbie Jones (Jacklyn Zeman). While Damian did seduce Bobbie (who fell for him), Lucy welshed on both ends of her bet.

7. The Jagged Edge

Lawyer Glenn Close falls in love with her client (Jeff Bridges), a man accused of murdering his wealthy wife. During the course of their affair, Close discovers evidence that makes her doubt Bridges's innocence.

On *Santa Barbara*: Julia Wainwright (Nancy Grahn) was hired to represent David Laurent (Brian Matthews), who had been accused of murdering his wealthy wife, Madeline (Terry Davis). During preparation for the trial, Julia ended up in bed with David. Although she fell in love with him, she was not altogether convinced of his innocence. In the end, he turned out to be innocent, but did not return her affection.

8. *The Most Dangerous Game*

The power-mad Count Zaroff (Leslie Banks) hunts down humans as prey on his private island.

On *Santa Barbara*: While investigating a case, Cruz wound up the prisoner of a crazed Dr. Willoughby, who hunted humans for fun. Willoughby took Eden hostage as well and hunted the two of them across his private island.

9. *Pocketful of Miracles*

Racketeer Dave the Dude (Glenn Ford) transforms down-and-out apple vendor Apple Annie (Bette Davis) into a lady of elegance to impress the daughter (Ann-Margaret) she has not seen in years.

On *Another World*: Mobster Tony the Tuna enlisted help from Cass Winthrop (Stephen Schnetzer) and Felicia Gallant (Linda Dano) to transform a homeless woman—also named Apple Annie (Lisa Eichorn)—into a lady to impress the daughter she had not seen in years.

10. *The Accused*

Jodie Foster won an Oscar for playing a party girl who is gang-raped after drunkenly flirting with a number of bar patrons. When she brings the men who raped her up on charges, the woman's less than noble reputation damages her case.

On *One Life to Live*: Susan Haskell won a Daytime Emmy for playing Marty Saybrooke, the town bad girl, who was gang-raped by three fraternity brothers during a party. When Marty pressed charges, her past history of lying, drinking, and sleeping around hindered her chances for a conviction.

10 ACTORS WHO HAVE APPEARED IN ALFRED HITCHCOCK FILMS

1. Macdonald Carey (Tom Horton, *Days of Our Lives*) in *Shadow of a Doubt*

2. Jane Wyman (Angela Channing, *Falcon Crest*) in *Stage Fright*

3. John Forsythe (Blake Carrington, *Dynasty*) in *Topaz* and *The Trouble with Harry*

4. Barbara Bel Geddes (Miss Ellie Ewing, *Dallas*) in *Vertigo*

5. Kim Novak (Kit Marlowe, *Falcon Crest*) in *Vertigo*

Note: Novak's storyline on *Falcon Crest*, in which she assumes the identity of her dead friend, bore a passing similarity to her role in *Vertigo*. *Falcon Crest* shot some scenes with Novak in the very same spots around San Francisco where *Vertigo* had been filmed.

6. Farley Granger (Earl Mitchell, *As the World Turns*; Dr. Will Vernon, *One Life to Live*) in *Rope* and *Strangers on a Train*

7. William Devane (Greg Sumner, *Knots Landing*) in *Family Plot*

8. Darlene Conley (Sally Spectra, *The Bold and the Beautiful*) in *The Birds*

9. Tippi Hedren (Helen MacLaine, *The Bold and the Beautiful*) in *The Birds* and *Marnie*

10. Melody Thomas Scott (Nikki Newman, *The Young and the Restless*) in *Marnie*

Note: Eight-year-old Scott made her film debut in *Marnie* playing Tippi Hedren's title role in a flashback scene.

10 ACTORS WHO HAVE APPEARED IN WOODY ALLEN FILMS

1. Louise Lasser (Mary Hartman, *Mary Hartman, Mary Hartman*) in *Bananas* and *Everything You Always Wanted to Know About Sex (But Were Afraid to Ask)*

Note: Lasser was also married to Allen.

2. Mia Farrow (Allison Mackenzie, *Peyton Place*) in several Woody Allen films, among them: *Purple Rose of Cairo, Zelig, Hannah and Her Sisters,* and *Radio Days.*

3. Mariel Hemingway (Stephanie Wells, *Central Park West*) in *Manhattan*

4. John Beck (Mark Graison, *Dallas*; David Raymond, *Santa Barbara*) in *Sleeper*

5. Dan Frazer (Mac McCloskey, *As the World Turns*) in *Take the Money and Run*

6. Lysette Anthony (Angelique, the prime-time *Dark Shadows*) in *Husbands and Wives*

7. Margaret Sophie Stein (Corvina Lang, *All My Children*) in *Bullets Over Broadway*
   Note: Stein has one of those don't-blink-you'll-miss-her parts.

8. Paul Anthony Stewart (Casey Bowman, *Loving*) in *Shadows and Fog*
   Note: Stewart's film debut.

9. Claire Bloom (Orlena Grimaldi, *As the World Turns*) in *Crimes and Misdemeanors* and *Mighty Aphrodite*

10. Paolo Seganti (Damian Grimaldi, *As the World Turns*) in Allen's as-yet-untitled 1996 film
    Note: Louise Sorel (Vivian Alamain, *Days of Our Lives*; Augusta Lockridge, *Santa Barbara*) worked with Allen in a pilot for a never-aired TV sitcom.

13 SOAP ACTORS WHO DID CAMEOS IN *YOUNG DOCTORS IN LOVE*

The popularity of General Hospital *in the early '80s spawned the 1982 film* Young Doctors in Love. Young Doctors *spoofed* General Hospital *in the same way that* Airplane *had spoofed the* Airport *movies—with a series of sight gags, physical humor, and short, skit-like scenes. The movie starred Michael McKean and Pamela Reed (who would both go on to star in the short-lived soap opera sitcom* Grand*), Dabney Coleman (who had starred on the soap opera spoof* Mary Hartman, Mary Hartman *as well as the serious soap* Bright Promise*), Sean Young, Harry Dean Stanton, and a pre-*Seinfeld *Michael Richards (Kramer). Richard Dean Anderson, who had played Jeff Webber on* General Hospital, *had a small role in the film as a drug dealer. The movie also featured cameos by 8* General Hospital *regulars and a handful of soap stars from* All My Children *and* The Young and the Restless.

From *General Hospital*

1. John Beradino (Dr. Steve Hardy)

2. Emily McLaughlin (Nurse Jessie Brewer)

3. Stuart Damon (Dr. Alan Quartermaine)

4. Chris Robinson (Dr. Rick Webber; currently Jack Hamilton, *The Bold and the Beautiful*)

5. Jacklyn Zeman (Bobbie Jones)

6. Demi Moore (Jackie Templeton)

7. Kin Shriner (Scotty Baldwin)

8. Janine Turner (Laura Templeton)

From *All My Children*

9. Susan Lucci (Erica Kane)

From *The Young and the Restless*

10. Michael Damian (Danny Romalotti)

11. Steve Ford (Andy Richards)

12. Jaime Lyn Bauer (Lauralee Brooks; currently Laura Horton, *Days of Our Lives*)

13. Tom Ligon (Lucas Prentiss)

13 SOAP ACTORS STALKED BY JASON IN *FRIDAY THE 13TH* MOVIES

Released in 1980, the slasher film Friday the 13th *began one of the most successful series in movie history. By 1993, thirteen years after the original movie was released, a total of eight sequels had been made. Many of these films featured soap opera actors. In the last few sequels, the role of Jason Voorhees, the hockey-masked killer, has been played by Kane Hodder, a former stunt man on* Days of Our Lives. *The killer in the first movie, though, was not Jason but his mother, played by Betsy Palmer, who would go on to play Valene Ewing's (Joan Van Ark) Aunt Ginny on* Knots Landing. *Among the victims in that first movie was a pre-Diner Kevin Bacon, who was still on* Guiding Light *at the time, playing alcoholic teen T. J. Werner.*

13 other soap stars have gone up against Jason at some point in their acting careers.

1. Lauren-Marie Taylor (Stacey Forbes, *Loving*)
   Taylor was stabbed to death in *Friday the 13th Part II*.
   Note: Stacey Forbes was the first victim of a mass murderer on *Loving*. The *Loving* killer, though, was far more gentle than Jason. Stacey was killed with a poisoned powder puff.

2. Russell Todd (Jamie Frame, *Another World*)
   Todd's throat was slashed while he was hanging upside down from a tree in Part II.

3. Amy Steel (Trudy Wilson, *Guiding Light*)
   Steel managed to evade Jason throughout Part II, in part by convincing him she was his dead mother.

4. Kimberly Beck (Julie Clegg, *Capitol*)
   Beck "killed" Jason in Part IV, which by title was supposed to be *The Final Chapter*.

5–6. Camilla and Carey Moore (Grace and Gillian Forrester, *Days of Our Lives*)
   In Part IV, one twin was speared to the side of a house; the other was pulled through a second-floor window and thrown to the ground below.

7. Peter Barton (Scott Grainger, *The Young and the Restless*)
   Jason crushed Barton's head in the shower in Part IV.

8. Michael Swan (Duncan McKechnie, *As the World Turns*)
   Like Peter Barton, Swan also got his head crushed two sequels later in Part VI—*Jason Lives*.

9. Renee Jones (Lexie Carver, *Days of Our Lives*)

Right before Jason crushed Michael Swan's head, he twisted Jones's head off her shoulders.

10. Lar Park Lincoln (Linda Fairgate, *Knots Landing*)

In an effort to give the series a new twist, a Carrie-like character played by Lincoln was introduced. Lincoln's ability to move objects with her mind kept her alive in Part VII—*The New Blood.*

Note: Ironically, Linda Fairgate met a *Friday the 13th*–style death on *Knots Landing*, having her throat slashed by a vengeful ex-lover.

11. Staci Greason (Isabella Toscanni, *Days of Our Lives*)

Greason, who was also in Part VII but whose character was not blessed with any supernatural powers of her own, took a tent stake through the neck.

12. Peter Mark Richman (Andrew Laird, *Dynasty*; C. C. Capwell, *Santa Barbara*)

Richman was dumped upside down into a barrel of toxic waste in Part VIII—*Jason Takes Manhattan.* Richman had been such a nuisance throughout the movie that people applauded Jason's actions.

13. Scott Reeves (Ryan McNeil, *The Young and the Restless*)

Reeves survived being chased around New York, both above ground and in the sewers in Part VIII.

12 SOAP OPERA ALUMNI WHO WON ACADEMY AWARDS

1. Tommy Lee Jones (Dr. Mark Toland, *One Life to Live*)
   1993's Best Supporting Actor for *The Fugitive*

2. Marisa Tomei (Marcy Thompson, *As the World Turns*)
   1992's Best Supporting Actress for *My Cousin Vinnie*

3. Kevin Kline (Woody Reed, *Search for Tomorrow*)
   1988's Best Supporting Actor for *A Fish Called Wanda*

4. Olympia Dukakis (Dr. Barbara Moreno, *Search For Tomorrow*)
   1987's Best Supporting Actress for *Moonstruck*

5. F. Murray Abraham (Joshua Browne, *How to Survive a Marriage*)
   1984's Best Actor for *Amadeus*

6. Beatrice Straight (Vinnie Phillips, *Love of Life*)
   1976's Best Supporting Actress for *Network*

7. Lee Grant (Rose Peterson, *Search for Tomorrow*)
   1975's Best Supporting Actress for *Shampoo*

8. Ellen Burstyn (Dr. Kate Bartok, *The Doctors*)
   1974's Best Actress for *Alice Doesn't Live Here Anymore*
   Note: Burstyn went by the name Ellen McRae when she was on *The Doctors* in 1965.

9. Sandy Dennis (Alice Holden, *The Guiding Light*)
   1966's Best Supporting Actress for *Who's Afraid of Virginia Woolf?*

10. Martin Balsam (Harold Matthews, *The Greatest Gift*; Joey Gordon, *Valiant Lady*)
    1965's Best Supporting Actor for *A Thousand Clowns*

11. Patty Duke (Ellen Dennis, *The Brighter Day*)
    1962's Best Supporting Actress for *The Miracle Worker*

12. Eva Marie Saint (Claudia Barbour, *One Man's Family*)
    1954's Best Supporting Actress for *On the Waterfront*

8 ACADEMY AWARD–WINNERS WHO APPEARED BRIEFLY ON THE SOAPS

1. Dustin Hoffman, 1988's Best Actor for *Rain Man*; 1979's Best Actor for *Kramer vs. Kramer*
   On *Search for Tomorrow*

2. Robert De Niro, 1980's Best Actor for *Raging Bull*; 1974's Best Supporting Actor for *The Godfather Part II*
    On *Search for Tomorrow*

3. Mercedes Ruehl, 1991's Best Supporting Actress for *The Fisher King*
    On *The Doctors*

4. Kathy Bates, 1990's Best Actress for *Misery*
    On *All My Children*

5. Warren Beatty, 1981's Best Director for *Reds*
    On *Love of Life*

6. Christopher Walken, 1978's Best Supporting Actor for *The Deer Hunter*
    On *The Guiding Light.*
    Note: Walken occasionally filled in for his brother Glenn as Mike Bauer.

7. Jack Lemmon, 1973's Best Actor for *Save the Tiger*
    On *The Brighter Day* and *The Road of Life*

8. Patricia Neal, 1963's Best Actress for *Hud*
    On *The Secret Storm*
    Note: Geraldine Page, 1985's Best Actress for *The Trip to Bountiful*, appeared on the prime-time movie that kicked off *Loving*.

15 ACADEMY AWARD–WINNERS WHO WENT ON TO DO SOAPS

1. Jane Wyman, 1948's Best Actress for *Johnny Belinda*
    Wyman starred as Angela Channing on *Falcon Crest.*

2. Charlton Heston, 1959's Best Actor for *Ben-Hur*
    Heston starred as Jason Colby on *The Colbys.*

3. Celeste Holm, 1947's Best Supporting Actress for *Gentleman's Agreement*

Holm played Anna Rossini on *Falcon Crest* in 1985. In 1987, she was nominated for a Daytime Emmy as Outstanding Guest Performer for playing Clara/Lydia Woodhouse on *Loving*. She rejoined the show in 1991, taking over the role of Isabelle Alden.

4. Joan Fontaine, 1941's Best Actress for *Suspicion*

Fontaine was nominated in 1980 for a Daytime Emmy for her cameo role as Page Williams on *Ryan's Hope*.

5. Cliff Robertson, 1968's Best Actor for *Charly*

Robertson played neurosurgeon Michael Ranson on *Falcon Crest* during the 1983–84 season.

6. George Kennedy, 1967's Best Supporting Actor for *Cool Hand Luke*

Kennedy joined *Dallas* in 1988 as rival-rancher-turned-rival-oil-company-owner Carter McKay. He stayed with the show till its cancellation in 1991.

7. Kim Hunter, 1951's Best Supporting Actress for *A Streetcar Named Desire*

Hunter was nominated in 1980 for a Daytime Emmy as Outstanding Actress for her role as actress Nola Madison on *The Edge of Night*.

8. Red Buttons, 1957's Best Supporting Actor for *Sayonara*

Buttons appeared as Al Baker on *Knots Landing* for half a dozen episodes in 1987. He romanced five-time Tony winner Julie Harris (Lilimae Clements), and the two left the show together.

9. José Ferrer, 1950's Best Actor for *Cyrano de Bergerac*

Ferrer played Reuben Marino on *Another World* in 1983.

10. Eileen Heckart, 1972's Best Supporting Actress for *Butterflies Are Free*

Nominated for a 1987 Daytime Emmy as Outstanding Guest Performer for her role as Ruth Perkins on *One Life to Live*, Heckart came back to *One Life to Live* in 1992 for a short-term role as Wilma Bern.

11. Theresa Wright, 1942's Best Supporting Actress for *Mrs. Miniver*

Wright played Grace Cummings on *Guiding Light* in 1986.

12–13. Anne Revere, 1945's Best Supporting Actress for *National Velvet,* and Gale Sondergaard, 1936's Best Supporting Actress for *Anthony Adverse*

Both actresses played Marguerite Beaulac on *Ryan's Hope* in 1976. (Sondergaard also played Amanda Key in *Best of Everything.*)

14. Dorothy Malone, 1956's Best Supporting Actress for *Written on the Wind*

Malone originated the role of Constance Mackenzie on *Peyton Place.*

15. Donna Reed, 1953's Best Supporting Actress for *From Here to Eternity*

Reed filled in for an ailing Barbara Bel Geddes as Miss Ellie on *Dallas* during the 1984–85 season.

11

And the Emmy Goes to . . .

THE 10 SOAPS THAT HAVE WON THE MOST MAJOR EMMYS

1. *All My Children* (24)

2. *Guiding Light* (23)

3. *The Young and the Restless* (20)

4. *One Life to Live* (18)

5–6. *Ryan's Hope* and *General Hospital* (15)

7. *Santa Barbara* (14)

8. *As the World Turns* (12)

9. *Another World* (10)

10. *Days of Our Lives* (9)

Note: Major Emmys include: Best Actor, Best Actress, Best Supporting Actor, Best Supporting Actress, Best Younger Actor, Best Younger Actress, Best Directing Team, Best Writing Team, and Outstanding Show. Trustee Awards, Special Recognitions, and one-time categories such as Best Cameo Performance were not counted.

THE 8 SOAPS NAMED OUTSTANDING SHOW MOST OFTEN

1. *The Young and the Restless*
   Five times: 1975, 1983, 1985, 1986, 1993

2. *Santa Barbara*
   Three times: 1988, 1989, 1990

3. *General Hospital*
   Three times: 1981, 1984, 1995

4. *The Doctors*
   Twice: 1972, 1974

5. *Ryan's Hope*
   Twice: 1977, 1979

6. *Guiding Light*
   Twice: 1980, 1982

7. *As the World Turns*
   Twice: 1987, 1991

8. *All My Children*
   Twice: 1992, 1994

THE 16 ACTORS AND ACTRESSES WHO HAVE WON THE MOST EMMY AWARDS FOR THEIR WORK ON THE SOAPS

Five Emmys

1. Justin Deas (Tom Hughes, *As the World Turns*; Keith Timmons, *Santa Barbara*; Buzz Cooper, *Guiding Light*)
   Outstanding Supporting Actor 1984 for *As the World Turns*; 1988, 1989 for *Santa Barbara*; and 1994 for *Guiding Light*; Outstanding Actor 1995 for *Guiding Light*

Four Emmys

2. David Canary (Adam and Stuart Chandler, *All My Children*)
   Outstanding Actor 1986, 1988, 1989, and 1993

3. Erika Slezak (Vicki Buchanan, *One Life to Live*)
   Outstanding Actress 1984, 1986, 1992, and 1995

Three Emmys

4. Helen Gallagher (Maeve Ryan, *Ryan's Hope*)
   Outstanding Actress 1976, 1977, and 1988

5. Kim Zimmer (Reva Shayne Lewis, *Guiding Light*)
   Outstanding Actress 1985, 1987, and 1990

Two Emmys

6. Macdonald Carey (Tom Horton, *Days of Our Lives*)
   Outstanding Actor 1974 and 1975

7. Larry Haines (Stu Bergman, *Search for Tomorrow*)
   Outstanding Actor 1976; Outstanding Supporting Actor 1981

8. Judith Light (Karen Wolek, *One Life to Live*)
   Outstanding Actress 1980 and 1981

9. Douglass Watson (Mac Cory, *Another World*)
    Outstanding Actor 1980 and 1981

10. Dorothy Lyman (Opal Gardner, *All My Children*)
    Outstanding Supporting Actress 1982; Outstanding Actress 1983

11. Darnell Williams (Jesse Hubbard, *All My Children*)
    Outstanding Supporting Actor 1983; Outstanding Actor 1985

12. Larry Bryggman (John Dixon, *As the World Turns*)
    Outstanding Actor 1984 and 1987

13. Michael E. Knight (Tad Martin, *All My Children*)
    Outstanding Younger Actor 1986 and 1987

14. John Wesley Shipp (Doug Cummings, *As the World Turns*; Martin Ellis, *Santa Barbara*)
    Outstanding Supporting Actor 1986 for *As the World Turns*; Outstanding Guest Performer 1987 for *Santa Barbara*

15. Ellen Wheeler (Victoria and Marley Love, *Another World*; Cindy Parker, *All My Children*)
    Outstanding Ingenue 1986 for *Another World*; Outstanding Supporting Actress 1988 for *All My Children*

16. Peter Bergman (Jack Abbott, *The Young and the Restless*)
    Outstanding Actor 1991 and 1992

THE 12 ACTORS AND ACTRESSES WHO HAVE GARNERED THE MOST DAYTIME EMMY NOMINATIONS WITHOUT WINNING ONE

Fifteen Nominations

1. Susan Lucci (Erica Kane, *All My Children*)

The SOAP OPERA BOOK of LISTS

Seven Nominations

2. James Mitchell (Palmer Cortlandt, *All My Children*)

Five Nominations

3. Lois Kibbee (Geraldine Whitney Saxon, *The Edge of Night*)
   Note: One nomination was for writing *The Edge of Night*.

Four Nominations

4. Jeanne Cooper (Katherine Chancellor, *The Young and the Restless*)

5. Nicholas Coster (Lionel Lockridge, *Santa Barbara*)

6. Stuart Damon (Alan Quartermaine, *General Hospital*)

7. Anthony Call (Herb Callison, *One Life to Live*)

8. Eileen Herlie (Myrtle Fargate, *All My Children*)

9. Terry Lester (Jack Abbott, *The Young and the Restless*)

10. Robin Mattson (Heather Webber, *General Hospital*; Gina Capwell, *Santa Barbara*)

11. Beverlee McKinsey (Iris Bancroft, *Another World*)

12. Susan Seaforth Hayes (Julie Williams, *Days of Our Lives*)

Note: Listed are the roles they were nominated for playing.

AND THE EMMY GOES TO . . .

12 POTENTIAL NOMINEES WHO AT ONE TIME OR ANOTHER HAVE CHOSEN NOT TO SUBMIT THEIR NAMES FOR CONSIDERATION

1. Beverlee McKinsey (Alexandra Spaulding, *Guiding Light*)
   Note: When she finally decided to submit her name in 1991, she was not nominated.

2. Tony Geary (Luke Spencer, *General Hospital*)

3. Julia Barr (Brooke English, *All My Children*)

4. Lane Davies (Mason Capwell, *Santa Barbara*)

5. Deidre Hall (Marlena Evans, *Days of Our Lives*)

6. Jay Hammer (Fletcher Reade, *Guiding Light*)

7. Peter Simon (Dr. Ed Bauer, *Guiding Light*)

8. Robert S. Woods (Bo Buchanan, *One Life to Live*)

9. Clint Ritchie (Clint Buchanan, *One Life to Live*)

10. Colleen Zenk Pinter (Barbara Ryan, *As the World Turns*)

11. Don Hastings (Bob Hughes, *As the World Turns*)

12. Kathryn Hays (Kim Hughes, *As the World Turns*)

8 SOAP ACTORS WHO WON DAYTIME EMMYS FOR WORK OUTSIDE THE SOAP FIELD

1. Douglass Watson (Mac Cory, *Another World*)
   Before winning his back-to-back Emmys as Best Actor in a Drama, Watson won

a 1978 Emmy for Outstanding Individual Achievement in Religious Programming for narrating "Continuing Creation."

2. Carolee Campbell (Carolee Simpson, *The Doctors*)

In 1978, Carolee Campbell also picked up an Outstanding Individual Achievement in Religious Programming for her work in "This Is My Son."

3. Rolanda Mendels (Molly Ordway, *Another World*)

In 1979, Rolanda Mendels won an Outstanding Individual Achievement in Religious Programming for her work in "Interrogation in Budapest."

4. Elizabeth Hubbard (Dr. Althea Davis, *The Doctors*; Lucinda Walsh, *As the World Turns*)

In 1974 Hubbard won Best Actress in a Daytime Drama for her work on *The Doctors*. Two years later, while still on the show, she won Outstanding Actress in a Daytime Drama Special for her work on *First Ladies' Diaries: Edith Wilson*.

5–6. Gerald Gordon (Dr. Nick Bellini, *The Doctors*) and James Luisi (Phil Wainwright, *Another World*)

Gerald Gordon and James Luisi tied for 1976's Outstanding Actor in a Daytime Drama Special. Gordon won for *First Ladies' Diaries: Rachel Jackson*; Luisi for *First Ladies' Diaries: Martha Washington*. Unprepared for a tie, the producers cut to a commercial after Gordon's acceptance speech and did not air Luisi's.

7. Maia Danziger (Glenda Toland, *Another World*)

Danziger won a 1980 Outstanding Individual Achievement in Children's Programming Emmy for the *ABC Afterschool Special* "The Late Great Me: Story of a Teenage Alcoholic."

8. Justin Whalin (A. J. Quartermaine, *General Hospital*)

Justin Whalin, who had played A. J. Quartermaine as a teen back in the late '80s, picked up the 1994 Emmy as Outstanding Performer in a Children's Special for playing the son of two lesbians in the CBS Schoolbreak Special *Other Mothers*. Also nominated for the award were Meredith Baxter Birney and Joanna Cassidy, who had played Whalin's mothers.

5 ACTORS AND ACTRESSES WHO WON EMMYS FOR PLAYING MULTIPLE ROLES—AND ONE SPECIAL CASE

1. David Canary for twin brothers Adam and Stuart Chandler, *All My Children*

2. Erika Slezak for split personality Vicki Buchanan/Nikki Smith et alii, *One Life to Live*

3. Ellen Wheeler for twins Vicky and Marley Love, *Another World*

4. Anne Heche also for playing Vicky and Marley, *Another World*

5. Julianne Moore for look-alike half-sisters/cousins Frannie and Sabrina Hughes, *As the World Turns*

And Tom Christopher (Carlo Hesser and Mortimer Bern, *One Life to Live*)

Christopher won the 1992 Best Supporting Actor Emmy for playing Carlo Hesser on *One Life to Live*. At the time, it was a single role for him. The character was killed, and Christopher came back as Mortimer Bern, who turned out to be Carlo's twin brother. Christopher was nominated for that role as well, but didn't win.

12 CURIOUS EMMY NOMINATIONS AND SURPRISING VICTORIES

1. 1962's Outstanding Continued Performance by an Actress in a Series (Lead)

In 1962, Mary Stuart (Joanne Gardner, *Search for Tomorrow*) became the first actor or actress to be recognized for work on a daytime soap opera. This was definitely a breakthrough for daytime actors, but Stuart stood out like the proverbial sore thumb among the list of nominees. Not only were the four actresses she was competing against prime-time stars, they were all starring in sitcoms: Shirley Booth (*Hazel*), Gertrude Berg (*The Gertrude Berg Show*), Cara Williams (*Pete and Gladys*), and *Dallas*'s future Miss Ellie, Donna Reed (*The Donna Reed Show*). The Emmy went to Booth.

2. 1967's Outstanding Performance by an Actress in a Supporting Role in a Drama

Ruth Warrick (Phoebe Tyler Wallingford, *All My Children*) had been nominated for her work as housekeeper Hannah Cord on *Peyton Place*. She lost out to Agnes Moorehead, who had been the producers' first choice for the role of Hannah. The loss was somewhat unfair because Moorehead won the Emmy for a one-shot guest appearance on *The Wild, Wild West* versus Warrick's continued work on *Peyton Place*. Even Moorehead felt the competition was lopsided and said on her way to receive the award, "I shouldn't be getting this."

3. 1973's Outstanding Achievement by an Individual in Daytime Drama

It is uncommon but not altogether absurd to see actors competing against actresses for an acting award. In 1973, however, Mary Fickett (Ruth Martin, *All My Children*) found herself competing not only against an actor—Macdonald Carey (Dr. Tom Horton, *Days of Our Lives*)—but against four directors, a scenic designer, and a set decorator as well. When Fickett won, someone backstage joked that the voting committee must have preferred her acting to the set decorator's drapes. By the following year, individual awards were given for Best Writing, Best Individual Director, Best Actor (which Macdonald Carey won), and Best Actress (which Mary Fickett was nominated for but which she lost to Elizabeth Hubbard, who was playing Dr. Althea Davis on *The Doctors*).

4. 1975's Outstanding Writing for a Daytime Drama

The odds weighed heavily in Bill Bell's favor for getting the Emmy for writing in 1975. There were only three nominations and two of them were his: one for his work on *The Young and the Restless* and one as part of the writing team on *Days of Our Lives*. Despite the favorable odds, the award went to the category's only other nominee, the writing team from *Another World*. The following year, Bell was double-nominated again for *The Young and the Restless* and *Days of Our Lives*. That year, he won for *Days of Our Lives*. He would not win a writing Emmy for *The Young and the Restless* until 1992.

5. 1978's Outstanding Actress

When Laurie Heinemann accepted her Emmy award, she said, "This is amazing." She wasn't the only one who felt so. Heinemann had been long gone from the show when she received her nomination. The tail end of her run on the show had fallen into the eligibility period. She squeezed into a list of nominees that had swelled to seven, including two others from *Another World*: Victoria Wyndham (Rachel Cory) and Beverlee McKinsey (Iris Carrington). Also on the list was Susan Lucci (Erica Kane, *All My Children*)—her first nomination. Despite the Emmy,

Heinemann was not brought back to *Another World*, nor did she find work on any other shows.

6. 1986's Outstanding Supporting Actress

In 1986, Uta Hagen's nomination for Outstanding Supporting Actress confused and angered a lot of soap fans and industry insiders. Despite the wealth of talent on daytime, Hagen earned her nomination on the basis of five days' worth of work on *One Life to Live*. In essence, she was nominated more on name recognition than anything else. As a famed acting teacher in New York, Hagen is known and respected throughout the theater community, many of whose members also work on daytime TV. In response to the controversy, the category Outstanding Guest Performer was created the following year to cover actors/actresses who, like Hagen, worked on the show a limited number of days. The Guest Performer category, like the Outstanding Cameo Appearance category in 1980, lasted only one year.

7. 1990's Outstanding Juvenile Male

Andy Dixon's bout with alcoholism on *As the World Turns* was hailed by *Soap Opera Digest* as 1990's best storyline, but it didn't yield an Emmy nomination for Andy's portrayer, Scott DeFreitas. Maybe that oversight would not have been so inexcusable if there had been more than *two* actors nominated for Outstanding Juvenile Male that year: DeFreitas's *As the World Turns* castmate Andy Kavovit (Paul Stenbeck), who won, and *Guiding Light*'s Bryan Buffinton (Little Billy Lewis).

8. 1992's Outstanding Supporting Actress

In 1992, Kimberlin Brown was nominated as Outstanding Supporting Actress for her work as the evil nurse Sheila Grainger on *The Young and the Restless*. During the eligibility period for the award, however, she had spent approximately nine months playing Sheila on *The Bold and the Beautiful*. That same year, Gerald Anthony won an Emmy for playing Marco Dane on *General Hospital*; he'd been nominated previously for playing Marco on *One Life to Live*, where he originated the role.

9. 1994's Outstanding Supporting Actor

Justin Deas may have won the Emmy award as Outstanding Supporting Actor in 1994, but many believe that he should have been running in the Best Actor category—despite his personal philosophy that all actors on soaps are essentially supporting each other. As Buzz Cooper, Deas had been the center of *Guiding Light.* The plots that didn't revolve around Buzz's return from "the dead" managed to include him in some way. To top it off, Deas's leading lady, Fiona Hutchison (Jenna Bradshaw), had been nominated as a lead actress. In 1995, Deas, for the first time, was nominated for an Emmy as Outstanding (Lead) Actor, which he won.

10–12. Outstanding Daytime Drama Series: 1976, 1980, 1983

It was the Daytime Emmy's purest example of a whole being greater than the sum of its parts: not only was *Another World* nominated as Outstanding Daytime Drama of 1976 without racking up one other nomination in either the acting, writing, or directing categories, it won the award. What some critics dismissed as a one-time fluke happened a second time in 1980 when *Guiding Light* was named Outstanding Drama Series, the only award it was up for. In 1983, *The Young and the Restless* pulled off the same trick despite an ABC stranglehold on the nominations—30 out of the 33 were for ABC shows. (Also nominated as Best Show that year was *Days of Our Lives*, its lone nomination.)

7 SOAP STARS WHO HAVE CO-HOSTED THE EMMY AWARDS

1. Susan Lucci (Erica Kane, *All My Children*)
   Note: Three times.

2. Walt Willey (Jackson Montgomery, *All My Children*)

3. Peter Bergman (Jack Abbott, *The Young and the Restless*)

4. Drake Hogestyn (John Black, *Days of Our Lives*)

5. James De Paiva (Max Holden, *One Life to Live*)

6. Deidre Hall (Marlena Evans, *Days of Our Lives*)

7. Robert Kelker-Kelly (Bo Brady, *Days of Our Lives*)

EMMY'S 6 MOST EMBARRASSING MOMENTS

1. *The Young and the Restless* Wrongly Named as Winner

In 1986, the Emmy for Outstanding Writing went to the team from *The Young and the Restless* headed by Bill Bell. It was the first Emmy the show had received for its writing. The very next morning, Bell got a phone call telling him that a mistake had been made. The wrong show's name had been written on the card. The Emmy was supposed to go to *Guiding Light*, not *The Young and the Restless*. In other words, Bell had to give the Emmy back. In 1992, *The Young and the Restless* finally won its first Emmy for writing. Upon accepting the award, Bell told the story of what had happened in 1986 and joked, "If the phone rings tomorrow morning, I'm not answering it."

2. *The New York Post* Reveals Winners before Ceremony

Prior to the 1984 award ceremony, the Academy had released the names of the winners to members of the press. Because the awards were being held at night and not televised, the Academy was trying to accommodate the deadline for newspapers on the East Coast. Rather than hold off naming the winners until the following morning, *The New York Post* decided to scoop the competition and reveal the winners' names in its late afternoon edition. (The newspaper defended its decision by saying that the press release read *For Immediate Release*.) As a result, many people—including some of the actors attending the ceremony—knew who all the winners were going to be before their names were even announced. Among those in the know was Robert Gentry (Ross Chandler, *All My Children*). He was seated at the same table with Susan Lucci, whose Emmy losing streak was already becoming legendary. He had to sit there throughout the ceremony, knowing that once again she was not going to get the Emmy.

3. No One Gets the Prize

One of the Academy's biggest slaps in the face to daytime certainly started out well enough. In 1968, the Academy decided to finally recognize daytime dramas with a category of their own: Individual Achievement in Daytime Programming. Nominated that year were Macdonald Carey (Dr. Tom Horton) for his work on *Days of Our Lives*, Joan Bennett (Elizabeth Collins) for her work on *Dark Shadows*, and Celeste Holm (the future Isabelle Alden, *Loving*) for a guest appearance on the Sunday morning religious show *Insight*. Because the category was an Area award, the Emmy could be given to as many as all or as few as none of the nominees. As it turned out, none of the three received the Emmy, which many took as a greater insult than if the category had not been created to begin with. It would be another four years before any individuals would be recognized for their work in the soaps.

4. NBC Refuses to Air Emmy Awards

In some ways, it sounded like a joke: The Daytime Emmys, an awards show celebrating television, would not be shown on television. Yet, in 1983, NBC, which was scheduled to air the ceremony, chose not to exercise its option. Although it cited poor ratings as the reason, many insiders believe that NBC was responding to the virtual stranglehold ABC had on the nominations: 30 out of 33 nominations for major Emmys that year had been given to ABC shows. Many felt that NBC, whose afternoon ratings were already lagging far behind ABC, did not want to spend two hours of its airtime promoting the glories of a rival network.

5. NBC Refuses to Participate in the Emmys

In 1984, NBC refused to participate at all in the Emmy nominating or electing process. Some felt that the network was still smarting from its shutout at the Emmys the year before. Even CBS, which had been nominated for only one major award, Outstanding Drama Series for *The Young and the Restless*, had won an Emmy. As its official reason for refusing to participate, NBC cited problems with the balloting procedure and with last-minute rule changes. Ironically, even though NBC refused to participate, it did manage to pick up four nominations, twice as many as it had the year before.

6. *As the World Turns* Presenters Cut from Program

Fans of *As the World Turns* certainly noticed the absence of presenters from the show at the 1994 awards ceremony. Michael Swan (Duncan McKechnie), Tamara Tunie (Jessica Griffin), and Margaret Reed (Shannon O'Hara) were supposed to introduce a series of clips featuring such newsmakers as Lorena Bobbitt, who had severed her husband's penis, and ice skater Tonya Harding, who was involved in a plot to cripple rival Nancy Kerrigan. Although the segment intended to be a truth-is-stranger-than-fiction joke, none of the three saw the segment as relevant to the soaps. Beyond that, they found their script demeaning to the intricacies of their storyline. When they complained, ABC pulled the segment but did not give them anything else to do. The *World Turns* contingent, it should be noted, were not the only ones who found fault with the ceremony. Several soap publications and one of the ceremony's hosts, Peter Bergman, criticized the show for focusing too heavily on the sex scenes and ignoring the social issues dealt with on the soaps.

12
The Cliffhanger

10 FINAL EPISODES THAT LEFT US HANGING

1. *Dallas*

Last airdate: May 3, 1991

Dallas ended its thirteen-year run with a demonic twist on the Jimmy Stewart classic *It's a Wonderful Life*. The episode opened with J. R. (Larry Hagman) drunk and depressed over losing Ewing Oil and having the majority of his family turn against him. When Joel Grey appeared as a figure named Adam, J. R. mistook him for his guardian angel. Adam showed J. R. what the lives of his family and enemies would have been like had he never been born. Some like ex-wife Sue Ellen (Linda Gray) and his archenemy, Cliff Barnes (Ken Kercheval), were better off while others like brother Bobby (Patrick Duffy) and ex-wife Cally (Cathy Podewell) weren't. The gimmick allowed for the return of such *Dallas* alumni as Linda Gray, Mary Crosby (as Kristin Shepard), Steve Kanaly (as Ray Krebbs), and *Knots Landing*'s Ted Shackleford and Joan Van Ark as Gary and Valene. In the final few moments, Grey's character revealed himself to be not an angel but a demon, who urged J. R. to kill himself. While a shot did ring out in J. R.'s bedroom, all the audience saw was brother Bobby (Patrick Duffy) coming into the scene. The show ended with a reaction shot of horror on Bobby's face. Whether J. R. shot himself or fired the gun in the air remains unknown. A reunion movie has been promised since the show went off the air, but has yet to materialize.

2. Dynasty

Last airdate: May 11, 1989

During the last few minutes of the show, five major character's lives were left in jeopardy. Fallon (Emma Samms) and baby sister Krystina (Jessica Player) had been trapped in a cave-in below the mansion; Alexis (Joan Collins) and Dex (Michael Nader) had been pushed off a balcony by Adam (Gordon Thomson); and Blake (John Forsythe) had been shot. It was almost two and a half years before ABC presented the four-hour movie to tie up the loose ends. Alexis survived by landing on Dex, whose exact fate was never quite made clear. "He didn't fare that well," was all that was said. Whether that means he died or was crippled was left open—probably to Nader's availability for future reunions. Blake did survive the gunshot and was sent to prison, framed by an international cartel of ruthless power brokers. Fallon and Krystina also survived the cave-in.

3. Soap

Last airdate: April 20, 1981

Soap's final episode found a number of core characters facing potentially violent deaths. Chester (Robert Mandan) was holding a gun on Danny (Ted Wass) whom he had caught in bed with his (Chester's) new wife. Police Chief Burt (Richard Mulligan) was ambushed by a gang of criminals. And Jessica (Katherine Helmond), who had gotten involved with a South American revolutionary, was left facing a firing squad.

Note: When Jessica's ghost popped up on a subsequent episode of the *Soap* spin-off *Benson*, her character was said to have died not by the firing squad but by a freak accident.

4. Capitol

Last airdate: March 20, 1987

Like *Soap*, Capitol also ended with its major heroine facing a firing squad. The producers were so angry at the show's cancellation that they refused to bring any of the storylines to a close. Sloane Denning (Debrah Farentino née Mullowney), who had married Prince Ali (Peter Lochran) from the fictional Middle Eastern country of Baracq, had been taken prisoner in his country. Despite efforts from the

State Department and her family, she had been condemned to death. The show ended with the words "Ready, aim . . . "

5. Dark Shadows

Last airdate: April 2, 1971

The end of *Dark Shadows* left viewers in the past and in parallel time. The show, which often moved characters into the past and into parallel worlds, did both in its final story arc. In a change of pace, the story moved to a parallel world in 1840 without linking any of the core characters into that dimension. For the first time, Jonathan Frid played a second role, Bramwell, who was in love with his brother's wife. The show ended at the conclusion of this storyline, never bringing the audience back to present-day Collinwood.

6. Love of Life

Last airdate: February 1, 1980

The producers had hoped that *Love of Life* would be picked up by another network. (Five years previously, ABC had picked up *The Edge of Night* after CBS cancelled it.) As such, the producers decided against wrapping everything up and proceeded with the storyline as planned. Ben Harper (Chandler Hill Harben) was on trial for assaulting his ex-wife Betsy Crawford (Margo McKenna); in reality, she'd been injured accidentally while he was rescuing her from a snake. In the final episode, Betsy left her hospital bed to testify in Ben's behalf. Although her testimony cleared him of the blame, she collapsed in the courtroom. Her life hung in the balance as the show went off the air. *Love of Life* was not picked up by ABC or NBC.

7. Peyton Place

Last airdate: June 2, 1969

By the time *Peyton Place* went off the air, its ratings had sunk almost to the bottom of the Neilsens. The show ranked eighty-second in its last season. Maybe because the audience had fallen off so dramatically, the producers didn't think anyone would care if plotlines were left hanging in the last episode. Dr. Michael Rossi (Ed Nelson), who had been with the show from the first episode, was left on trial for the murder of Fred Russell (Joe Maross). The final episode also left audience favorite Rodney Harrington (Ryan O'Neal) paralyzed in a wheelchair. While a daytime version *Return to Peyton Place* came to TV in 1972, the audience could not truly trust the continuity of its storylines from its prime-time predecessor. Among the cast of characters was Martin Peyton, who had died and was buried in 1968.

8. *Generations*

Last airdate: January 25, 1991

Because there was talk that *Generations* might be picked up for first-run syndication, storylines were not wrapped up. Core couple Ruth and Henry Marshall (Joan Pringle and James Reynolds) remained at odds with each other. The night Ruth debuted as a singer at the Music Box, Henry wound up in a hotel room with Doreen Jackson (Jonelle Allen). Nothing happened between them because Henry suffered a heart attack. The show ended with Henry's son Adam (Kristoff St. John) being let into the hotel room and finding Doreen trying to revive Henry. Despite expectations, the show did not get picked up for first-run syndication. It did, however, air in reruns on the cable channel BET.

9. *Grand*

Last airdate: December 27, 1990

Like *Soap, Grand* was a soap opera spoof that often traveled into areas the soaps didn't usually touch upon. In its final weeks, *Grand*'s lead heroine Janice Passetti (Pamela Reed) was unwittingly being lured into a cult of devil-worshippers. While the producers had the episode taped which would have brought her story to a conclusion, NBC chose not to air the episode because it didn't want to start the first week of a new year with the last episode of a dying series.

10. *Twin Peaks*

Last airdate: June 10, 1991

The final episode left a number of core characters' lives in jeopardy. Audrey Horne (Sherilyn Fenn) was among those in a bank when a bomb exploded, while her father, Ben (Richard Beymer), had been knocked against a fireplace and possibly killed during a fight with Doc Hayward (Warren Frost). The real cliffhanger, though, surrounded FBI agent Dale Cooper (Kyle MacLachlan), who had recently traveled into an otherwordly dimension called the Black Lodge. When he looked in the mirror during the last few minutes, the audience saw the demon BOB's (Frank Silva) reflection staring back, signifying that Agent Cooper was possessed by the same demon that had murdered Laura Palmer. Although the film *Twin Peaks: Fire Walk with Me* was supposed to resolve the cliffhangers, the film took place before Laura Palmer's murder and left all the cliffhangers still up in the air.

Bibliography

(or 25 Books Every Soap Fan's Library Should Include)

Bonderoff, Jason. *Soap Opera Babylon.* New York: Putnam, 1987.

Bronson, Fred. *The Billboard Book of Number One Hits.* New York: Billboard, 1985.

Brooks, Tim, and Earle Marsh. *The Complete Directory to Prime-Time Network TV Shows 1946–Present* (Fifth Edition). New York: Ballantine, 1992.

Carey, Macdonald. *The Days of My Life.* New York: St. Martin's Press, 1991.

Copeland, Mary Ann. *Soap Opera History.* Lincolnwood, IL: Publications International, Ltd., 1991.

Fulton, Eileen with Brett Bolton. *How My World Turns.* New York: Warner Books, 1970.

Kalter, Suzy. *The Complete Book of Dallas: Behind the Scenes at the World's Favorite Television Show.* New York: Abrams, 1986.

LaGuardia, Robert. *Soap World.* New York, Arbor House, 1983.

Lemay, Harding. *Eight Years in Another World.* New York: Atheneum, 1981.

Lofman, Ron. *Celebrity Vocals.* Iola, WI: Krause Publications, 1994.

McNeil, Alex. *Total Television: A Comprehensive Guide to Programming from 1948 to the Present* (Third Edition). New York: Penguin, 1991.

Meyers, Richard. *The Illustrated Soap Opera Companion.* New York: Drake Publishers, 1977.

O'Neil, Thomas. *The Emmys: Star Wars, Showdowns, and the Supreme Test of TV's Best.* New York: Penguin, 1992.

Schemering, Christopher. *Guiding Light: A 50th Celebration*. New York: Ballantine, 1987.

Schemering, Christopher. *The Soap Opera Encyclopedia* (Second Edition). New York: Ballantine, 1987.

Scott, Kathryn Leigh. *My Scrapbook Memories of Dark Shadows*. Los Angeles: Pomegranate Press, 1987.

Scott, Kathryn Leigh. *The Dark Shadows Companion: Twenty-fifth Anniversary Collection*. Los Angeles: Pomegranate Press, 1987.

Siegel, Barbara and Scott Siegel. *Susan Lucci: The Woman Behind Erica Kane*. New York: St. Martin's Press, 1986.

Stallings, Peggy. *Forbidden Channels: The Truth They Hide from TV Guide*. New York: HarperPerennial, 1991.

Stuart, Mary. *Both of Me*. New York: Doubleday, 1980.

Wakefield, Dan. *All Her Children*. Garden City, NY: Doubleday, 1976.

Warner, Gary. *All My Children: The Complete Family Scrapbook*. Los Angeles: General Publishing Group, 1994.

Warrick, Ruth. *The Confessions of Phoebe Tyler*. Englewood Cliffs, NJ: Prentice Hall, 1980.

Weiner, Ed & the Editors of *TV Guide*. *The TV Guide TV Book*. New York: HarperPerennial, 1992.

Whitburn, Joel. *The Billboard Book of Top 40 Hits*. New York: Billboard, 1989.

My research also relied heavily on:

5 PUBLICATIONS EVERY SOAP FAN SHOULD SUBSCRIBE TO

Soap Opera Digest

Soap Opera Magazine

Soap Opera Update

Soap Opera Weekly

TV Guide

GERARD J. WAGGETT has been following soap operas for almost twenty years. He is a frequent contributor to *Soap Opera Weekly* and has also written about the soaps for *Soap Opera Update* and *TV Guide*. A graduate of Harvard University, where he spent as much time in front of a television as he did in class, he now lives in Boston where he is working on his next two soap books for HarperPaperbacks.